D0567805

A SHORT HISTORY OF THE MIDDLE AGES

A SHORT HISTORY OF THE MIDDLE AGES

THIRD EDITION

VOLUME II: FROM *c.*900 TO *c.*1500

BARBARA H. ROSENWEIN

University of Toronto Press

Copyright © University of Toronto Press Incorporated 2009

www.utphighereducation.com

All rights reserved. The use of any part of this publication reproduced, transmitted in any form or by any means, electronic, mechanical, photocopying, recording, or otherwise, or stored in a retrieval system, without prior written consent of the publisher—or in the case of photocopying, a licence from Access Copyright (Canadian Copyright Licensing Agency), One Yonge Street, Suite 1900, Toronto, Ontario M5E 1E5—is an infringement of the copyright law.

Second edition published by Broadview Press 2004.

LIBRARY AND ARCHIVES CANADA CATALOGUING IN PUBLICATION

Rosenwein, Barbara H.
  A short history of the Middle Ages / Barbara H. Rosenwein.—3rd ed.

Includes bibliographical references and index.
Contents: v. 1. From c.300 to c.1150 – v. 2. From c.900 to c.1500.
ISBN 978-1-4426-0122-2 (v. 1).—ISBN 978-1-4426-0123-9 (v. 2)

    1. Middle Ages. 2. Europe—History—476-1492. I. Title.

D117.R67 2009a   940.1   C2009-902059-9

We welcome comments and suggestions regarding any aspect of our publications— please feel free to contact us at news@utphighereducation.com or visit our internet site at www.utphighereducation.com.

North America
5201 Dufferin Street
Toronto, Ontario, Canada, M3H 5T8

2250 Military Road
Tonawanda, New York, USA, 14150

ORDERS PHONE: 1-800-565-9523
ORDERS FAX: 1-800-221-9985
ORDERS EMAIL: utpbooks@utpress.utoronto.ca

UK, Ireland, and continental Europe
NBN International
Estover Road, Plymouth, PL6 7PY, UK
TEL: 44 (0) 1752 202301
FAX ORDER LINE: 44 (0) 1752 202333
enquiries@nbninternational.com

The University of Toronto Press acknowledges the financial support for its publishing activities of the Government of Canada through the Book Publishing Industry Development Program (BPIDP).

Designed by Daiva Villa, Chris Rowat Design.

Printed in Canada

To Jason and Ariana, my dear new children-in-law

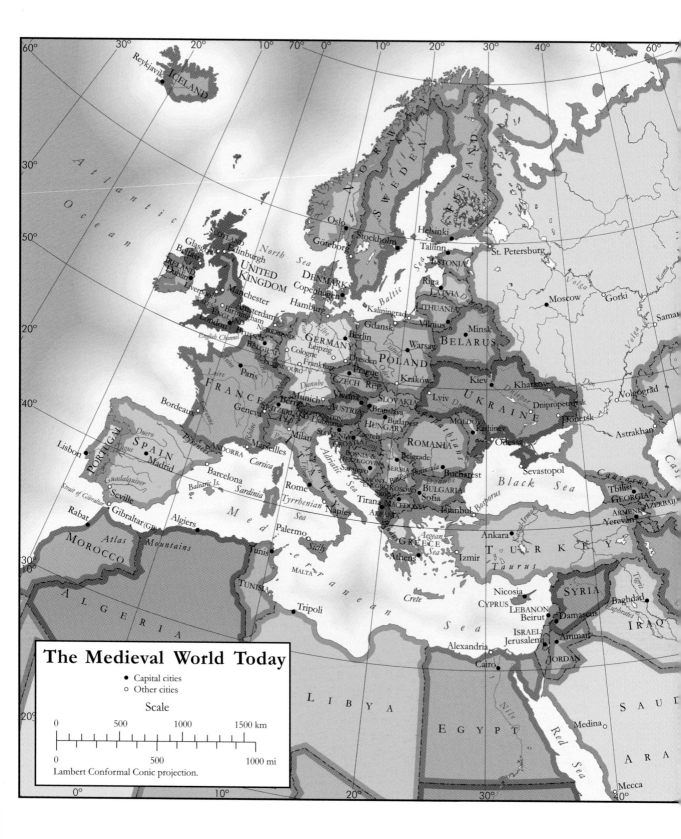

The Medieval World Today

- ● Capital cities
- ○ Other cities

Scale

0   500   1000   1500 km

0   500   1000 mi

Lambert Conformal Conic projection.

THE UNION of the Roman empire was dissolved; its genius was humbled in the dust; and armies of unknown barbarians, issuing from the frozen regions of the North, had established their victorious reign over the fairest provinces of Europe and Africa.

Edward Gibbon,
The Decline and Fall of the Roman Empire

IT MAY very well happen that what seems for one group a period of decline may seem to another the birth of a new advance.

Edward Hallett Carr,
What is History?

CONTENTS

MAPS

PLATES

Seeing the Middle Ages

GENEALOGIES

FIGURES

LISTS

ABBREVIATIONS, CONVENTIONS, WEBSITES

ABBREVIATIONS

  c. circa. Used in dates to mean that they are approximate.
cent. century
  d. date of death
emp. emperor
  fl. flourished. This is given when even approximate birth and death dates are unknown.
  pl. plural. The plural form of a noun.
  r. rule. Indicates the dates of rule.
 sing. singular. The singular form of a noun.

DATE CONVENTIONS

All dates are C.E./A.D. unless otherwise noted (the two systems are interchangeable). The dates of popes are not preceded by *r.* because popes took their papal names upon accession to office, and the dates after those names apply only to their papacies.

WEBSITES

www.rosenweinshorthistory.com = The website for this book, which has practice short-answer and essay questions (with sample answers provided), as well as Maps, Genealogies, and Links to other medieval web resources.

http://labyrinth.georgetown.edu = The Labyrinth: Resources for Medieval Studies sponsored by Georgetown University.

http://www.roman-emperors.org = *De Imperatoribus Romanis*: An Online Encyclopedia of Roman Rulers and Their Families (to 1453).

PREFACE TO THE ORIGINAL EDITION OF VOLUME TWO

At the beginning of the first volume of his long and learned trilogy, *Suicide in the Middle Ages*, Alexander Murray remarks amiably, "Unconventionally long, the book remains, to the author's certain knowledge, 'a mere introduction.'" Well, if *that* is just an introduction (and it undoubtedly is), then what is *this* book?

It is meant to be an easy pass through a dense thicket. It has been written so that you, the reader, may know enough about the second half of the Middle Ages to move on, after reading it, to meatier fare connected to that period: to "secondary sources" (so called not because they are "second best" but because they are present-day interpretations of the past) and to "primary sources," the texts, pictures, artefacts, and other bits and pieces of their lives and thought that early medieval people left behind.

There are five chapters in this book, taking you from the aftermath of the Carolingian empire to the Renaissance and the eve of the Reformation. If you are in college, your course will last between ten to fifteen weeks. This means that you will probably read a chapter every other week or so and have plenty of time for supplementary material. If you are not a student, you may nevertheless wish to interleave your reading with some of the materials cited in the footnotes here (all primary sources) or in the bibliographies (which list relevant secondary sources). This book has lots of maps, genealogies, lists, and plates to help you figure out the context of the other things that you will need or want to study. The index is a handy way to look up names (which are followed by dates where possible), events, and places. Some technical words are explained in a glossary. The lists of Key Events at the end of each chapter are meant to help you review the material. A web site at Broadview Press allows for map searches and other useful study aids.

Volume Two of *A Short History* looks at the Byzantine and Islamic worlds, but its focus is Europe, broadly understood. I have tried to write not only political history but also social, economic, and cultural history. There is, however, a conscious emphasis on political history, deriving from my twofold conviction that (1) politics tells us a good deal about the uses and distribution of power, always important if we wish to consider general conditions of life; and (2) politics, with its decisive events, provides a nice, clear grid for everything else. The book is organized chronologically because I am persuaded that everything in a period—intellectual life, religious feelings and aspirations, even methods of rulership—is interconnected.

While preparing this revised text I have incurred many debts that I wish to acknowledge. I thank Giles Constable, Adam Kosto, Graham Loud, and Michael Morony for pointing out errors and suggesting changes to the first edition. Monique Bourin, Samuel Leturcq, Rosamond Mack, R.I. Moore, and Anders Winroth generously contributed their expertise to particular sections. Thomas Head shared some of his photographs. Maureen Miller was, as always, a wonderful resource and sounding-board. I am indebted to my students in History 310; I wish to thank Jamie McGowan, Eric Nethercott, Susie Newman, and Suzette Vela for their thoughtful suggestions. Paul Heersink prepared new maps with his customary professionalism; George Kirkpatrick worked his own magic with the design. Finally I am grateful to the people at Broadview Press—especially Barbara Conolly, Don Le Pan, and Mical Moser (an invaluable advisor)—for their help and support.

PREFACE TO THIS EDITION

For this new edition I had the opportunity to coordinate the text more closely with my sourcebook, *Reading the Middle Ages: Sources from Europe, Byzantium, and the Islamic World*, Vol. 2; to update information; and to choose a few illustrations for extended discussion in a new feature entitled "Seeing the Middle Ages." I have one new piece of advice for student readers: turn first to the Glossary to get the definitions of possibly unfamiliar terms. Then read the book.

I am grateful to Loyola University Chicago and particularly to Dean Isiaah Crawford for financing my trip to Istanbul and Ephesus to see monuments still standing and others under excavation. I thank Paul Cobb, Maureen Miller, Piroska Nagy, Dionysios Stathakopoulos, Anders Winroth, and many anonymous reviewers for their careful reading of the earlier edition and their thoughtful suggestions for this one. I have benefited enormously from the help, advice, suggestions, and expertise of Maria Aurenhammer, Karl Brunner, Neil Christie, Andrew Donnelly, Ross Brooke Ettle, Elina Gertsman, Zouhair Ghazzal, Mark Humphries, Simon James, Fritz Krinzinger, Sabine Ladstätter, Kristen B. Neuschel, and Christian Sapin. Bert Roest was the ideal fact-checker: immensely erudite, thorough, and zealous. I am grateful to the people at and associated with the University of Toronto Press: Martin Boyne, Laura Cardiff, Judith Earnshaw, Natalie Fingerhut, Melissa Goertzen, Christopher Griffin, Michael Harrison, Tara Lowes, Chris Rowat, and Daiva Villa.

FOUR

POLITICAL COMMUNITIES REORDERED (*c*.900–*c*.1050)

The large-scale centralized governments of the ninth century dissolved in the tenth. The fission was least noticeable at Byzantium, where, although important landowning families emerged as brokers of patronage and power, the primacy of the emperor was never effectively challenged. Quite the opposite happened in the Islamic world, where new dynastic groups established themselves as regional rulers. In Western Europe, Carolingian kings ceased to control land and men, while new political entities—some extremely local and weak, others quite strong and unified—emerged in their wake. Everywhere political reordering brought new military elites to the fore.

BYZANTIUM: THE STRENGTHS AND LIMITS OF CENTRALIZATION

By 1025 the Byzantine Empire once again shadowed the Danube and touched the Euphrates. To the north it had a new and restless neighbor: Kievan Rus. The emperors at Constantinople maintained the traditional cultural importance of the capital city by carefully orchestrating the radiating power of the imperial court. Nevertheless, the centralized model of the Byzantine state was challenged by powerful men in the countryside, who gobbled up land and dominated the peasantry.

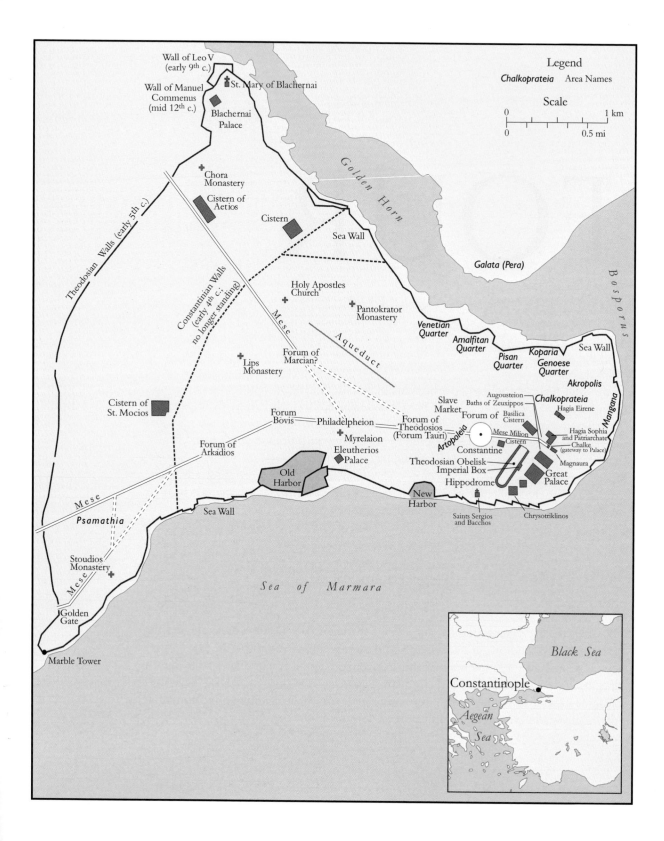

Legend

Chalkoprateia Area Names

Scale

0   1 km
0   0.5 mi

Wall of Leo V
(early 9th c.)

Wall of Manuel
Commenus
(mid 12th c.)

St. Mary of Blachernai

Blachernai
Palace

Golden Horn

Chora
Monastery

Cistern of
Aetios

Cistern

Sea Wall

Galata (Pera)

Bosporus

Theodosian Walls (early 5th c.)

Constantinian Walls
(early 4th c.;
no longer standing)

Holy Apostles
Church

Pantokrator
Monastery

*Venetian
Quarter*

*Amalfitan
Quarter*

*Pisan
Quarter*

Koparia

*Genoese
Quarter*

Sea Wall

Mese

Aqueduct

Forum of
Marcian?

Lips
Monastery

Akropolis

Slave
Market

Augousteion
Baths of Zeuxippos

Chalkoprateia

Hagia Eirene

Cistern of
St. Mocios

Forum of
Theodosios
(Forum Tauri)

Forum of
Bovis

Philadelpheion

Myrelaion

Eleutherios
Palace

Artopoleia

Forum of
Mese Milion

Basilica
Cistern

Hagia Sophia
and Patriarchate

Cistern

Chalke
(gateway to Palace)

Mangana

Constantine

Forum of
Arkadios

Old
Harbor

Theodosian Obelisk
Imperial Box

Hippodrome

New
Harbor

Saints Sergios
and Bacchos

Magnaura

Great
Palace

Chrysotriklinos

Mese

Psamathia

Sea Wall

Mese

Stoudios
Monastery

Sea of Marmara

Golden
Gate

Marble Tower

Black Sea

Constantinople

*Aegean
Sea*

The Imperial Court

The Great Palace of Constantinople, a sprawling building complex begun under Constantine, was expanded, redecorated, and fortified under his successors. (See Map 4.1.) It was more than the symbolic emplacement of imperial power; it was the central command post of the empire. Servants, slaves, and grooms; top courtiers and learned clergymen; cousins, siblings, and hangers-on of the emperor and empress lived within its walls. Other courtiers—civil servants, officials, scholars, military men, advisers, and other dependents—lived as near to the Palace as they could manage. They were "on call" at every hour. The emperor had only to give short notice and all were to assemble for impromptu but nevertheless highly choreographed ceremonies. These were in themselves instruments of power; the emperors manipulated courtly formalities to indicate new favorites or to signal displeasure.

Map 4.1 (facing page): Constantinople, *c.* 1100

The court was mainly a male preserve, but there were women's quarters at the Great Palace as well—and sometimes powerful women. Consider Zoe (*d.* 1050), the daughter of Constantine VIII. Contemporaries acknowledged her right to rule through her imperial blood. But they were happier when she was married, her blood-right legitimizing the rule of her husband. In most cases, though, the emperors themselves boasted the hereditary bloodline, and their wives were the ones to marry into the imperial family. In that case the empress normally could exercise power only as a widow acting on behalf of her children.

There was also a "third gender" at the Great Palace: eunuchs—men who had been castrated, normally as children, and raised to be teachers, doctors, or guardians of the women at court. Their status began to rise in the tenth century. Originally foreigners, they were increasingly recruited from the educated upper classes in the Byzantine Empire itself. In addition to their duties in the women's quarter, some of them accompanied the emperor during his most sacred and vulnerable moments—when he removed his crown; when he participated in religious ceremonies; even when he dreamed, at night. They hovered by his throne, like the angels in Mary's icon in Plate 1.12 on p. 55 of volume 1. No one, it was thought, was as faithful, trustworthy, or spiritually pure as a eunuch. Small wonder that in the tenth century Basil the Nothos, the castrated bastard son of one emperor, rose to become grand chamberlain (responsible for internal affairs) at the court of another.

About a century later, the grand chamberlain was not a eunuch but rather a professor, Michael Psellus (1018-*c.* 1092). The Macedonian Renaissance, which had begun in the ninth century, continued apace in the tenth and eleventh, bringing people like Psellus to the fore. Under his direction a new school of philosophy at Constantinople, founded by Constantine IX (*r.* 1042-1055), began to flourish. Beyond his philosophical interests, Psellus was a moralist, keen to explore the character and emotional life of powerful men and women. In his hands, a new sort of historical writing was born: not a universal chronicle covering Creation to the present, as had been the style, but rather an opinionated account of recent events, personalities, and well-oiled political networks:

> [Basil II] surrounded himself with favorites who were neither remarkable for brilliance of intellect, nor of noble lineage, nor too learned. To them were entrusted the imperial rescripts [laws written in response to particular cases], and with them he was accustomed to share the secrets of State.[1]

The impression that Psellus gives of a self-indulgent emperor presiding over a frivolous court is only part of the story, however. As Psellus himself recognized, Basil was a successful centralizer, amassing enormous wealth through taxes, confiscations, and tribute. Above all—something that Psellus only hinted at—Basil was a tough military man whose rule reshaped the geography of Byzantium.

Map 4.2: The Byzantine Empire, *c.*1025

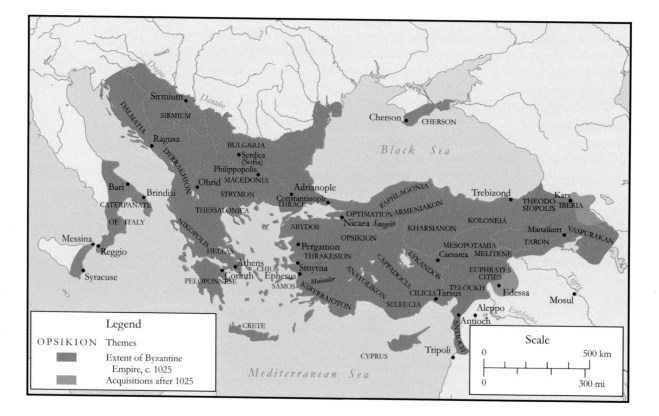

A Wide Embrace and Its Tensions

The expansion of the Byzantine Empire, so cautiously begun in the ninth century, quickened under the tenth-century soldier-emperors Nicephorus Phocas and John Tzimisces. (See Map 4.2.) Crete, lost to the Muslims in the ninth century, was retaken in 961; Cyprus was reconquered in 965; Antioch, portal to Syria, in 969. Most importantly, under Basil II (r.963-1025), Bulgaria, a thorn in Byzantium's side since the seventh century, was at last definitively defeated (1018). The entire region was put under Byzantine rule, its territory divided into themes.

Certainly Basil's nickname, the "Bulgar Slayer," was apt. Nevertheless, it hid the fact that the same emperor was also busy setting up protectorates against the Muslims on his eastern front and that at the end of his life he was preparing an expedition to Sicily. By 1025 the Byzantine army was no longer focused on the interior but was rather mobilized at the peripheries of the empire.

This empire was no longer the tight fist centered on Anatolia that it had been in the dark days of the eighth century. On the contrary, it was an open hand: sprawling, multi-ethnic, and multilingual. To the east it embraced Armenians, Syrians, and Arabs; to the north it included Slavs and Bulgarians (by now themselves Slavic speaking) as well as Pechenegs, a Turkic group that had served as allies of Bulgaria; to the west, in the Byzantine toe of Italy, it contained Lombards, Italians, and Greeks. There must have been Muslims right in the middle of Constantinople: a mosque was built for them there in 1027. Russian soldiers from the region of Kiev formed the backbone of Basil's "Varangian Guard," his elite troops; by the mid-eleventh century, Byzantine mercenaries included "Franks" (mainly from Normandy), Arabs, and Bulgarians as well. In spite of ingrained prejudices, Byzantine princesses had occasionally been married to foreigners before the tenth century, but in Basil's reign this happened to a sister of the emperor himself.

All this openness went only so far, however. In the tenth century, the emperors expelled the Jews from Constantinople, severely curtailing their participation in the silk trade (their traditional profession), and forcing them into the degrading labor of tanners. Some of these restrictions were lifted in the course of the eleventh century, but Jews were never integrated into Byzantine society. Similarly, the annexation of Armenia did not lead to the assimilation of Armenians, who kept their Monophysite beliefs (see p. 29 of volume 1), heretical to many Orthodox Byzantines.

Ethnic diversity was in part responsible for new regional political movements that threatened centralized imperial control. More generally, however, regional revolts were the result of the rise of a new class of wealthy provincial landowners, the *dynatoi* (sing. *dynatos*), "powerful men." Benefiting from a general quickening in the economy and the rise of new urban centers, they took advantage of unaccustomed wealth, buying

Scale

0   500 km

0   300 mi

Lake Ladoga

Gulf of Finland

Kingdom of Sweden

Kingdom of Denmark

Baltic Sea

LITHUANIANS

PRUSSIANS

Vistula

Novgorod

Lake Ilmen

Volga

Vladimir

Suzdal

Kievan Rus

Western Dvina

Polatsk

Smolensk

Kolobrzeg

Wolin

Radgošč

Poznań

Gniezno

Plock

Poland

Oder

Bautzen

Wroclaw

Cracow

Czerwien

Volodymyr

Przemyśl

Halych

Chernigov

Kiev

Pereiaslav

Dnieper

PECHENEGS

Vienna

Nitra

Esztergom

Székesfehérvár

Hungary

Zagreb

Kalocsa

Pannonia

Dniester

PECHENEGS

Sea of Azov

Croatia

Split

Doclea
(Serbian Kingdom)

Ragusa
(Dubrovnik)

Duklja

Adriatic Sea

Bari

Brindisi

Dyrrhachium

Danube

Serdica

Philippopolis

Preslav

Odessos

Black Sea

Byzantine   **Empire**

land from still impoverished peasants as yet untouched by the economic upswing. In his *Novel* (New Law) of 934, Emperor Romanus I Lecapenus (r.920-944) bewailed the "intrusion" of the rich

> into a village or hamlet for the sake of a sale, gift, or inheritance.... For the domination of these persons has increased the great hardship of the poor ... [and] will cause no little harm to the commonwealth unless the present legislation puts an end to it first. For the settlement of the population demonstrates the great benefit of its function—contribution of taxes and fulfillment of military obligations—which will be completely lost should the common people disappear.[2]

Map 4.3 (facing page): Kievan Rus, c.1050

The *dynatoi* also made military men their clients (even if they were not themselves military men) and often held positions in government. The Dalasseni family was fairly typical of this group. The founder of the family was an army leader and governor of Antioch at the end of the tenth century. One of his sons, Theophylact, became governor of "Iberia"—not Spain but rather a theme on the very eastern edge of the empire. Another, Constantine, inherited his father's position at Antioch. With estates scattered throughout Anatolia and a network of connections to other powerful families, the Dalasseni at times could defy the emperor and even coordinate rebellions against him. From the end of the tenth century, imperial control had to contend with the decentralizing forces of provincial *dynatoi* such as these. But the emperors were not dethroned, and a man like Basil II could triumph over the families that challenged his reign to emerge even stronger than before.

The rise of the provincial aristocracy and the prestige of the soldier emperors worked a change in Byzantine culture: from civilian to military ideals. The emperor had long ceased to be "declared" by his troops; but in the eleventh century artists insisted on portraying the emperor hoisted on a shield, symbol of military power. Military saints, such as George, became increasingly popular, especially in their roles as arms-wielding knights on horseback. An epic poem, *Digenis Akritis*, begun in the tenth century and probably put into its final form in the twelfth, depicts Digenis Akritis, a twin-blooded hero (half Greek, half Muslim), winning single-handed battles on the Byzantine frontier.

The Formation of Rus

Digenis plied his trade in Anatolia, but his talents would have served equally well to the north. There, well before the ninth century, fur traders from Scandinavia—in the

West known as Vikings—had settled east of the Gulf of Finland, in the regions of Lake Ladoga and Lake Ilmen (see Maps 4.3 and 4.5). Once settled, they took advantage of river networks and other trade routes that led as far south as Iraq and as far west as Austria. Other peoples in the region were doing the same, above all the Khazars, whose powerful state straddling the Black and Caspian Seas dominated part of the silk road. (See Map 3.2 on p. 109 of volume 1 for the location of the Khazar Empire.) A Turkic-speaking group whose elites converted to Judaism in the ninth century, the Khazars were ruled by a khagan, much like the Avars and the Bulgars. Scandinavians had no khagans, but they were influenced enough by Khazar culture to adopt the title for the ruler of their own fledgling ninth-century state at Novgorod, the first Rus polity.

Soon northern Rus had an affiliate in the south—in the region of Kiev—very close to the Khazars, to whom it likely at first paid tribute. While on occasion attacking both Khazars and Byzantines, Rus rulers saw their greatest advantage in good relations with the Byzantines, who wanted their fine furs, wax, honey, and—especially—slaves. In the course of the tenth century, with the blessing of the Byzantines, Rus brought the Khazar Empire to its knees.

Nurtured through trade and military agreements, good relations between Rus and Byzantium were sealed through religious conversion. In the mid-tenth century quite a few Christians lived in Rus (indeed, one Rus princess converted, calling herself Helena, after Constantine's mother). But the conversion of Rus to Christianity was ultimately the work of Vladimir (r.c.978-1015). Ruler of Rus by force of conquest (though from a princely family), Vladimir was anxious to court the elites of both Novgorod and Kiev. He did so through wars with surrounding peoples that brought him and his troops plunder and tribute—but never enough to satisfy. Losing faith in the traditional gods, Vladimir sought something better. In 988, wooed by the Byzantines, he adopted the Byzantine form of Christianity, took the name "Basil" in honor of Emperor Basil II, and married Anna, the emperor's sister. Christianization of the general population seems to have followed quickly. In any event, the *Russian Primary Chronicle*, a twelfth-century text based in part on earlier materials, reported that under Vladimir's son Yaroslav the Wise (r.1019-1054), "the Christian faith was fruitful and multiplied, while the number of monks increased, and new monasteries came into being."[3]

Vladimir's conversion was part of a larger movement of the tenth and eleventh centuries in which most of the remaining non-monotheistic peoples of the western Eurasian land mass adopted one of the four dominant monotheisms: Islam, Roman Catholicism, Byzantine Orthodoxy, or Judaism. Given its geographic location, it was anyone's guess which way Rus would go. On its western flank was Poland, where in 966, Mieszko I (r.963-992), leader of the tribe known as the Polanians, accepted baptism into the Roman Catholic faith. Eventually (in 991) he placed his realm under the protection of the pope. The experience of Hungary, just south of Poland, was similar: there Géza (*r.c.*972-997) converted to Roman Catholicism and, according to a potent legend, his son, Stephen I (*r.*997-1038), accepted a royal crown from the pope in the year 1000 or 1001. Further north the Scandinavians were also turning to Catholic Christianity: the king of the Danes, for example, was baptized around 960. But to the east Rus had other models: the Khazars, as we have seen, were Jewish; the Volga Bulgars converted to Islam in the early tenth century. Why, then, did Vladimir choose the Byzantine form of Christianity? Perhaps because he could drive the hardest bargain with Basil, who badly needed troops from Rus for his Varangian Guard.

That momentary decision left lasting consequences. Rus, ancestor of Russia, became the heir of the Byzantine church, customs, art, and political ideology. Choosing Christianity linked Russia to the West, but choosing the Byzantine form guaranteed that Russia would always stand apart from Western Europe.

DIVISION AND DEVELOPMENT IN THE ISLAMIC WORLD

While at Byzantium the forces of decentralization were feeble, they carried the day in the Islamic world. Where once the caliph at Baghdad or Samarra could boast collecting taxes from Kabul (today in Afghanistan) to Benghazi (today in Libya), in the eleventh century a bewildering profusion of regional groups and dynasties divided the Islamic world. Yet this was in general a period of prosperity and intellectual blossoming.

The Emergence of Regional Powers

The Muslim conquest had never eliminated all local powers or regional affiliations. It had simply papered over them. While the Umayyad and Abbasid caliphates remained strong, they imposed their rule through their governors and army. But when the caliphate became weak, as it did in the tenth and eleventh centuries, old and new regional interests came to the fore.

A glance at a map of the Islamic world *c.*1000 (Map 4.4) shows, from east to west, the main new groups that emerged: the Samanids, Buyids, Hamdanids, Fatimids, and Zirids. But the map hides the many territories dominated by smaller independent rulers. North of the Fatimid Caliphate, al-Andalus had a parallel history. Its Umayyad ruler took the title of caliph in 929, but in the eleventh century, he too was unable to stave off political fragmentation.

The key cause of the weakness of the Abbasid caliphate was lack of revenue. When landowners, governors, or recalcitrant military leaders in the various regions of the Islamic world refused to pay taxes into the treasury, the caliphs had to rely on the rich farmland of Iraq, long a stable source of income. But a deadly revolt lasting from 869 to 883 by the Zanj—black slaves from sub-Saharan Africa who had been put to work to turn marshes into farmland—devastated the Iraqi economy. Although the revolt was put down and the head of its leader was "displayed on a spear mounted in front of [the winning general] on a barge," there was no chance for recovery.[4] In the tenth century the Qaramita (sometimes called the "Carmathians"), a sect of Shi'ites based in Arabia, found Iraq easy prey. The result was decisive: the caliphs could not pay their troops. New men—military leaders with their own armies and titles like "commander of commanders"—took the reins of power. They preserved the Abbasid line, but they reduced the caliph's political authority to nothing.

The new rulers represented groups that had long awaited their new power. The Buyids, for example, belonged to ancient warrior tribes from the mountains of Iran. Even in the tenth century, most were relatively new converts to Islam. Bolstered by long-festering local discontent, one of them became "commander of commanders" in 945. Thereafter, the Buyids, with the help from their own Turkish mercenaries,

Map 4.4: Fragmentation of the Islamic World, *c*.1000

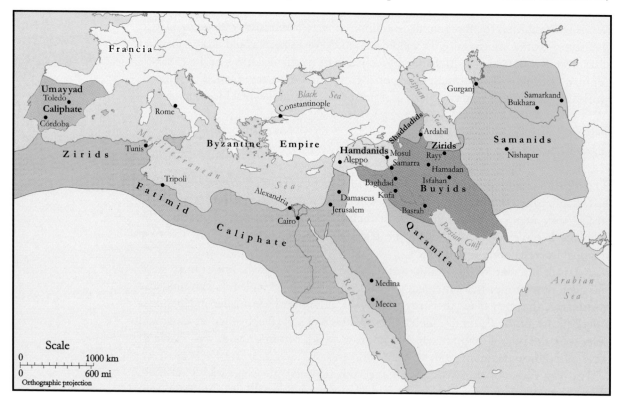

dominated the region south of the Caspian Sea, including Baghdad (once again the home of the caliphs) itself. Yet already by the end of the tenth century, their own power was challenged by still more local men, in a political process—the progressive regionalization and fragmentation of power—echoed elsewhere in the Islamic world and in parts of Western Europe as well.

The most important of the new regional rulers were the Fatimids. They, like the Qaramita (and, increasingly in the course of time, the Buyids), were Shi'ites, taking their name from Muhammad's daughter Fatimah, wife of Ali. The Fatimid leader claimed to be not only the true *imam*, descendant of Ali, but also the *mahdi*, the "divinely guided" messiah, come to bring justice on earth. Because of this, the Fatimids were proclaimed "caliphs" by their followers—the true "successors" of the Prophet. (See the list of Fatimid caliphs on p. 363.) Allying with the Berbers in North Africa, the Fatimids established themselves as rulers by 909 in what is today Tunisia and Libya. Within a half-century they had moved eastward (largely abandoning the Maghreb to the Zirids), to rule Egypt, southern Syria, and the western edge of the Arabian Peninsula.

The Fatimids looked east rather than west because the east was rich and because the west was dominated by Sunnis, hostile to Shi'ite rule. The most important of the Sunni rulers were the Umayyads at Córdoba. Abd al-Rahman III (r.912–961) took the title caliph in 929 as a counterweight to the Fatimids, although he claimed to rule only all of al-Andalus, not the whole Islamic world. An active military man backed by an army made up mainly of Slavic slaves, al-Rahman defeated his rivals and imposed his rule not only on southern Iberia (as his predecessors had done) but also in northern regions (near the Christian kingdoms) and in the Maghreb. Under al-Rahman and his immediate successors, al-Andalus became a powerful centralized state. But regional Islamic rulers there worked to undermine the authority of the Umayyads, so that between 1009 and 1031 bitter civil war undid the dynasty's power. After 1031, al-Andalus was split into small emirates called *taifas*, ruled by local strongmen.

Thus in the Islamic world, far more decisively than at Byzantium, newly powerful regional rulers came to the fore. Nor did the fragmentation of power end at the regional level. To pay their armies, rulers often resorted to granting their commanders *iqta*—lands and villages from which the *iqta*-holder was expected to gather revenues and pay their troops. As we shall see, this was a bit like the Western institution of the fief. It meant that even minor commanders could act as local governors, tax-collectors, and military leaders. But there was a major difference between this institution and the system of fiefs and vassals in the West: while vassals were generally tied to one region and one lord, the troops under Islamic local commanders were often foreigners and former slaves, unconnected to any particular place and easily wooed by rival commanders.

At Byzantium the ascendancy of the military classes led poets and artists to praise warriors in general. In the Islamic world as well, a few writers proudly portrayed old Persian and Bedouin heroes as model fighting men. In the *Shahnama* (*Book of Kings*) by the poet Firdawsi (*c.*935–*c.*1020), the hero slays demons and saves kings. But on the whole, poets and writers continued to laud "civilian" life and to embroider the old themes of *adab* literature.

Cultural Unity, Religious Polarization

In fact, the emergence of local strongmen meant not the end of Arab court culture but a multiplicity of courts, each attempting to out-do one another in brilliant artistic, scientific, theological, and literary productions. Consider Cairo, for example, which was founded by the Fatimids. Already by 1000 it was a huge urban complex. Imitating the Abbasids, the Fatimid caliphs built mosques and palaces, fostered court ceremonials, and turned Cairo into a center of intellectual life. One of the Fatimid caliphs, al-Hakim (*r.*996–1021), founded the *dar al-ilm*, a sort of theological college plus public library.

Even more impressive was the Umayyad court at Córdoba, the wealthiest and showiest city of the West. It boasted 70 public libraries in addition to the caliph's private library of perhaps 400,000 books. The Córdoban Great Mosque was a center for scholars from the rest of the Islamic world (the caliph paid their salaries), while nearly 30 free schools were set up throughout the city.

Córdoba was noteworthy not only because of the brilliance of its intellectual life but also because of the role women played in it. Elsewhere in the Islamic world there were certainly a few unusual women associated with cultural and scholarly life. But at Córdoba this was a general phenomenon: women not only were doctors, teachers, and librarians but also worked as copyists for the many books so widely in demand.

Male scholars were, however, everywhere the norm, and they moved easily from court to court. Ibn Sina (980–1037), known to the West as Avicenna, began his career serving the ruler at Bukhara in Central Asia, and then moved westward to Gurganj, Rayy, and Hamadan before ending up for thirteen years at the court of Isfahan in Iran. Sometimes in favor and sometimes decidedly not so (he was even briefly imprisoned), he nevertheless managed to study and practice medicine and write numerous books on the natural sciences and philosophy. His pioneering systematization of Aristotle laid the foundations of future philosophical thought in the field of logic:

> There is a method by which one can discover the unknown from what is known. It is the science of logic. Through it one may know how to obtain

the unknown from the known. This science is also concerned with the different kinds of valid, invalid, and near valid inferences.[5]

Despite its political disunity, then, the Islamic world of the tenth and eleventh centuries remained in many ways an integrated culture. This was partly due to the model of intellectual life fostered by the Abbasids, which even in decline was copied by the new rulers, as we have just seen. It was also due to the common Arabic language, the glue that bound the astronomer at Córdoba to the philosopher at Cairo. Finally, integration was the result of open trade networks. With no national barriers to commerce and few regulations, merchants regularly dealt in far-flung, various, and sometimes exotic goods. From England came tin, while salt and gold were imported from Timbuktu in west-central Africa; from Russia came amber, gold, and copper; slaves were wrested from sub-Saharan Africa, the Eurasian steppes, and Slavic regions.

Although Muslims dominated these trade networks, other groups were involved in commerce as well. We happen to know a good deal about one Jewish community living at Fustat, about two miles south of Cairo. It observed the then-common custom of depositing for eventual ritual burial all worn-out papers containing the name of God. For good measure, the Jews in this community included everything written in Hebrew letters: legal documents, fragments of sacred works, marriage contracts, doctors' prescriptions, and so on. By chance, the materials that they left in their *geniza* (depository) at Fustat were preserved rather than buried. These sources reveal a cosmopolitan, middle-class society. Many were traders, for Fustat was the center of a vast and predominately Jewish trade network that stretched from al-Andalus to India. Consider the Tustari brothers, Jewish merchants from southern Iran. By the early eleventh century, the brothers had established a flourishing business in Egypt. Informal family networks offered them many of the same advantages as branch offices: friends and family in Iran shipped the Tustaris fine textiles to sell in Egypt, while they exported Egyptian fabrics back to Iran.

Only Islam, ironically, pulled Islamic culture apart. In the tenth century the split between the Sunnis and Shi'ites widened to a chasm. At Baghdad, al-Mufid (*d.*1022) and others turned Shi'ism into a partisan ideology that insisted on publicly cursing the first two caliphs, turning the tombs of Ali and his family into objects of veneration, and creating an Alid caliph by force. Small wonder that the Abbasid caliphs soon became ardent spokesmen for Sunni Islam, which developed in turn its own public symbols. Many of the new dynasties — the Fatimids and the Qaramita especially — took advantage of the newly polarized faith to bolster their power.

THE WEST: FRAGMENTATION AND RESILIENCE

Fragmentation was the watchword in Western Europe in many parts of the shattered Carolingian Empire. Historians speak of "France," "Germany," and "Italy" in this period as a shorthand for designating broad geographical areas. But there were no national states, only regions with more or less clear borders and rulers with more or less authority. In some places—in parts of "France," for example—regions as small as a few square miles were under the control of different lords who acted, in effect, as independent rulers. Yet this same period saw both England and Scotland become unified kingdoms. And to the east, in Saxony, a powerful royal dynasty, the Ottonians, emerged to rule an empire stretching from the North Sea to Rome.

Map 4.5 (facing page): Viking, Muslim, and Hungarian Invasions, Ninth and Tenth Centuries

The Last Invaders of the West

Three groups invaded Western Europe during the ninth and tenth centuries: the Vikings, the Muslims, and the Magyars (called Hungarians by the rest of Europe). (See Map 4.5.) In the short run, they wreaked havoc on land and people. In the long run, they were absorbed into the European population and became constituents of a newly prosperous and aggressive European civilization.

THE VIKINGS

At the same time as they made their forays into Russia, the Vikings were raiding the coasts of France, England, Scotland, and Ireland. In their longships—often traveling as families with husbands, wives, children, and slaves—they crossed the Atlantic, making themselves at home in Iceland and Greenland and, in about 1000, touching on the North American mainland. They settled as well in Ireland, Scotland, England, and Normandy (giving their name to the region: Norman = Northman, or Viking).

In Ireland, where the Vikings settled in the east and south, the newcomers added their own claims to rule an island already fragmented among four or five competing dynasties. In Scotland, however, in the face of Norse settlements in the north and west, the natives drew together under kings who—in a process we have seen elsewhere—allied themselves with churchmen and other powerful local leaders. Cináed mac Ailpín (Kenneth I MacAlpin) (*d*.858) established a hereditary dynasty of kings that ruled over two hitherto separate native peoples. By *c*.900, the separate identities were gone, and most people in *Alba*, the nucleus of the future Scotland, shared a common sense of being Scottish.

England underwent a similar process of unification. Initially divided into small

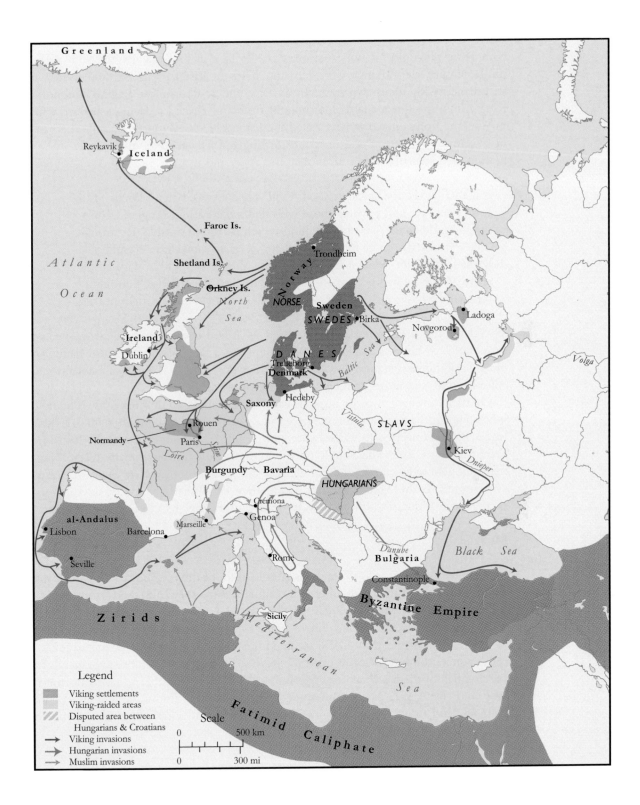

Greenland

Reykavik • **Iceland**

Atlantic

Ocean

Faroe Is.

Shetland Is.

Orkney Is.
*North
Sea*

Ireland

Dublin •

Norway

Trondheim

NORSE

Sweden

SWEDES • Birka

• Ladoga

Novgorod •

Volga

D A N E S

Trelleborg
Denmark

*Baltic
Sea*

Saxony

• Hedeby

S L A V S

Rouen

Normandy

Paris •

Seine

Loire

Kiev •

Dnieper

Burgundy   **Bavaria**

HUNGARIANS

al-Andalus

• Lisbon

Barcelona •

Marseille •

Cremona •

Genoa •

• Rome

Vistula

Danube

Bulgaria

Black   Sea

• Seville

Constantinople •

Byzantine   Empire

Z i r i d s

Sicily

Mediterranean

Sea

F a t i m i d   C a l i p h a t e

Legend

■ Viking settlements

▨ Viking-raided areas

▨ Disputed area between
    Hungarians & Croatians

→ Viking invasions

→ Hungarian invasions

→ Muslim invasions

Scale

0 ┤─┼─┼─┼─┤ 500 km

0 ┤──┼──┼──┤ 300 mi

competing kingdoms, it was weak prey in the face of invasion. By the end of the ninth century, the Vikings were plowing fields in eastern England and living in accordance with their own laws. In Wessex, the southernmost English kingdom, King Alfred the Great (r.871–899) bought time and peace by paying a tribute with the income from a new tax, later called the Danegeld. (It eventually became the basis of a relatively lucrative taxation system in England.) Even more importantly, in 878 he mustered an army and, as his biographer, Asser, put it,

> gained the victory through God's will. He destroyed the Vikings with great slaughter, and pursued those who fled as far as the stronghold, hacking them down; he seized everything which he found outside the stronghold—men (whom he killed immediately), horses, and cattle—and boldly made camp in front of the gates of the Viking stronghold with all his army. When he had been there for fourteen days the Vikings, thoroughly terrified by hunger, cold and fear, and in the end by despair, sought peace.[6]

Thereafter the pressure of invasion eased as Alfred reorganized his army, set up strongholds of his own (called *burhs*), and created a fleet of ships—a real navy. An uneasy stability was achieved, with the Vikings dominating the east of England and Alfred and his successors gaining control over most of the rest.

On the Continent, too, the invaders came to stay, above all in Normandy. The new inhabitants of the region were integrated into the political system when, in 911, their leader Rollo converted to Christianity and received Normandy as a duchy from the Frankish king Charles the Simple (or Straightforward). Although many of the Normans adopted sedentary ways, some of their descendants in the early eleventh century ventured to the Mediterranean, where they established themselves as rulers of petty principalities in southern Italy. By mid-century they had their eyes on Sicily.

MUSLIMS

Sicily, once Byzantine, was the rich and fertile plum of the conquests achieved by the Muslim invaders of the ninth and tenth centuries. That they took the island attests to the power of a new Muslim navy developed by the dynasty that preceded the Fatimids in Ifriqiya. After 909, Sicily came under Fatimid rule, but by mid-century it was controlled by independent Islamic princes, and Muslim immigrants were swelling the population.

Elsewhere the new Muslim presence in western Europe was more ephemeral. In the first half of the tenth century, Muslim raiders pillaged southern France, northern Italy, and the Alpine passes. But these were quick expeditions, largely attacks on churches and monasteries. Some of these Muslims did establish themselves at La

Garde-Freinet, in Provence, becoming landowners in the region and lords of Christian serfs. They even hired themselves out as occasional fighters for the wars that local Christian aristocrats were waging against one another. But they made the mistake of capturing for ransom the holiest man of his era, Abbot Majolus of Cluny. Outraged, the local aristocracy finally came together and ousted the Muslims from their midst.

HUNGARIANS

By contrast, a new kingdom was created by the Hungarians. ("Magyar" was and remains their name for themselves, but the rest of Europe called them "Hungarians," from the Slavonic for "Onogurs," a people already settled in the Danube basin in the eighth and ninth centuries.) The Hungarians were originally nomads who raised (and rode) horses, speaking a language unrelated to any other in Europe (except Finnish). Known as effective warriors, they were employed by Arnulf, king of the East Franks (887-899), during his war against the Moravians and by the Byzantine emperor Leo VI (886-912) during his struggle against the Bulgars. In 894, taking advantage of their position, the Hungarians conquered much of the Danube basin for themselves.

From there, for over fifty years, the Hungarians raided into Germany, Italy, and even southern France. At the same time, however, they worked for various western rulers. Until 937 they spared Bavaria, for example, because they were allies of its duke. Gradually they made the transition from nomads to farmers, and their polity coalesced into the Kingdom of Hungary. This is no doubt a major reason for the end of their attacks. At the time, however, the cessation of their raids was widely credited to the German king Otto I (r.936-973), who won a major victory over a Hungarian marauding party at the battle of Lechfeld in 955.

Polytheists at the time of their entry into the West, the majority of the Hungarians were peasants, initially specializing in herding but soon busy cultivating vineyards, orchards, and grains. Above them was a warrior class, and above the warriors were the elites, whose richly furnished graves reveal the importance of weapons, jewelry, and horses to this society. Originally organized into tribes led by dukes, by the mid-tenth century the Hungarians recognized one ruling house — that of Géza.

Determined to put his power on a new footing, Géza accepted baptism, probably by a bishop from Germany, and pledged to convert all his subjects. His son, Stephen I, consolidated the change to Christianity: he built churches and monasteries, and required everyone to attend church on Sundays. Establishing his authority as sole ruler, Stephen had himself crowned king in the year 1000 (or possibly 1001). Around the same time, "governing our monarchy by the will of God and emulating both ancient and modern caesars [emperors]," he issued a code of law that put his kingdom in step with other European powers.[7]

Public Power and Private Relationships

The invasions left new political arrangements in their wake. Unlike the Byzantines and Muslims, Western rulers had no mercenaries and no salaried officials. They commanded others by ensuring personal loyalty. The Carolingian kings had had their *fideles*—their faithful men. Tenth-century rulers were even more dependent on ties of dependency: they needed their "men" (*homines*), their "vassals" (*vassalli*). Whatever the term, all were armed retainers who fought for a lord. Sometimes these subordinates held land from their lord, either as a reward for their military service or as an inheritance for which services were due. The term for such an estate, fief (*feodum*), gave historians the word "feudalism" to describe the social and economic system created by the relationships among lords, vassals, and fiefs. Some recent historians argue that the word "feudalism" has been used in too many different and contradictory ways to mean anything at all: is it a mode of exploiting the land that involves lords and serfs? A state of anarchy and lawlessness? Or a state of ordered gradations of power, from the king on down? All of these definitions have been given. Ordinarily we may dispense with the word feudalism, though it can be very useful as a "fuzzy category" when contrasting, for example, the political, social, and economic organization of Antiquity with that of the Middle Ages.

Lords and Vassals

The key to tenth- and eleventh-century society was personal dependency. This took many forms. Of the three traditional "orders" recognized by writers in the ninth through eleventh centuries—those who pray (the *oratores*), those who fight (the *bellatores*), and those who work (the *laboratores*)—the top two were free. The pray-ers (the monks) and the fighters (the nobles and their lower-class cousins, the knights) participated in prestigious kinds of subordination, whether as vassals, lords, or both. Indeed, they were usually both: a typical warrior was lord of several vassals and the vassal of another lord. Monasteries normally had vassals to fight for them, while their abbots in turn were vassals of a king or other lord. At the low end of the social scale, poor vassals looked to their lords to feed, clothe, house, and arm them. At the upper end, vassals looked to their lords to enrich them with still more fiefs.

Some women were vassals, and some were lords (or, rather, "ladies," the female counterpart). Many upper-class laywomen participated in the society of warriors and monks as wives and mothers of vassals and lords and as landowners in their own right. Others entered convents and became *oratores* themselves. Through its abbess or a man standing in for her, a convent was itself often the "lord" of vassals.

Vassalage was voluntary and public. In some areas, it was marked by a ceremony:

the vassal-to-be knelt and, placing his hands between the hands of his lord, said, "I promise to be your man." This act, known as "homage," was followed by the promise of "fealty"—fidelity, trust, and service—which the vassal swore with his hand on relics or a Bible. Then the vassal and the lord kissed. In an age when many people could not read, a public moment such as this represented a visual and verbal contract, binding the vassal and lord together with mutual obligations to help one another. On the other hand, these obligations were rarely spelled out, and a lord with many vassals, or a vassal with many lords, needed to satisfy numerous conflicting claims. "I am a loser only because of my loyalty to you," Hugh of Lusignan told his lord, William of Aquitaine, after his expectations for reward were continually disappointed.[8]

LORDS AND PEASANTS

At the lowest end of the social scale were those who worked: the peasants. In many regions of Europe, as power fell into the hands of local rulers, the distinction between "free" and "unfree" peasants began to blur; many peasants simply became "serfs," dependents of lords. This was a heavy dependency, without prestige or honor. It was hereditary rather than voluntary: no serf did homage or fealty to his lord; no serf and lord kissed.

Indeed, the upper classes barely noticed the peasants—except as sources of labor and revenue. In the tenth century, the three-field system became more prevalent, and the heavy moldboard plows that could turn wet, clayey northern soils came into wider use. Such plows could not work around fences, and they were hard to turn: thus was produced the characteristic "look" of medieval agriculture—long, furrowed strips in broad, open fields. (Peasants knew very well which strips were "theirs" and which belonged to their neighbors. See the late medieval lands of Toury in Map 7.7 on p. 298.) A team of oxen was normally used to pull the plow, but horses (more efficient than oxen) were sometimes substituted. The result was surplus food and a better standard of living for nearly everyone.

In search of still greater profits, some lords lightened the dues and services of peasants temporarily to allow them to open up new lands by draining marshes and cutting down forests. Other lords converted dues and labor services into money payments, providing themselves with ready cash. Peasants benefited from these rents as well because their payments were fixed despite inflation. As the prices of agricultural products went up, peasants became small-scale entrepreneurs, selling their chickens and eggs at local markets and reaping a profit.

In the eleventh century, and increasingly so in the twelfth, peasant settlements gained boundaries and focus: they became real villages. (For the example of Toury, see Map 7.6 on p. 297.) The parish church often formed the center, around which was the cemetery. Then, normally crowded right onto the cemetery itself, were the houses, barns, animals, and tools of the living peasants. Boundary markers—sometimes simple stones, at other times real fortifications—announced not only the physical limit of the village but also its sense of community. This derived from very practical concerns: peasants needed to share oxen or horses to pull their plows; they were all dependent on the village craftsmen to fix their wheels or shoe their horses.

Variety was the hallmark of peasant society for this period of history across the regions of Europe. In Saxony and other parts of Germany free peasants prevailed. In France and England most were serfs. In Italy peasants ranged from small independent landowners to leaseholders; most were both, owning a parcel in one place and leasing another nearby.

Where the power of kings was weak, peasant obligations became part of a larger system of local rule. As landlords consolidated their power over their manors, they collected not only dues and services but also fees for the use of their flour mills, bake houses, and breweries. In some regions—parts of France and in Catalonia, for example—some lords built castles and exercised the power of the "ban": the right to collect taxes, hear court cases, levy fines, and muster men for defense. These lords were "castellans." Guillem Guifred, a castellan in Catalonia (and a bishop, too, for good measure), for example, received "half of the revenue of the courts [at Sanahuja], without deceit. From the market, half.... Of the oven, half. Of rights on minting, half."[9]

WARRIORS AND BISHOPS

Although the developments described here did not occur everywhere simultaneously (and in some places hardly at all), in the end the social, political, and cultural life of the West came to be dominated by landowners who saw themselves as both military men and regional leaders. These men and their armed retainers shared a common lifestyle, living together, eating in the lord's great hall, listening to bards sing of military exploits, hunting for recreation, competing with one another in military games. They fought in groups as well—as cavalry, riding on horses. In the month of May, when the grasses were high enough for their mounts to forage, the war season began. To be sure, there were powerful vassals who lived on their own fiefs and hardly ever saw their lord—except for perhaps forty days out of the year, when they owed him military duty. But they themselves were lords of knightly vassals who were not married and who lived and ate and hunted with them.

The marriage bed, so important to the medieval aristocracy from the start, now took on new meaning. Long before, in the seventh and eighth centuries, aristocratic families had been large, diffuse, loosely organized kin groups. (Historians often use the German word *Sippe*—clan—to refer to them.) These families were not tied to any particular estate, for they had numerous estates, scattered all about. With wealth enough to go around, the rich practiced partible inheritance, giving land (though not in equal amounts) to all of their sons and daughters. The Carolingians "politicized" these family relations. As some men were elevated to positions of dazzling power, they took the opportunity to pick and choose their "family members," narrowing the family circle. They also became more conscious of their male line, favoring sons over daughters. In the eleventh century, family definitions tightened even further. The claims of one son, often the eldest, overrode all else; to him went the family inheritance. (This is called "primogeniture"; but there were regions in which the youngest son was privileged, and there were also areas in which more equitable inheritance practices continued in place.) The heir in the new system traced his lineage only through the male line, backward through his father and forward through his own eldest son.

What happened to the other sons? Some of them became knights, others monks. Nor should we forget that some became bishops. In many ways the interests of bishops and lay nobles were similar: they were men of property, lords of vassals, and faithful to patrons, such as kings, who appointed them to their posts. In some cities, bishops wielded the powers of a count or duke. We have seen that Bishop Guillem Guifred was a castellan at Sanahuja—and that was only one of his properties. Nevertheless, bishops were also "pastors," spiritual leaders charged with shepherding their flock. The "flock" included the priests and monks in the diocese, a district that gained clear definition in the eleventh century. The flock also included the laity, among them the very warriors from whose class the bishops came.

As episcopal power expanded and was clarified in the course of the eleventh century, some bishops in southern France sought to control the behavior of the knightly class through a movement called the "Peace of God," which developed apace from 989 onwards. Their forum was the regional church council, where the bishops galvanized popular opinion, attracting both lords and peasants to their gatherings. There, drawing upon bits and pieces of defunct Carolingian legislation, the bishops declared the Peace, and knights took oaths to observe it. At Bourges a particularly enthusiastic archbishop took the oath himself: "I Aimon ... will wholeheartedly attack those who steal ecclesiastical property, those who provoke pillage, those who oppress monks, nuns, and clerics."[10] In the Truce of God, which soon supplemented the Peace, warfare between armed men was prohibited from Lent to Easter, while at other times of the year it was forbidden on Sunday (because that was the Lord's Day), on Saturday (because that was a reminder of Holy Saturday), on Friday (because it symbolized Good Friday), and on Thursday (because it stood for Holy Thursday).

The bishops who promulgated the Peace were ambivalent about warriors. There were the bad ones who broke the Peace, but there were also others who were righteous upholders of church law. Soon the Peace and Truce were taken up by powerful lay rulers, eager to sanctify their own warfare and control that of others.

The new importance of the fighting man in the West gave rise to a military ethos mirrored in art and literature. In *The Battle of Maldon* the hero, Byrhtnoth, inspires the English to face the Danes:

> Then Byrhtnoth began to martial his men.
> He rode about, issuing instructions
> As to how they should stand firm, not yielding an inch,
> And how they should tightly grip their shields
> Forgetting their qualms and pangs of fear.[11]

The parallels with developments in the Byzantine and Islamic worlds are striking: everywhere a military class, more or less local, rose to power.

Equally important, however, are the differences: in no place but Europe were overlapping lordships the rule. Nowhere else was fealty so important. Nowhere else were rural enclaves the normal centers of power.

CITIES AND MERCHANTS

Though ruralism was the norm in the West, it was not invariable. In Italy the power structure reflected, if feebly, the political organization of ancient Rome. Whereas in France great landlords built their castles in the countryside, in Italy they often constructed their family seats within the walls of cities. From these perches the nobles, both lay and religious, dominated the *contado*, the rural area around the city.

In Italy, most peasants were renters, paying cash to urban landowners. Peasants depended on city markets to sell their surplus goods; their customers were not only bishops and nobles but also middle-class shopkeepers, artisans, and merchants. At Milan, for example, the merchants were prosperous enough to own houses in both the city center and the *contado*.

Rome, although exceptional in size, was in some ways a typical Italian city. Large and powerful families built their castles within its walls and controlled the churches and monasteries in the vicinity. The population depended on local producers for their food, and merchants brought their wares to sell within its walls. Yet Rome was special apart from its size: it was the "see"—the seat—of the pope, the most important bishop in the West. The papacy did not control the church, but it had great prestige, and powerful families at Rome fought to place one of their sons at its head.

Outside of Italy cities were less prevalent in the West. Yet even so we can see the rise of a new mercantile class. This was true less in the heartland of the old Carolingian empire than on its fringes. In the north, England, northern Germany, Denmark, and the Low Countries bathed in a sea of silver coins; commercial centers such as

Haithabu reached their grandest extent in the mid-tenth century. Here merchants bought and sold slaves, honey, furs, wax, and pirates' plunder. Haithabu was a city of wood, but a very rich one indeed.

In the south of Europe, beyond the Pyrenees, Catalonia was equally commercialized, but in a different way. It imitated the Islamic world of al-Andalus (which was, in effect, in its backyard). The counts of Barcelona minted gold coins just like those at Córdoba. The villagers around Barcelona soon got used to selling their wares for money, and some of them became prosperous. They married into the aristocracy, moved to Barcelona to become city leaders, and lent money to ransom prisoners of the many wars waged to their south.

New-style Kingships

In such a world, what did kings do? At the least, they stood for tradition; they served as symbols of legitimacy. At the most, they united kingdoms and maintained a measure of law and order. (See Map 4.6.)

ENGLAND

Alfred was a king of the second sort. In the face of the Viking invasions, he developed new mechanisms of royal government, creating institutions that became the foundation of strong English kingship. We have already seen his military reforms: the system of *burhs* and the creation of a navy. Alfred was interested in religious and intellectual reforms as well. These were closely linked in his mind: the causes of England's troubles (in his view) were the sins—many due to ignorance—of its people. Alfred intended to educate "all free-born men." He brought scholars to his court and embarked on an ambitious program to translate key religious works from Latin into Anglo-Saxon (or Old English). This was the vernacular, the spoken language of the people. As Alfred wrote in his prose preface to the Anglo-Saxon translation of *The Pastoral Care* of Gregory the Great,

> I recalled how the Law was first composed in the Hebrew language, and thereafter, when the Greeks learned it, they translated it all into their own language, and all other books as well. And so too the Romans, after they had mastered them, translated them all through learned interpreters into their own language.... Therefore it seems better to me ... that we too should turn into the language that we can all understand certain books which are the most necessary for all men to know.[12]

Scale

0 _____ 500 km

0 _____ 300 mi

N o r t h

S e a

N O R W A Y

S w e d e n

Baltic

Sea

Scotland

Denmark

• Haithabu

Ireland

• Durham

England

Wales

P o l a n d

Atlantic

Ocean

London •

Saxony

Magdeburg •

Frisia

Lower

Lotharingia

Hildesheim •

Cologne •

G E R M A N

Montreuil
Ponthieu

Flanders

Picardy

Vermandois

Beauvais

Normandy **Vexin**

Franconia

Trier

Upper

Lotharingia

Worms •

B o h e m i a

Moravia

Brittany

Maine

Paris •

Ile-de-France

Blois

Troyes

Gatinais

Auxerre •

K i n g d o m

Swabia

Bavaria

Anjou

Touraine

Nevers •

Autun •

Alsace

H u n g a r y

Bourges •

Burgundy

Châteauroux •

Cluny •

Carinthia

Aquitaine

Auvergne

Kingdom

of

Burgundy

I t a l y

Venice •

Venice

C r o a t i a

Adriatic

Sea

Gevaudan

Santiago de Compostela •

Gascony

Toulouse

Marseille •

Pisa •

Patrimony
of St Peter

Spoleto

B y z a n t i n e

Doclea

León

Navarre

Aragon

Castile

Barcelona

Barcelona •

Corsica
(Pisan
*c.*1020)

Rome •

South Italian
principalities

E m p i r e

I s l a m i c

T a i f a s

Sardinia
(Pisan
*c.*1050)

Córdoba •

M e d i t e r r a n e a n

S e a

Those "certain books" included the Psalter and writings by the Church Fathers—Gregory the Great and Saint Augustine—as well as Boethius. Soon Anglo-Saxon was being used in England not only for literature but for official administrative purposes as well, in royal "writs" that kings and queens directed to their officials. England was not alone in its esteem for the vernacular: in Ireland, too, the vernacular language was a written one. But the British Isles *were* unusual by the standards of Continental Europe, where Latin alone was the language of scholarship and writing.

As Alfred harried the Danes who were pushing south and westward, he gained recognition as king of all the English not under Viking rule. His law code, issued in the late 880s or early 890s, was the first by an English king since 695. Unlike earlier codes, which had been drawn up for each separate kingdom, Alfred's contained laws from and for all the English kingdoms in common. The king's inspiration was the Mosaic law of the Bible. Alfred believed that God had made a new covenant with the victors over the Vikings; as leader of his people, Alfred, like the Old Testament patriarch Moses, should issue a law for all.

Map 4.6 (facing page): Europe, *c.* 1050

His successors, beneficiaries of that covenant, rolled back the Viking rule in England. (See Genealogy 4.1: Alfred and His Progeny.) "Then the Norsemen made off in their nailed boats,/ Saddened survivors shamed in battle," wrote one poet about a battle lost by the Vikings in 937.[13] But, as we have seen, many Vikings remained. Converted to Christianity, their great men joined Anglo-Saxons to attend the English king at court. The whole kingdom was divided into districts called "shires" and "hundreds," and in each shire, the king's reeve—the sheriff—oversaw royal administration.

Alfred's grandson Edgar (*r.c.*959-975) commanded all the possibilities early medieval kingship offered. The sworn lord of all the great men of the kingdom, he also controlled appointments to the English church and sponsored monastic reform. In 973, following the Continental fashion, he was anointed. Master of *burhs* and army, Edgar asserted hegemony over many of the non-Anglo-Saxon rulers in Britain. He extended Alfred's legal reforms by proclaiming certain crimes—arson and theft—to be under royal jurisdiction.

From the point of view of control, however, Edgar had nowhere near the power over England that, say, Basil II had over Byzantium at about the same time. The *dynatoi* might sometimes chafe at the emperor's directives and rebel, but the emperor had his Varangian guard to put them down and an experienced, professional civil service to do his bidding. The king of England depended less on force and bureaucracy than on consensus. The great landowners adhered to the king because they found it in their interest to do so. When they did not, the kingdom easily fragmented, becoming prey to civil war. Disunity was exacerbated by new attacks from the Danes. One Danish king, Cnut (or Canute), even became king of England for a time (*r.*1016-1035). Yet under Cnut, English kingship did not change much. He kept intact much of the administrative, ecclesiastical, and military apparatus already established. By Cnut's time, Scandinavia had been Christianized and its traditions had largely merged with those of the rest of Europe. The Vikings were no longer an alien culture.

GERMANY

The king of Germany was as effective as the English king—and additionally worked with a much wider palette of territories, institutions, and possibilities. It is true that at first Germany seemed ready to disintegrate into duchies: five emerged in the late Carolingian period, each held by a military leader who exercised quasi-royal powers. But, in the face of their own quarrels and the threats of outside invaders, the dukes needed and wanted a strong king. With the death in 911 of the last Carolingian king in Germany, Louis the Child, they crowned one of themselves. Then, as attacks by the Hungarians increased, the dukes gave the royal title to their most powerful member,

Genealogy 4.1: Alfred and His Progeny

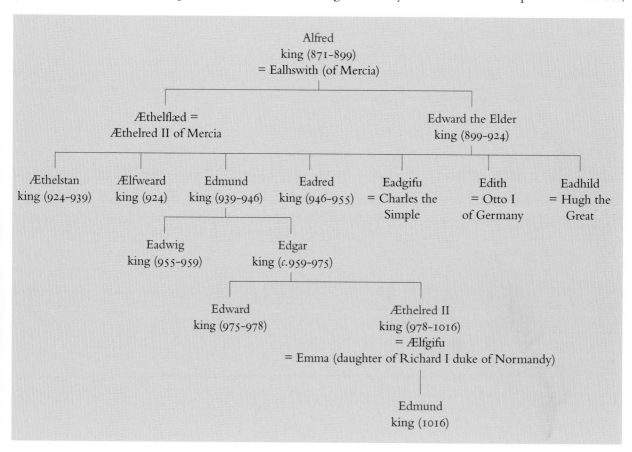

the duke of Saxony, Henry I (r.919-936), who proceeded to set up fortifications and reorganize his army, crowning his efforts with a major defeat of the Hungarians in 933.

Henry's son Otto I (r.936-973) defeated rival family members, rebellious dukes, and Slavic and Hungarian armies soon after coming to the throne. Through astute marriage alliances and appointments, he was eventually able to get his family members to head up all of the duchies. In 951, Otto marched into Italy and took the Lombard crown. He was thus king of Germany and Italy, and soon (in 962) he received the imperial crown that recognized his far-flung power. Both to himself and to contemporaries he recalled the greatness of Charlemagne. Meanwhile, Otto's victory at Lechfeld in 955 (see p. 155) ended the Hungarian threat. In the same year, Otto defeated a Slavic incursion, and for about a half-century the Slavs of central and eastern Europe came under German hegemony.

Victories such as these brought tribute, plum positions to disburse, and lands to give away, ensuring Otto a following among the great men of the realm. His successors,

Genealogy 4.2: The Ottonians

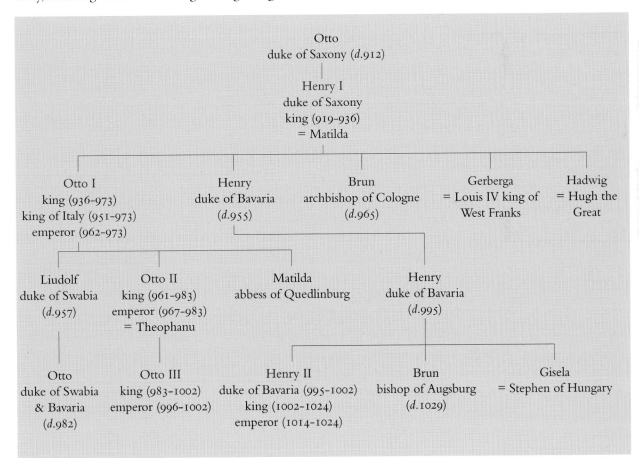

Otto II, Otto III—hence the dynastic name "Ottonians"—and Henry II, built on his achievements. (See Genealogy 4.2: The Ottonians.) Granted power by the magnates, they gave back in turn: they gave away lands and appointed their aristocratic supporters to duchies, counties, and bishoprics. Always, however, their decisions were tempered by hereditary claims and plenty of lobbying by influential men at court and at the great assemblies that met with the king to hammer out policies. The role of kings in filling bishoprics and archbishoprics was particularly important because, unlike counties and duchies, these positions could not be inherited. Otto I created a ribbon of new bishoprics in newly converted regions along his eastern border, endowing them with extensive lands and subjecting the local peasantry to episcopal overlordship. Throughout Germany bishops gained the power of the ban, with the right to collect revenues and call men to arms. Once the king chose the bishop (usually with at least the consent of the clergy of the cathedral over which he was to preside), he "invested" the new prelate in his post by participating in the ceremony that installed him into office. Bishop Thietmar of Merseburg, for example, reported on his own experience:

Plate 4.1 (facing page): The Raising of Lazarus, Egbert Codex (977-993). This miniature is one of 51 gospel illustrations in a Pericopes, a book of readings arranged for the liturgical year. The story of the Raising of Lazarus, which is recounted in John 11:1-45, is read during the week before Easter. Of the many elements of this story, the artist chose a few important moments, arranging them into a unified scene.

> The archbishop [Tagino of Magdeburg, Thietmar's sponsor] led me to Bishop Bruno's chapel [Bruno was the king's brother], where the king [Henry II] awaited him. After preparing for the celebration of the mass, he commended me into the hands of the king. I was elected by those who were present, and the king committed the pastoral office to me with the staff.[14]

With wealth coming in from their eastern tributaries, Italy, and the silver mines of Saxony (discovered in the time of Otto I), the Ottonians presided over a brilliant intellectual and artistic efflorescence. As in the Islamic world, much of this was dispersed; in Germany the centers of culture included the royal court, the great cathedral schools, and women's convents.

The most talented young men crowded the schools at episcopal courts at Trier, Cologne, Magdeburg, Worms, and Hildesheim. Honing their Latin, they studied classical authors such as Cicero and Horace as well as Scripture, while their episcopal teachers wrote histories, saints' lives, and works on canon law. One such was the *Decretum* (*c.*1020) by Burchard, bishop of Worms, a widely influential collection that (much like the compilations of *hadith* produced about a century before in the Islamic world) winnowed out the least authoritative canons and systematized the contradictory ones. The men at the cathedral schools were largely in training to become courtiers, administrators, and bishops themselves.

Bishops appreciated art as well as scholarship. Some, such as Egbert, archbishop of Trier (*r.*977-993), patronized artists and fine craftsworkers. Plate 4.1, an illustration of the Raising of Lazarus from the Egbert Codex (named for its patron) is a good example of

Plate 4.2: Christ Asleep, Hitda Gospels (*c*.1000–1020). The moral of the story (which is told in Matt. 8:23–26) is right in the picture: as the apostles look anxiously toward the mast to save them from the stormy sea, one (in the exact center) turns to rouse the sleeping Christ, the real Savior.

what is called the "Ottonian style" at the end of the tenth century. Drawing above all on the art of the late antique "Renaissance" (see p. 40 and Plate 1.9 of volume 1) nevertheless, the Egbert Codex artists achieved an effect all their own. Utterly unafraid of open space, which was rendered in otherworldly pastel colors, their focus was on the figures, who gesture like actors on a stage. In Plate 4.1 the apostles are on the left-hand side, their arms raised and hands wide open with wonder at Christ. He has just raised the dead Lazarus from the tomb, and one of the Jews, on the right, holds his nose. Two women—Mary and Martha, the sisters of Lazarus—fall at Christ's feet, completing the dramatic tableau.

At around the same time, in convents that provided them with comfortable private apartments, noblewomen were writing books and (in the case of Hrotsvitha of Gandersheim) Roman-style plays. Ottonian noblewomen also supported other artists and scholars. Plate 4.2 is from a manuscript made at Cologne between c.1000 and c.1020 for Abbess Hitda of Meschede. It draws on Byzantine and Carolingian models as well as the palette of the Egbert Codex to produce a calm Christ, asleep during a wild storm on the Sea of Galilee that ruffles the sails of the ship and seems to toss it into sheer air. The marriage of Otto II to a Byzantine princess, Theophanu, helps account for the Byzantine influence.

Among the most active patrons of the arts were the Ottonian kings themselves. In a Gospel book made for Otto III—a work fit for royal consumption—the full achievement of Ottonian culture is made clear. Plate 4.3 shows one of 29 full-page miniatures in this manuscript, whose binding alone—set with countless gems around a Byzantine carved ivory—was worth a fortune. The figure of the evangelist Luke emerges from a pure gold-leaf background, while the purple of his dress and the columns that frame him recall imperial majesty. At the same time, Luke is clearly of another world, and his Gospels have here become a theological vision.

FRANCE

By contrast with the English and German kings, those in France had a hard time coping with invasions. Unlike the English kings, who started small and built slowly, the French kings had half an empire to defend. Unlike the Ottonians, who asserted their military prowess in decisive battles such as the one at Lechfeld, the French kings generally had to let local men both take the brunt of the attacks and reap the prestige and authority that came with military leadership. Nor did the French kings have the advantage of Germany's tributaries, silver mines, or Italian connections. Much like the Abbasid caliphs at Baghdad, the kings of France saw their power wane. During most of the tenth century, Carolingian kings alternated on the throne with kings from a family that would later be called the "Capetians." At the end of that century

EONE PATRU DUCTAS BOS AGNIS ELICIT UNDA

SEEING THE MIDDLE AGES

Plate 4.3 (facing page):
Saint Luke, Gospel Book of Otto III (998–1001)

This is a complicated picture. How can we tease out its meaning? We know that the main subject is the evangelist Saint Luke, first because this illustration precedes the text of the Gospel of Saint Luke in the manuscript, and second because of the presence of the ox (who is labeled "Luc"). Compare Plate 2.4 on p. 91 of volume 1, which shows the same symbol and also includes the label "Agios Lucas"— Saint Luke. In that plate, Luke is writing his gospel. Here Luke is doing something different. But what?

An important hint is at the bottom of the page: the Latin inscription there says, "From the fountain of the Fathers, the ox draws water for the lambs." So Luke (the ox) draws water, or nourishment, from the Fathers for the "lambs," who are in fact shown drinking from the stream. Who are the lambs? In the same manuscript, the page depicting the evangelist Saint Matthew, which precedes his own Gospel, shows men, rather than lambs, drinking from the streams: clearly the lambs signify the Christian people.

Above Luke's head are the "Fathers." They are five of the Old Testament prophets, each provided with a label; the one to Luke's right, for example, is "Abacuc"— Habakkuk. Behind each prophet is an angel (David, at the very top, is accompanied by two), and each is surrounded by a cloud of glory, giving off rays of light that appear like forks jutting into the sky. The artist was no doubt thinking of Paul's Epistle to the Hebrews (12:1) where, after naming the great Old Testament prophets and their trials and tribulations, Paul calls them a "cloud of witnesses over our head" who help us to overcome our sins. But the artist must also have had in mind Christ's Second Coming, when, according to Apoc. 4:2–3, Christ will be seated on a "throne set in heaven" with "a rainbow round about the throne." In our plate, Luke sits in the place of Christ.

Thus this picture shows the unity of the Gospel of Luke with both the Old Testament and the final book of the Bible, the Apocalypse. Luke is the continuator and the guardian of the prophets, whose books are piled on his lap.

There is more. The figure of Luke forms the bottom half of a cross, with the ox in the center. The lamb and the ox were both sacrificial animals, signifying Christ himself, whose death on the cross redeemed mankind. Thus Luke not only "draws water for the lambs" from the Fathers, but he prefigures the Second Coming of Christ himself, the moment of salvation. The mandorla—the oval "halo" that surrounds him—was frequently used to portray Christ in glory.

Why would Emperor Otto III want to own a Gospel book of such theological sophistication? It is very likely because he saw *himself* as part of the divine order. He called himself the "servant of Jesus Christ," and he appears in one manuscript within a mandorla, just like Luke. (See the illustration below.) In this depiction, the symbols of the evangelists hold up the scarf of heaven that bisects the emperor: his feet touch the ground (note the cringing figure of Earth holding him up), while his head touches the cross of Christ, whose hand places a crown on his head.

Otto III Enthroned, Aachen Gospels (c.996).
Otto III saw himself—much like Christ (and Luke)— as mediating between the people and God.

Further Reading
Mayr-Hartung, Henry. *Ottonian Book Illumination: An Historical Study*. 2nd rev. ed. London, 1999.
Nees, Lawrence. *Early Medieval Art*. Oxford, 2002.

the most powerful men of the realm, seeking to stave off civil war, elected Hugh Capet (r.987-996) as their king. The Carolingians were displaced, and the Capetians continued on the throne until the fourteenth century. (See Genealogy 5.4: The Capetian Kings of France, on p. 202.)

The Capetians' scattered but substantial estates lay in the north of France, in the region around Paris. Here the kings had their vassals and their castles. This "Ile-de-France" (which was all there was to "France" in the period; see Map 4.6) was indeed an "island," surrounded by independent castellans. In the sense that he, too, had little more military power than a castellan, Hugh Capet and his eleventh-century successors were similar to local strongmen. But the Capetian kings had the prestige of their office. Anointed with holy oil, they represented the idea of unity and God-given rule inherited from Charlemagne. Most of the counts and dukes — at least those in the north of France — swore homage and fealty to the king, a gesture, however weak, of personal support. Unlike the German kings, the French could rely on vassalage to bind the great men of the realm to them.

★   ★   ★   ★

Political fragmentation did not mean chaos. It simply betokened a new order. At Byzantium, in any event, even the most centrifugal forces were focused on the center; the real trouble for Basil II, for example, came from *dynatoi* who wanted to be emperors, not from people who wanted to be independent regional rulers. In the Islamic world fragmentation largely meant replication, as courts patterned on or competitive with the Abbasid model were set up by Fatimid caliphs and other rulers. In the West, the rise of local rulers was accompanied by the widespread adoption of forms of personal dependency — vassalage, serfdom — which could be (and were) manipulated even by kings, such as the Capetians, who seemed to have lost the most from the dispersal of power.

The *real* fragmentation was among the former heirs of the Roman Empire. They did not speak the same language, they were increasingly estranged by their religions, and they knew almost nothing about one another. In the next century, Christian Europeans, newly prosperous and self-confident, would go on the offensive. Henceforth, without forgetting about the Byzantine and Islamic worlds, we shall focus on this aggressive and dynamic new society.

*c.*790–*c.*950	Invasions into Europe by Vikings, Muslims, and Hungarians
869–883	Zanj revolt in Iraq
871–899	Reign of King Alfred the Great of England
*c.*909	Fatimids (in North Africa) establish themselves as caliphs
929	Abd al-Rahman III (at Córdoba in al-Andalus) takes title of caliph
955	Victory of Otto I over Hungarians at Lechfeld
962	Otto I crowned emperor
980–1037	Ibn Sina (Avicenna)
988	Conversion of Vladimir, Rus ruler, to Byzantine Christianity
989	Beginning of "Peace of God" movement
991	Mieszko I puts Poland under papal protection
1000 (OR 1001)	Stephen I crowned king of Hungary
1025	Death of Basil II the Bulgar Slayer
*c.*1031	Al-Andalus splits into *taifas*

NOTES

1. Michael Psellus, *Portrait of Basil II,* in *Reading the Middle Ages: Sources from Europe, Byzantium, and the Islamic World,* ed. Barbara H. Rosenwein (Peterborough, ON, 2006), pp.228–29.

2. Romanus Lecapenus, *Novel,* in *Reading the Middle Ages,* pp.205–6.

3. *The Russian Primary Chronicle,* in *Reading the Middle Ages,* p.237.

4. Al-Tabari, *The Defeat of the Zanj Revolt,* in *Reading the Middle Ages,* p.204.

5. Ibn Sina (Avicenna), *Treatise on Logic,* in *Reading the Middle Ages,* p.235.

6. "Asser's Life of King Alfred," in *Alfred the Great: Asser's "Life of King Alfred" and Other Contemporary Sources,* trans. Simon Keynes and Michael Lapidge (Harmondsworth, 1983), pp.84–85.

7. King Stephen, *Laws,* in *Reading the Middle Ages,* p.239.

8. *Agreements between Count William of the Aquitanians and Hugh of Lusignan,* in *Reading the Middle Ages,* p.215.

9. *Charter of Guillem Guifred,* in *Reading the Middle Ages,* p.221.

10. Andrew of Fleury, *The Miracles of St. Benedict,* in *Reading the Middle Ages,* p.220.

11. *Battle of Maldon,* in *Reading the Middle Ages,* p.258.

12. *Prefaces to Gregory the Great's Pastoral Care,* in *Reading the Middle Ages,* p.257.

13. *The Battle of Brunanburh,* in *The Battle of Maldon and Other Old English Poems,* trans. Kevin Crossley-Holland, ed. Bruce Mitchell (London & New York, 1966), p.42.

14. *Ottonian Germany: The Chronicon of Thietmar of Merseburg,* trans. David A. Warner (Manchester, 2001), p.265.

FURTHER READING

Abels, Richard. *Alfred the Great: War, Kingship and Culture in Anglo-Saxon England*. Harlow, Essex, 1998.

Berkey, Jonathan P. *The Formation of Islam: Religion and Society in the Near East, 600-1800*. Cambridge, 2003.

Bowman, Jeffrey A. *Shifting Landmarks: Property, Proof, and Dispute in Catalonia around the Year 1000*. Ithaca, NY, 2004.

Engel, Pál. *The Realm of St. Stephen: A History of Medieval Hungary, 895-1526*. Trans. Tamás Pálosfalvi. London, 2001.

Franklin, Simon, and Jonathan Shepard. *The Emergence of Rus, 750-1200*. London, 1996.

Jayyusi, Salma Khadra, ed. *The Legacy of Muslim Spain*. 2 vols. Leiden, 1994.

Kazhdan, A.P., and Ann Wharton Epstein. *Change in Byzantine Culture in the Eleventh and Twelfth Centuries*. Berkeley, 1985.

Lev, Yaacov. *State and Society in Fatimid Egypt*. Leiden, 1991.

Maguire, Henry, ed. *Byzantine Court Culture from 829 to 1204*. Washington, 1997.

Moore, R.I. *The First European Revolution, c. 970-1215*. Oxford, 2000.

Neville, Leonora. *Authority in Byzantine Provincial Society, 950-1100*. Cambridge, 2004.

Reuter, Timothy. *Germany in the Early Middle Ages, c. 800-1056*. London, 1991.

Reynolds, Susan. *Fiefs and Vassals: The Medieval Evidence Reinterpreted*. Oxford, 1994.

Richards, Julian D. *The Vikings: A Very Short Introduction*. Oxford, 2005.

Ringrose, Kathryn M. *The Perfect Servant: Eunuchs and the Social Construction of Gender in Byzantium*. Chicago, 2003.

Stafford, Pauline. *Unification and Conquest: A Political and Social History of England in the Tenth and Eleventh Centuries*. London, 1989.

Walter, Christopher. *The Warrior Saints in Byzantine Art and Tradition*. Aldershot, 2003.

▄►◄►◄►◄►◄►◄►◄►◄►◄►◄►▄

**To test your knowledge of this chapter, please go to
www.rosenweinshorthistory.com
and click "Study Questions."**

FIVE

THE EXPANSION OF EUROPE
(*c*.1050-*c*.1150)

Europeans gained muscle in the second half of the eleventh century. They built cities, reorganized the church, created new varieties of religious life, expanded their intellectual horizons, pushed aggressively at their frontiers, and even waged war over 1400 miles away, in what they called the Holy Land. Expanding population and a vigorous new commercial economy lay behind all this. So, too, did the weakness, disunity, and beckoning wealth of their neighbors, the Byzantines and Muslims.

THE SELJUKS

In the eleventh century the Seljuk Turks, a new group from outside the Islamic world, entered and took over its eastern half. Eventually penetrating deep into Anatolia, they took a great bite out of Byzantium. Soon, however, the Seljuks themselves split apart, and the Islamic world fragmented anew under the rule of dozens of emirs.

From the Sultans to the Emirs

Pastoralists on horseback, the Turkish peoples called the "Seljuks" (after the name of their most enterprising leader) crossed from the region east of the Caspian Sea into

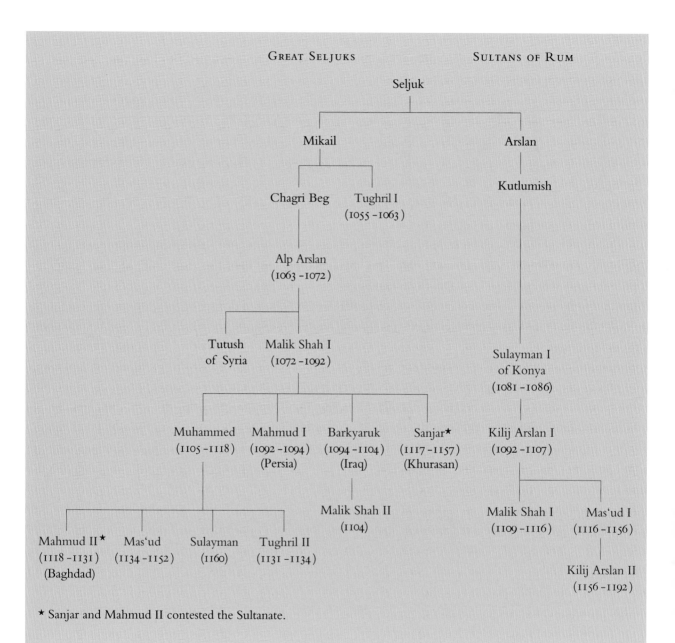

GREAT SELJUKS   SULTANS OF RUM

Seljuk

Mikail   Arslan

Chagri Beg   Tughril I   Kutlumish
              (1055-1063)

Alp Arslan
(1063-1072)

Tutush   Malik Shah I   Sulayman I
of Syria (1072-1092)   of Konya
                                (1081-1086)

Muhammed   Mahmud I   Barkyaruk   Sanjar★   Kilij Arslan I
(1105-1118) (1092-1094) (1094-1104) (1117-1157) (1092-1107)
           (Persia)   (Iraq)   (Khurasan)

                       Malik Shah II   Malik Shah I   Mas'ud I
                       (1104)   (1109-1116)   (1116-1156)

Mahmud II★   Mas'ud   Sulayman   Tughril II   Kilij Arslan II
(1118-1131) (1134-1152) (1160)   (1131-1134)   (1156-1192)
(Baghdad)

★ Sanjar and Mahmud II contested the Sultanate.

Iran in about the year 1000. Within a little over fifty years, they had allied themselves with the caliphs as upholders of Sunni orthodoxy, defeated the Buyids, taken over the cities, and started collecting taxes. Between 1055 and 1092, a succession of formidable Seljuk leaders—Tughril I, Alp Arslan, and Malik Shah (see Genealogy 5.1: The Early Seljuks)—proclaimed themselves rulers, "sultans," of a new state. Bands of herdsmen followed in their wake, moving their sheep into the very farmland of Iran (disrupting agriculture there), then continuing westward, into Armenia, which had been recently annexed by Byzantium. Meanwhile, under Alp Arslan (*r*.1063–1072), the Seljuk army (composed precisely of such herdsmen but also, increasingly, of other Turkish tribesmen recruited as slaves or freemen) harried Syria. This was Muslim territory, but it was equally the back door to Byzantium. Thus the Byzantines got involved, and throughout the 1050s and 1060s they fought numerous indecisive battles with the Seljuks. Then in 1071 a huge Byzantine force met an equally large Seljuk army at Manzikert (today Malazgirt, in Turkey). The battle ended with the Byzantines defeated and Anatolia open to a flood of militant nomads. (See Map 5.1.)

The Seljuks of Anatolia set up their own sultanate and were effectively independent

Genealogy 5.1 (facing page): The Early Seljuks

Map 5.1: The Byzantine Empire and the Seljuk World, *c.*1090

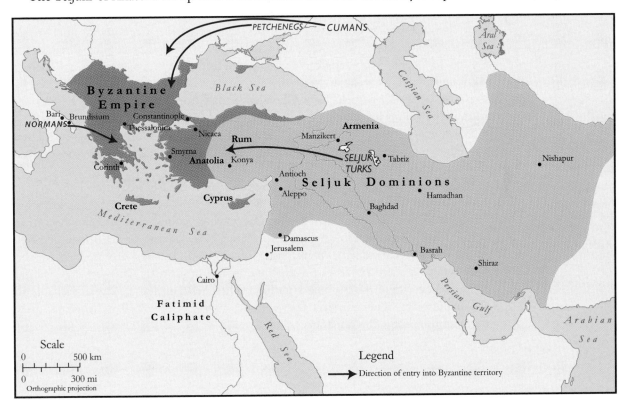

of the Great Seljuks who ruled (and disputed among themselves) elsewhere. The Anatolian Seljuks did not so much declare themselves rulers of the region as simply take it over; for them this once-central Byzantine province was Rum, "Rome." Meanwhile, other Seljuks took off on their own, hiring themselves out (as Turks long had done) as military leaders. Atsiz ibn Uwaq is a good example. For a while he worked for Alp Arslan, but in 1070 he was called in by the Fatimid caliph at Egypt to help shore up the crumbling rule of the Fatimids against their own military leaders. Seizing his chance, Atsiz turned the tables to become emir himself of a region that stretched from Jerusalem to Damascus.

Atsiz was the harbinger of a new order. After the death of Malik Shah I in 1092, the Seljuks could no longer maintain any sort of centralized rule over the Islamic world, even though they still were valued, if only to confer titles like "emir" on local rulers who craved legitimacy. Nor could the Fatimids prevent their own territories from splintering into tiny emirates, each centered on one or a few cities. Some emirs were from the Seljuk family; others were military men who originally served under them. We shall see that the tiny states set up by the crusaders who conquered the Levant in 1099 were, in size, not so very different from their neighboring Islamic emirates.

In the western part of North Africa, the Maghreb, Berber tribesmen (camel breeders rather than sheep herders) forged a state similar to that of the Seljuks. Fired (as the Seljuks had been) with religious fervor on behalf of Sunni orthodoxy, the Berber Almoravids took over north-west Africa in the 1070s and 1080s. In 1086, invited by the ruler of Seville to help fight Christian armies from the north, they sent troops into al-Andalus. This military "aid" soon turned into conquest. By 1094 all of al-Andalus not yet conquered by the Christians was under Almoravid control. Their hegemony over the western Islamic world ended only in 1147, with the triumph of the Almohads, a rival Berber group.

Together the Seljuks and Almoravids rolled back the Shi'ite wave. They kept it back through a system of schools, the *madrasas*. These centers of higher learning, which were attached to mosques, were places where young men attended lessons in religion, law, and literature. Sometimes visiting scholars arrived to debate at lively public displays of intellectual brilliance. More regularly, teachers and students carried on a quiet regimen of classes on the Qur'an and other texts. In the face of Sunni retrenchment, some Shi'i scholars modified their teachings to be more palatable to the mainstream. The conflicts between the two sects receded as Muslims drew together to counter the crusaders.

Byzantium: Bloodied but Unbowed

There would have been no crusaders if Byzantium had remained strong. But the once triumphant state of Basil II was unable to sustain its successes in the face of Turks and Normans. We have already discussed the triumph of the Turks in Anatolia; meanwhile, in the Balkans, the Turkic Pechenegs raided with ease. The Normans, some of whom (as we saw on p. 154) had established themselves in southern Italy, began attacks on Byzantine territory there (see Map 4.2 on p. 142), conquering its last stronghold, Bari, in 1071. Ten years later Norman knights were making penetrating attacks on Byzantine territory in the Balkans. In 1130 the Norman Roger II became king of a territory that ran from southern Italy to Palermo—the Kingdom of Sicily. It was a persistent thorn in Byzantium's side.

Clearly the Byzantine army was no longer very effective. Few themes were still manned with citizen-soldiers, and the emperor's army was also largely made up of mercenaries—Turks and Russians, as had long been the case, and increasingly Normans and Franks as well. But the Byzantines were not entirely dependent on armed force; in many instances they turned to diplomacy to confront the new invaders. When Emperor Constantine IX Monomachos (r.1042-1055) was unable to prevent the Pechenegs from entering the Balkans, he shifted policy, welcoming them, administering baptism, conferring titles, and settling them in depopulated regions. Much the same process took place in Anatolia, where the emperors at times welcomed the Turks to help them fight rival *dynatoi*. Here the invaders were sometimes also welcomed by Christians who did not adhere to Byzantine orthodoxy; the Monophysites of Armenia and Syria (see p. 143) were glad to have new Turkish overlords. The Byzantine grip on its territories loosened and its frontiers became nebulous, but Byzantium still stood.

There were changes at the imperial court as well. The model of the "public" emperor ruling alone with the aid of a civil service gave way to a less costly, more "familial" model of government. To be sure, for a time competing *dynatoi* families swapped the imperial throne. But Alexius I Comnenus (r.1081-1118), a Dalassenus on his mother's side, managed to bring most of the major families together through a series of marriage alliances. (The Comneni remained on the throne for about a century; see Genealogy 5.2: The Dynasty of Comnenus.) Until her death in c.1102, Anna Dalassena, Alexius's mother, held the reins of government while Alexius occupied himself with military matters. At his revamped court, which he moved to the Blachernai palace area, at the northwestern tip of the city (see Map 4.1 on p. 140), his relatives held the highest positions. Many of them received *pronoiai* (sing. *pronoia*), temporary grants of imperial lands that they administered and profited from.

Altogether, Byzantine rulers were becoming more like European ones, holding a relatively small amount of territory, handing some of it out in grants that worked a bit

Genealogy 5.2: The Dynasty of Comnenus

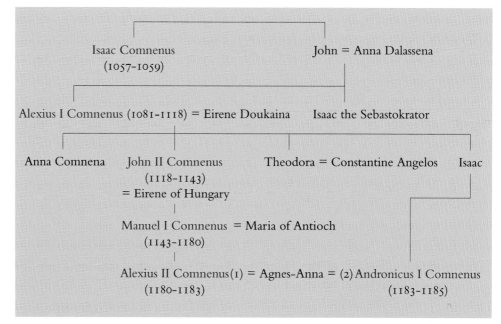

like fiefs, spending most of their time in battle to secure a stronghold here, a city there. Meanwhile, Western rulers were becoming less regional in focus, muscling their way, for example, into Byzantine territory and (as we shall see) attacking the Islamic world as well.

THE QUICKENING OF THE EUROPEAN ECONOMY

Behind the new European expansion was a new economy. Draining marshes, felling trees, setting up dikes: this was the backbreaking work that brought new land into cultivation. With their heavy, horse-drawn plows, peasants were able to reap greater harvests; using the three-field system, they raised more varieties of crops. Great landowners, the same "oppressors" against whom the Peace of God fulminated (see p. 159), could also be efficient economic organizers. They set up mills to grind grain, forced their tenants to use them, and then charged a fee for the service. It was in their interest that the peasants produce as much grain as possible. Some landlords gave peasants special privileges to settle on especially inhospitable land: the bishop of Hamburg was generous to those who came from Holland to work soil that was "uncultivated, marshy, and useless."[1]

As the countryside became more productive, people became healthier, their fertility increased, and there were more mouths to feed. Even so, surprising surpluses made possible the growth of old and the development of new urban centers. Within a generation or two, city dwellers, intensely conscious of their common goals, elaborated new instruments of commerce, self-regulating organizations, and forms of self-government.

Towns and Cities

Around castles and monasteries in the countryside or at the walls of crumbling ancient towns, merchants came with their wares and artisans set up shop. At Bruges (today in Belgium; for all the places mentioned in this section, see Map 5.3), it was the local lord's castle that served as a magnet. As one late medieval chronicler put it,

> To satisfy the needs of the people in the castle at Bruges, first merchants with luxury articles began to surge around the gate; then the wine-sellers came; finally the inn-keepers arrived to feed and lodge the people who had business with the prince.... So many houses were built that soon a great city was created.[2]

Churches and monasteries were the other centers of town growth. Recall Tours as it had been in the early seventh century (Map 1.4 on p. 46 of volume 1), with its semi-permanent settlements around the church of Saint-Martin, out in the cemetery, and its lonely cathedral nestling against one of the ancient walls. By the twelfth century (see Map 5.2), Saint-Martin was a monastery, the hub of a small town dense enough to boast eleven parish churches, merchant and artisan shops, private houses, and two markets. To the east, the episcopal complex was no longer alone: a market had sprung up outside the old western wall, and private houses lined the street leading to the bridge. Smaller than the town around Saint-Martin, the one at the foot of the old city had only two parish churches, but it was big and rich enough to warrant the construction of a new set of walls to protect it.

Early cities developed without prior planning, but some later ones were "chartered," that is, declared, surveyed, and plotted out. A marketplace and merchant settlement were already in place at Freiburg im Breisgau when the duke of Zähringen chartered it, promising each new settler there a house lot of 5000 square feet for a very small yearly rent. The duke had fair hopes that commerce would flourish right at his back door and yield him rich revenues.

The look and feel of medieval cities varied immensely from place to place. Nearly all included a marketplace, a castle, and several churches. Most were ringed by walls.

(See Map 7.4, p. 271, for the successive walls of Piacenza, evidence of the growth of population there.) Within the walls lay a network of streets—narrow, dirty, dark, smelly, and winding—made of packed clay or gravel. Most cities were situated near waterways and had bridges; the one at Tours was built in the 1030s. Many had to adapt to increasingly crowded conditions. At the end of the eleventh century in Winchester, England, city plots were still large enough to accommodate houses parallel to the street; but soon those houses had to be torn down to make way for narrow ones, built at right angles to the street. The houses at Winchester were made of wattle and daub—twigs woven together and covered with clay. If they were like the stone houses built in the late twelfth century (about which we know a good deal), they had two stories: a shop or warehouse on the lower floor and living quarters above. Behind this main building were the kitchen, enclosures for livestock, and a garden. Even city dwellers clung to rural pursuits, raising much of their food themselves.

Although commercial centers developed throughout Western Europe, they grew fastest and most densely in regions along key waterways: the Mediterranean coasts of Italy, France, and Spain; northern Italy along the Po River; the river system of Rhône-Saône-Meuse; the Rhineland; the English Channel; the shores of the Baltic Sea. During the eleventh and twelfth centuries, these waterways became part of a single, interdependent economy. At the same time, new roads through the countryside linked urban centers to rural districts and stimulated the growth of fairs (regular, short-term, often lively markets). (See Map 7.3 on p. 268 for a depiction of the trade routes and urban centers of a somewhat later period.)

Map 5.2: Tours in the Eleventh and Twelfth Centuries

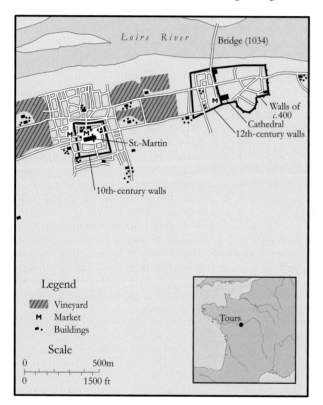

Business Arrangements

The revival of urban life and the expansion of trade, together dubbed the "commercial revolution" by historians, was sustained and invigorated by merchants. They were a varied lot. Some were local traders, like one monk who supervised a manor twenty miles south of his monastery and sold its surplus horses and grain at a local market. Others—mainly Jews and Italians—were long-distance traders, much in demand because they supplied fine wines, spices, and fabrics to the aristocracy. Some Jews had long been involved at least part time in long-distance trade as vintners. In the eleventh century, as lords reorganized the countryside, Jewish landowners were driven out and forced into commerce and urban trades full time. Other long-distance traders came from Italy. The key players were from Genoa, Pisa, Amalfi, and Venice. Regular merchants at Constantinople, their settlements were strung like pearls along the Golden Horn (see Map 4.1 on p. 140).

Italian traders found the Islamic world nearly as lucrative as the Byzantine. Establishing bases at ports such as Tunis, they imported Islamic wares—ceramics, textiles, metalwork—into Europe. Near Pisa, for example, the façade of the cathedral of San Miniato (Plate 5.1) was decorated with shiny bowls (Plate 5.2) imported by Pisan traders from North African artisans. In turn, merchants from the West exported wood, iron, and woolen cloth to the East.

Merchants invented new forms of collective enterprises to pool their resources and finance large undertakings. The Italian *commenda*, for example, was a partnership established for ventures by sea. A *compagnia* was created by investing family property in trade. Contracts for sales, exchanges, and loans became common, with the interest on loans hidden in the fiction of a penalty for "late payment" in order to avoid the church's ban on usury.

Pooled resources made large-scale productive enterprises possible. A cloth industry began, powered by water mills. New deep-mining technologies provided Europeans with hitherto untapped sources of metals. Forging techniques improved, and iron was for the first time regularly used for agricultural tools and plows, enhancing food production.

Whether driven by machines or handwork, the new economy was sustained by the artisans, financiers, and merchants of the cities. They formed guilds to regulate and protect themselves. In these social, religious, and economic associations, guild members prayed for and buried one another, agreed on quality standards for their products, and regulated their work hours, materials, and prices. Guilds guaranteed their members—mostly male—a place in the market by controlling production within each city. They represented the social and economic counterpart to urban walls, giving their members protection, shared identity, and recognized status.

The political counterpart to the walls was the "commune"—town self-government. City dwellers—keenly aware of their special identity in a world dominated by knights and peasants—recognized their mutual interest in reliable coinage, laws to facilitate commerce, freedom from servile dues and services, and independence to buy and sell as the market dictated. They petitioned the political powers that ruled them—bishops, kings, counts, castellans, dukes—for the right to govern themselves.

Collective movements for urban self-government were especially prevalent in Italy, France, and Germany. Already Italy's political life was city-centered; communes

there were attempts to substitute the power of one group (the citizens) for another (the nobles and bishops). At Milan in the second half of the eleventh century, for example, popular discontent with the archbishop, who effectively ruled the city, led to numerous armed clashes that ended, in 1097, with the transfer of power from the archbishop to a government of leading men of the city. Outside of Italy movements for urban independence—sometimes violent, as at Milan, at other times peaceful—took place within a larger political framework. For example, King Henry I of England (r. 1100–1135) freed the citizens of London from numerous customary taxes while granting them the right to "appoint as sheriff from themselves whomsoever they may choose, and [they] shall appoint from among themselves as justice whomsoever they choose to look after the pleas of my crown."[3] The king's law still stood, but it was carried out by the Londoners' officials.

Plate 5.1 (facing page): San Miniato (late 12th cent.). The façade of San Miniato was once decorated with *bacini*, bowls that sparkled in the Italian sun. In this picture you can see the small round cavities where they once belonged. The *bacino* in Plate 5.2 was slightly above and just to the left (from the viewer's point of view) of the oculus (the round window). The *bacini* were, in effect, cheap and attractive substitutes for marble or mosaics.

Plate 5.2: Bowl, North Africa (late 12th cent.). This earthenware bowl (*bacino*), imported from North Africa, and decorated with pseudo-Arabic writing, once adorned the façade of San Miniato. Such bowls, evidence of lively trade between the Islamic world and the West, were in great demand by Italians, not only for the façades of their churches but also for their kitchens. (See Plate 3.3, p. 111 of volume 1, for a far more sophisticated bowl from the Abbasid period.)

CHURCH REFORM AND ITS AFTERMATH

Disillusioned citizens at Milan denounced their archbishop not only for his tyranny but also for his impurity; they wanted their pastors to be untainted by sex and by money. In this they were supported by a new-style papacy, keen on reform in the church and society. The "Gregorian Reform," as this movement came to be called, broke up clerical marriages, unleashed civil war in Germany, changed the procedure for episcopal elections, and transformed the papacy into a monarchy. It began as a way to free the church from the world; but in the end the church was deeply involved in the new world it had helped to create.

The Coming of Reform

Freeing the church from the world: what could it mean? In 910 the duke and duchess of Aquitaine founded the monastery of Cluny with some unusual stipulations. They endowed the monastery with property (normal and essential if it were to survive), but then they gave it and its worldly possessions to Saints Peter and Paul. In this way they put control of the monastery into the hands of the two most powerful heavenly saints. They designated the pope, as the successor of Saint Peter, to be the monastery's worldly protector if anyone should bother or threaten it. The whole notion of "freedom" at this point was very vague. But Cluny's prestige was great because of the influence of its founders, the status of Saint Peter, and the fame of the monastery's elaborate round of prayers. The Cluniac monks fulfilled the role of "those who pray" in dazzling manner. Through their prayers, they seemed to guarantee the salvation of all Christians. Rulers, bishops, rich landowners, and even serfs (if they could) gave Cluny donations of land, joining their contributions to the land of Saint Peter. Powerful men and women called on the Cluniac abbots to reform new monasteries along the Cluniac model.

The abbots of Cluny came to see themselves as reformers of the world as well as the cloister. They believed in clerical celibacy, preaching against the prevailing norm in which parish priests and even bishops were married. They also thought that the laity could be reformed, become more virtuous, and cease its oppression of the poor. In the eleventh century, the Cluniacs began to link their program to the papacy. When they disputed with bishops or laypeople about lands and rights, they called on the popes to help them out.

The popes were ready to do so. A parallel movement for reform had entered papal circles via a small group of influential monks and clerics. Mining canon (church) law for their ammunition, these churchmen emphasized two abuses: nicolaitism (clerical marriage) and simony (buying church offices). The new patrilineal family taught them the importance of limiting offspring; in their eyes, celibate priests had higher status than men who procreated. The new profit economy sensitized them to the crass commercial meanings of gifts; in their eyes, churchmen should not give gifts in return for their offices.

Initially, the reformers got imperial backing. In the view of German king and emperor Henry III (r.1039-1056), as the anointed of God he was responsible for the well-being of the church in the empire. (For Henry and his dynasty, see Genealogy 5.3: The Salian Kings and Emperors.) Henry denounced simony and personally refused to accept money or gifts when he appointed bishops to their posts. He presided over the Synod of Sutri which, in 1046, deposed three papal rivals and elected another. When that pope and his successor died, Henry appointed Bruno of Toul, a member of the royal family, seasoned courtier, and reforming bishop. Taking the name Leo IX (1049-1054), the new pope surprised his patron: he set out to reform the church under papal, not imperial, control.

Leo revolutionized the papacy. He had himself elected by the "clergy and people" to satisfy the demands of canon law. Unlike earlier popes, Leo left Rome often to preside over church councils and make the pope's influence felt outside Italy, especially in France and Germany. To the papal curia Leo brought the most zealous church reformers of his day: Peter Damian, Hildebrand (later Pope Gregory VII), and Humbert of Silva Candida. They put new stress on the passage in Matthew's gospel

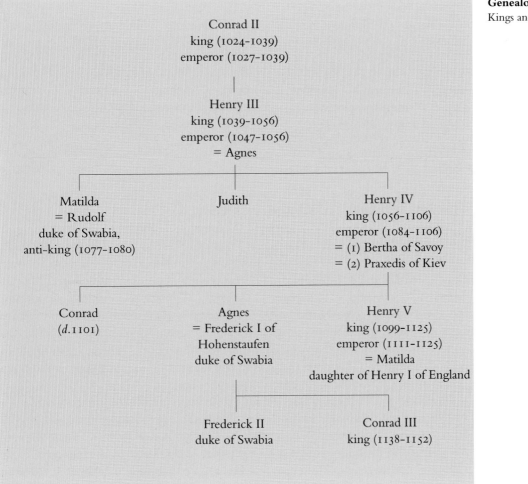

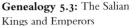

Genealogy 5.3: The Salian Kings and Emperors

(Matt. 16:19) in which Christ tells Peter that he is the "rock" of the Church, with the keys to heaven and the power to bind (impose penance) and loose (absolve from sins). As the successor to the special privileges of Saint Peter, the Roman church, headed by the pope, was "head and mother of all churches." What historians call the doctrine of "papal supremacy" was thus announced.

Its impact was soon felt at Byzantium. On a mission at Constantinople in 1054 to forge an alliance with the emperor against the Normans and, at the same time, to "remind" the patriarch of his place in the church hierarchy, Humbert ended by excommunicating the patriarch and his followers. In retaliation, the patriarch excommunicated Humbert and his fellow legates. Clashes between the Roman and Byzantine churches had occurred before and had been patched up, but this one, though not recognized as such at the time, marked a permanent schism. After 1054, the Roman Catholic and Greek Orthodox churches largely went their separate ways.

More generally, the papacy began to wield new forms of power. It waged unsuccessful war against the Normans in southern Italy and then made the best of the situation by granting them parts of the region—and Sicily as well—as a fief, turning former enemies into vassals. It supported the Christian push into the *taifas* of al-Andalus, transforming the "*reconquista*"—the conquest of Islamic Spain—into a holy war: Pope Alexander II (1061-1073) forgave the sins of the Christians on their way to the battle of Barbastro.

The Investiture Conflict and its Effects

The papal reform movement is associated particularly with Pope Gregory VII (1073-1085), hence the term "Gregorian reform." A passionate advocate of papal primacy (the theory that the pope is the head of the church), Gregory was not afraid to clash directly with the king of Germany, Henry IV (r.1056-1106), over church leadership. In Gregory's view—an astonishing one at the time, given the religious and spiritual roles associated with rulers—kings and emperors were simple laymen who had no right to meddle in church affairs. Henry, on the other hand, brought up in the traditions of his father, Henry III, considered it part of his duty to appoint bishops and even popes to ensure the well-being of church and empire together.

The pope and the emperor first clashed over the appointment of the archbishop of Milan. Gregory disputed Henry's right to "invest" the archbishop (put him into his office). In the investiture ritual, the emperor or his representative symbolically gave the church and the land that went with it to the bishop or archbishop chosen for the job. This was, for example, the role that Henry II played in Thietmar of Merseburg's episcopal installation (see above, p. 166.) In the case of Milan, two rival candidates for archiepiscopal office (one supported by the pope, the other by the emperor) had been at loggerheads for several years when, in 1075, Henry invested his own candidate. Gregory immediately called on Henry to "give more respectful attention to the master of the Church," namely Peter and his living representative — Gregory himself.[4] In reply, Henry and the German bishops called on Gregory, that "false monk," to resign. This was the beginning of what historians delicately call the "Investiture Conflict" or "Investiture Controversy." In fact it was war. In February of 1076, Gregory called a synod that both excommunicated Henry and suspended him from office:

> I deprive King Henry [IV], son of the emperor Henry [III], who has rebelled against [God's] Church with unheard-of audacity, of the government over the whole kingdom of Germany and Italy, and I release all Christian men from the allegiance which they have sworn or may swear to him, and I forbid anyone to serve him as king.[5]

The last part of this decree gave it real punch: anyone in Henry's kingdom could rebel against him. The German "princes" — the aristocrats — seized the moment and threatened to elect another king. They were motivated partly by religious sentiments — many had established links with the papacy through their support of reformed monasteries — and partly by political opportunism, as they had chafed under strong German kings who had tried to keep their power in check. Some bishops, too, joined with Gregory's supporters, a major blow to Henry, who needed the troops that they supplied.

Attacked from all sides, Henry traveled in the winter of 1077 to intercept Gregory, barricaded in a fortress at Canossa, high in the Appennines (see Map 5.3). It was a refuge provided by the staunchest of papal supporters, Countess Matilda of Tuscany. In an astute and dramatic gesture, the king stood outside the castle (in cold and snow) for three days, barefoot, as a penitent. Gregory was forced, as a pastor, to lift his excommunication and to receive Henry back into the church, precisely as Henry intended. For his part, the pope had the satisfaction of seeing the king humiliate himself before the papal majesty. Although it made a great impression on contemporaries, the whole episode solved nothing. The princes elected an anti-king, and bloody civil war continued intermittently until 1122.

The Investiture Conflict ended with a compromise. The Concordat of Worms (1122) relied on a conceptual distinction between two parts of investiture — the spiritual (in which the bishop-to-be received the symbols of his office) and the secular (in which he received the symbols of the material goods that would allow him to function). Under the terms of the Concordat, the ring and staff, symbols of church office, would be given by a churchman in the first part of the ceremony. Then the

Scale

0   500 km

0   300 mi

Sweden

NORWAY

North Sea

Denmark

Baltic Sea

Scotland

Ireland

England

Durham

Wales

Oxford

London

Sherborne

Hastings

Winchester

Bruges

Flanders

Crécy

Vermandois

Germany

Prague

Bohemia

Laon

Reims

Normandy

Paris

Metz

Worms

Champagne

Chartres

Blois

Speyer

Brittany

Auxerre

Fontenay

The Empire

Anjou

Vézelay

Cîteaux

Freiburg im Breisgau

Loire

Nevers

Tours

Bourbon

Clairvaux

Aquitaine

Cluny

La Grande

Auvergne

Chartreuse

Italy

Venice

Milan

Kingdom of Burgundy

Po

Atlantic Ocean

Meuse

Mosel

Rhine

Île-de-France

Seine

Thames

Burgundy

Santiago de Compostela

Gascony

Toulouse

Gothia (Septimania)

Montpellier

Marseille

Genoa

Pisa

Canossa

Bologna

Adriatic Sea

Navarre

Aragon

León-Castile

Zaragoza

Barcelona

Sant Tomàs de Fluvià

Barcelona

Papal States

Rome

Garonne

Rhône

Amalfi

Salerno

Córdoba

Mediterranean Sea

Palermo

Norman Kingdom of Sicily (1130)

Almoravid Empire

emperor or his representative would touch the bishop with a scepter, signifying the land and other possessions that went with his office. Elections of bishops in Germany would take place "in the presence" of the emperor — that is, under his influence. In Italy, the pope would have a comparable role.

In the end, then, secular rulers continued to matter in the appointment of churchmen. But just as the new investiture ceremony broke the ritual into spiritual and secular halves, so too it implied a new notion of kingship separate from the priesthood. The Investiture Conflict did not produce the modern distinction between church and state — that would develop only very slowly — but it set the wheels in motion. At the time, its most important consequence was to shatter the delicate balance among political and ecclesiastical powers in Germany and Italy. In Germany, the princes consolidated their lands and powers at the expense of the king. In Italy, the communes came closer to their goals: it was no accident that Milan gained its independence in 1097. And everywhere the papacy gained new authority: it had become a "papal monarchy."

Map 5.3 (facing page): Western Europe, *c.*1100

Papal influence was felt at every level. At the abstract level of canon law, papal primacy was enhanced by the publication *c.*1140 of the *Decretum*, written by a teacher of canon law named Gratian. Collecting nearly two thousand passages from the decrees of popes and councils as well as the writings of the Church Fathers, Gratian set out to demonstrate their essential agreement. In fact, the book's original title was *Harmony of Discordant Canons*. If he found any "discord" in his sources, Gratian usually imposed the harmony himself by arguing that the conflicting passages dealt with different situations. A bit later another legal scholar revised and expanded the *Decretum*, adding Roman law to the mix. At a more local level, papal denunciations of married clergy made inroads on family life. At Verona, for example, "sons of priests" disappeared from the historical record in the twelfth century. At the mundane level of administration, the papal claim to head the church helped turn the curia at Rome into a kind of government, complete with its own bureaucracy, collection agencies, and law courts. It was the teeming port of call for litigious churchmen disputing appointments and for petitioners of every sort.

The First Crusade

On the military level, the papacy's proclamations of holy wars led to bloody slaughter, tragic loss, and tidy profit. We have already seen how Alexander II encouraged the *reconquista* in Spain; it was in the wake of his call that the *taifa* rulers implored the Almoravids for help. An oddly similar chain of events took place at the other end of the Islamic world. Ostensibly responding to a request from the Byzantine Emperor Alexius for mercenaries to help retake Anatolia from the Seljuks, Pope Urban II

(1088-1099) turned the enterprise into something new: a pious pilgrimage to the Holy Land to be undertaken by an armed militia—one commissioned like those of the Peace of God, but thousands of times larger—under the leadership of the papacy. "Enter upon the road to the Holy Sepulcher," Urban exhorted the crowd at Clermont in 1095, "Wrest that land from the wicked race, and subject it to yourselves." On all sides the cry went up: "God wills it!"[6]

The event that historians call the First Crusade (1096-1099) mobilized a force of some 50,000-60,000 combatants, not counting women, children, old men, and hangers-on. The armies were organized not as one military force but rather as separate militias, each authorized by the pope and commanded by a different individual.

Several motley bands were not authorized by the pope. Though called collectively the "Peasants' (or People's) Crusade," these irregular armies included nobles. They were inspired by popular preachers, especially the eloquent Peter the Hermit, who was described by chroniclers as small, ugly, barefoot, and—partly because of those very characteristics—utterly captivating. Starting out before the other armies, the Peasants' Crusade took a route to the Holy Land through the Rhineland in Germany.

This indirect route was no mistake. The crusaders were looking for "wicked races" closer to home: the Jews. Under Henry IV many Jews had gained a stable place within the cities of Germany, particularly along the Rhine River. The Jews received protection from the local bishops (who were imperial appointees) in return for paying a tax. Living in their own neighborhoods, the Jews valued their tightly-knit communities focused on the synagogue, which was a school and community center as well as a place of worship. Nevertheless, Jews also participated in the life of the larger Christian community. For example, Archbishop Anno of Cologne made use of the services of the Jewish money-lenders in his city, and other Jews in Cologne were allowed to trade their wares at the fairs there.

Although officials pronounced against the Jews from time to time, and although Jews were occasionally (temporarily) expelled from some Rhineland cities, they were not persecuted systematically until the First Crusade. Then the Peasants' Crusade, joined by some local nobles and militias from the region, threatened the Jews with forced conversion or death. Some relented when the Jews paid them money; others, however, attacked. Beleaguered Jews occasionally found refuge with bishops or in the houses of Christian friends, but in many cities—Metz, Speyer, Worms, Mainz, and Cologne—they were massacred:

> Oh God, insolent men have risen against me
> They have sorely afflicted us from our youth
> They have devoured and destroyed us in their wrath against us
> Saying, let us take their inheritance for ourselves.[7]

So wrote Rabbi Eliezer ben Nathan, mourning and celebrating the Jewish martyrs who perished at the hands of the crusaders.

Leaving the Rhineland, some of the irregular militias disbanded, while others sought out the Holy Land via Hungary, at least one stopping off at Prague to massacre more Jews there. Only a handful of these armies continued on to Anatolia, where most of them were quickly slaughtered.

From the point of view of Emperor Alexius at Constantinople, even the "official" crusaders were potentially dangerous. One of the crusade's leaders, the Norman Bohemond, had, a few years before, tried to conquer Byzantium itself. Hastily forcing oaths from Bohemond and the other lords that any previously Byzantine lands conquered would be restored to Byzantium, Alexius shipped the armies across the Bosporus.

The main objective of the First Crusade—to conquer the Holy Land—was accomplished largely because of the disunity of the Islamic world and its failure to consider the crusade a serious military threat. Spared by the Turks when they first arrived in Anatolia, the crusaders first made their way to the Seljuk capital, Nicaea. Their armies were initially uncoordinated and their food supplies uncertain, but soon they organized themselves, setting up a "council of princes" that included all the great crusade leaders, while the Byzantines supplied food at a nearby port. Surrounding Nicaea and besieging it with catapults and other war machines, the crusaders took the city on June 18, 1097, dutifully handing it over to Alexius in accordance with their oath.

Gradually, however, the crusaders forgot their oath to the Byzantines. While most went toward Antioch, which stood in the way of their conquest of Jerusalem, one leader went off to Edessa, where he took over the city and its outlying area, creating the first of the Crusader States: the County of Edessa. Meanwhile the other crusaders remained stymied before the thick and heavily fortified walls of Antioch for many months. Then, in a surprise turn-around, they entered the town but found themselves besieged by Muslim armies from the outside. Their mood grim, they rallied when a peasant named Peter Bartholomew reported that he had seen in many visions the Holy Lance that had pierced Christ's body—it was, he said, buried right in the main church in Antioch. (Antioch had a flourishing Christian population even under Muslim rule.) After a night of feverish digging, the crusaders believed that they had discovered the Holy Lance, and, fortified by this miracle, they defeated the besiegers.

From Antioch, it was only a short march to Jerusalem, though disputes among the leaders delayed that next step for over a year. One leader claimed Antioch. Another eventually took charge—provisionally—of the expedition to Jerusalem. His way was eased by quarrels among Muslim rulers, and an alliance with one of them allowed free passage through what would have been enemy territory. In early June 1099, a large crusading force amassed before the walls of Jerusalem and set to work to build siege engines. In mid-July they attacked, breaching the walls and entering the city. "The Franks slaughtered more than 70,000 people .... [they] stripped the Dome of the Rock of more than forty silver candelabra," dryly noted a later Islamic historian looking back on the event.[8]

RULERS WITH CLOUT

While the papacy was turning into a monarchy, other rulers were beginning to turn their territories into states. They discovered ideologies to justify their hegemony, hired officials to work for them, found vassals and churchmen to support them. Some of these rulers were women.

The Crusader States

In the Holy Land, the leaders of the crusade set up four tiny states, European colonies in the Levant. Two (Tripoli and Edessa) were counties, Antioch was a principality, Jerusalem a kingdom. (See Map 5.4.) The region was habituated (as we have seen) to multi-ethnic and multi-religious territories ruled by a military elite; apart from the religion of that elite, the Crusader States were no exception. Yet, however much they engaged with their neighbors, the Europeans in the Levant saw themselves as a world apart, holding on to their western identity through their political institutions and the old vocabulary of homage, fealty, and Christianity.

The states won during the First Crusade lasted—tenuously—until 1291, though many new crusades had to be called in the interval to shore them up. Created by conquest, these states were treated as lordships. The new rulers carved out estates to give as fiefs to their vassals, who, in turn, gave portions of their holdings in fief to their own men. The peasants continued to work the land as before, and commerce boomed as the new rulers encouraged lively trade at their coastal ports. Italian merchants—the Genoese, Pisans, and Venetians—were the most active, but others—Byzantines and Muslim traders—participated as well. Enlightened lordship dictated that the mixed population of the states—Muslims, to be sure, but also Jews, Greek Orthodox Christians, Monophysite Christians, and others—be tolerated for the sake of production and trade. Most Europeans had gone home after the First Crusade; those left behind were obliged to maintain the inhabitants that remained.

The main concerns of the crusader states' rulers were military, and these could be guaranteed as well by a woman as by a man. Thus Melisende (r.1131–1152), oldest daughter of King Baldwin II of Jerusalem, was declared ruler along with her husband, Fulk, formerly count of Anjou, and their infant son. Taking the reins of government into her own hands after Fulk's death, she named a constable to lead her army and made sure that the greatest men in the kingdom sent her their vassals to do military service. Vigorously asserting her position as queen, she found supporters in the church, appointed at least one bishop to his see, and created her own chancery, where her royal acts were drawn up.

But vassals alone, however well commanded, were not sufficient to defend the fragile Crusader States, nor were the stone castles and towers that bristled in the countryside. Knights had to be recruited from Europe from time to time, and a new and militant kind of monasticism developed in the Levant: the Knights Templar. Vowed to poverty and chastity, the Templars at the same time devoted themselves to war. They defended the town garrisons of the Crusader States and ferried money from Europe to the Holy Land. Even so, they could not prevent a new Seljuk leader, Zengi, from taking Edessa in 1144. The slow but steady shrinking of the Crusader States began at that moment. The Second Crusade (1147–1149), called in the wake of Zengi's victory, came to a disastrous end. After only four days of besieging the walls of Damascus, the crusaders, whose leaders could not keep the peace among themselves, gave up and went home.

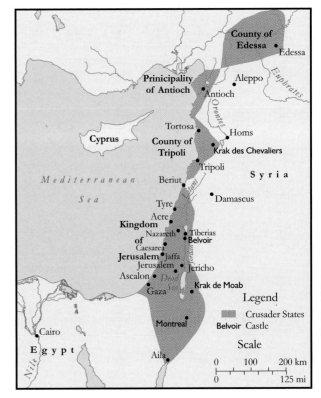

Map 5.4: The Crusader States, c.1140

England under Norman Rule

Anglo-Saxon England was early linked to the Continent by the Vikings, who settled in England's eastern half. In the eleventh century it was further tied to Scandinavia under the rule of Cnut (r.1016–1035), king of a state that extended from England to Denmark, Norway, and part of Sweden. But it was with its conquest by William, duke of Normandy, that England was drawn inextricably into the Continental orbit. (See Map 5.3.)

William the Conqueror, duke of Normandy, carried a papal banner with him when he left his duchy in 1066 to dispute the crown of the childless King Edward the Confessor. The one-day battle of Hastings was decisive, and William was crowned the first Norman king of England. (See Genealogy 6.1: The Norman and Angevin Kings of England, on p. 224.) Treating his conquest like booty (as the crusader leaders would do a few decades later in the Levant), he kept about 20 per cent of the land for himself and divided the rest, distributing it in large but scattered fiefs to a relatively small number of his barons—his elite followers—and family members, lay and ecclesiastical, as well as to some lesser men, such as personal servants and soldiers. In turn, these men maintained their own vassals; they owed the king military service (and the service of a fixed number of their vassals) along with certain dues, such as reliefs (money paid upon inheriting a fief) and aids (payments made on important occasions).

These were noble obligations; William expected their servile counterparts from the peasantry. In 1086, he ordered a survey of the land and landholders of England. Quickly dubbed "Domesday Book" because, like the records of people judged at doomsday, it provided facts that could not be appealed, it was the most extensive inventory of land, livestock, taxes, and people that had ever been compiled anywhere in medieval Europe. According to a chronicler of the time, William

> sent his men over all England into every shire and had them find out how many hundred hides [a measure of land] there were in the shire, or what land and cattle the king himself had in the country, or what dues he ought to receive every year from the shire.... So very narrowly did he have the survey to be made that there was no single hide nor a yard of land, nor indeed .... one ox or one cow or one pig left out.[9]

The surveys were made by the king's men by consulting Anglo-Saxon tax lists and by taking testimony from local jurors, men sworn to answer a series of formal questions truthfully. Summarized in Domesday, the answers gave William what he needed to know about his kingdom and the revenues—including the Danegeld, which was now in effect a royal tax—that could be expected from it.

Communication with the Continent was constant. The Norman barons spoke a brand of French; they talked more easily with the peasants of Normandy (if they bothered) than with those tilling the land in England. They maintained their estates on the Continent and their ties with its politics, institutions, and culture. English wool was sent to Flanders to be turned into cloth. The most brilliant intellect of his day, Saint Anselm of Bec (or Canterbury; 1033-1109), was born in Italy, became abbot of a Norman monastery, and was then appointed archbishop in England. English adolescent boys were sent to Paris and Chartres for schooling. The kings of England often spent more time on the Continent than they did on the island. When, on the death of William's son, King Henry I (*r.*1100–1135), no male descendent survived to take the throne, two counts from the Continent—Geoffrey of Anjou and Stephen of Blois—disputed it as their right through two rival females of the royal line. (See Genealogy 6.1 again.)

Christian Spain

While initially the product of defeat, Christian Spain in the eleventh and twelfth centuries turned the tables and became, in effect, the successful western counterpart of the Crusader States. The disintegration of al-Andalus into *taifas* opened immense opportunities to the Spanish princes of the north. Wealth flowed into their coffers not only from plundering raids and the confiscation of lands and cities but also (until the Almoravids put an end to it) from tribute, paid in gold by *taifa* rulers to stave off attacks.

Not just the rulers were enriched. When Rodrigo Díaz de Vivar, the Cid (from the Arabic *sidi*, lord), fell out of favor with his lord, King Alfonso VI (*r.*1065–1109) of León-Castile, he and a band of followers found employment with al-Mutamin, ruler of Zaragoza. There the Cid defended the city against Christian and Muslim invaders alike. In 1090, he struck out on his own, taking his chances in Valencia:

> My Cid knew well   that God was his strength.
> There was great fear   in the city of Valencia
> It grieves those of Valencia.   Know, they are not pleased
> They took counsel   and came to besiege him.[10]

Thus were the two sides depicted in the *Poem of the Cid*, written perhaps a century later: beleaguered inhabitants versus an army of God, even though the Cid had just come from serving a Muslim ruler. In the end, the Cid took Valencia in 1094 and ruled there until his death in 1099. He was a Spaniard, but other opportunistic armies sometimes came from elsewhere. The one that Pope Alexander II authorized to besiege Barbastro in 1064 was made up of Frenchmen.

The French connection was symptomatic of a wider process: the Europeanization of Spain. Initially the Christian kingdoms had been isolated islands of Visigothic culture. But already in the tenth century, pilgrims from France, England, Germany, and Italy were clogging the roads to the shrine of Saint James (Santiago de Compostela); in the eleventh century, monks from Cluny and other reformed monasteries arrived to colonize Spanish cloisters. Alfonso VI actively reached out beyond the Pyrenees, to Cluny—where he doubled the annual gift of 1000 gold pieces that his father, Fernando I, had given in exchange for prayers for his soul—and to the papacy. He sought recognition from Pope Gregory VII as "king of Spain," and in return he imposed the Roman liturgy throughout his kingdom, stamping out the traditional Visigothic music and texts.

In 1085 Alfonso made good his claim to be more than the king of León-Castile by conquering Toledo. (See Map 5.5.) After his death, his daughter Queen Urraca (r. 1109-1126) ruled in her own right a realm larger than England. Her strength came from many of the usual sources: control over land, which, though granted out to counts and others, was at least in theory revocable; church appointments; an army — everyone was liable to be called up once a year, even arms-bearing slaves — and a court of great men to offer advice and give their consent.

Praising the King of France

Map 5.5: Spain at the Death of Alfonso VI (1109)

Not all rulers had opportunities for grand conquest. How did they maintain themselves? The example of the kings of France reveals the possibilities. Reduced to bat-

tling a few castles in the vicinity of the Ile-de-France, the Capetian kings nevertheless wielded many of the same instruments of power as their conquering contemporaries: vassals, taxes, commercial revenues, military and religious reputations. Louis VI the Fat (r. 1108-1137), so heavy that he had to be hoisted onto his horse by a crane, was nevertheless a tireless defender of royal power. (See Genealogy 5.4: The Capetian Kings of France.)

Louis's virtues were amplified and broadcast by his biographer, Suger (1081-1152), the abbot of Saint-Denis, a monastery just outside Paris. A close associate of the king, Suger was his chronicler and propagandist. When Louis set himself the task of consolidating his rule in the Ile-de-France, Suger portrayed the king as a righteous hero. He was more than a lord with rights over the French nobles as his vassals; he was a peacekeeper with the God-given duty to fight unruly strongmen. Careful not to claim that Louis was head of the church, which would have scandalized the papacy and its supporters, Suger nevertheless emphasized Louis's role as protector of the church and the poor and insisted on the sacred importance of the royal dignity. When a pope happened to arrive in France, Louis, not yet king, and his father, Philip I (r. 1060-1108), bowed low, but (wrote Suger) "the lord pope lifted them up and made them sit before him like devout sons of the apostles. In the manner of a wise man acting wisely, he conferred with them privately on the present condition of the church."[11] Here the pope was shown needing royal advice. Meanwhile, Suger stressed Louis's piety and active defense of the faith:

Helped by his powerful band of armed men, or rather by the hand of God, he abruptly seized the castle [of Crécy] and captured its very strong tower as if it were simply the hut of a peasant. Having startled those criminals [Thomas of Marle, a regional castellan, and his retinue], he piously slaughtered the impious, cutting them down without mercy because he found them to be merciless.[12]

When Louis VI died in 1137, Suger's notion of the might and right of the king of France reflected reality in an extremely small area. Nevertheless, Louis laid the groundwork for the gradual extension of royal power. As the lord of vassals, the king could call upon his men to aid him in times of war (though the great ones could defy him). As king and landlord, he collected dues and taxes with the help of his officials, called *prévôts*. Revenues came from Paris as well, a thriving commercial and cultural center. With money and land, Louis could employ civil servants while dispensing the favors and giving the gifts that added to his prestige and power.

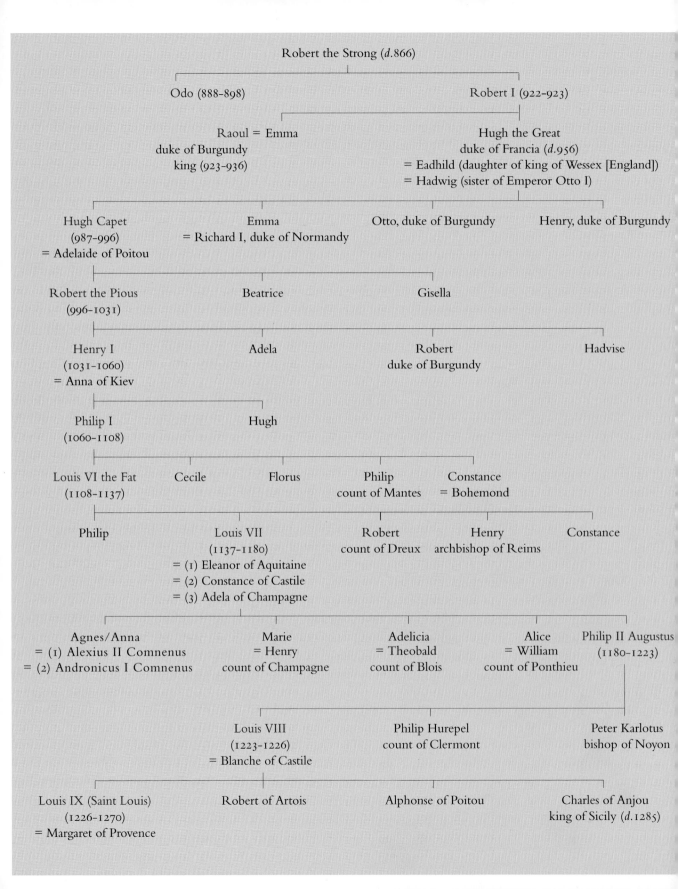

Robert the Strong (*d*.866)

Odo (888–898) Robert I (922–923)

Raoul = Emma Hugh the Great
duke of Burgundy duke of Francia (*d*.956)
king (923–936) = Eadhild (daughter of king of Wessex [England])
= Hadwig (sister of Emperor Otto I)

Hugh Capet Emma Otto, duke of Burgundy Henry, duke of Burgundy
(987–996) = Richard I, duke of Normandy
= Adelaide of Poitou

Robert the Pious Beatrice Gisella
(996–1031)

Henry I Adela Robert Hadvise
(1031–1060) duke of Burgundy
= Anna of Kiev

Philip I Hugh
(1060–1108)

Louis VI the Fat Cecile Florus Philip Constance
(1108–1137) count of Mantes = Bohemond

Philip Louis VII Robert Henry Constance
(1137–1180) count of Dreux archbishop of Reims
= (1) Eleanor of Aquitaine
= (2) Constance of Castile
= (3) Adela of Champagne

Agnes/Anna Marie Adelicia Alice Philip II Augustus
= (1) Alexius II Comnenus = Henry = Theobald = William (1180–1223)
= (2) Andronicus I Comnenus count of Champagne count of Blois count of Ponthieu

Louis VIII Philip Hurepel Peter Karlotus
(1223–1226) count of Clermont bishop of Noyon
= Blanche of Castile

Louis IX (Saint Louis) Robert of Artois Alphonse of Poitou Charles of Anjou
(1226–1270) king of Sicily (*d*.1285)
= Margaret of Provence

NEW FORMS OF LEARNING AND RELIGIOUS EXPRESSION

The commercial revolution, the newly reorganized church, close contact with the Islamic world, and the revived polities of the early twelfth century paved the way for the growth of schools and new forms of scholarship. Money, learning, and career opportunities attracted many to the new centers. On the other hand, the cities and the schools repelled others, who retreated from the world to seek poverty and solitude. Yet the new learning and the new money had a way of seeping into the cracks and crannies of even the most resolutely separate institutions.

Schools and the Liberal Arts

Genealogy 5.4 (facing page): The Capetian Kings of France

Connected to monasteries and cathedrals since the Carolingian period, schools had traditionally trained young men to become monks or priests. Some schools were better endowed than others with books and masters (teachers); a few developed reputations for particular expertise. By the end of the eleventh century, the best schools were those connected to cathedrals in the larger cities: Reims, Paris, Bologna, Montpellier.

Eager students sampled nearly all of them. The young monk Gilbert of Liège was typical: "Instilled with an insatiable thirst for learning, whenever he heard of somebody excelling in the arts, he rushed immediately to that place and drank whatever delightful potion he could draw from the master there."[13] For Gilbert and other students, a good lecture had the excitement of the theater. Teachers at some schools were sometimes forced to find larger halls to accommodate the crush of students. Other teachers simply declared themselves "masters" and set up shop by renting a room. If they could prove their mettle as lecturers, they had no trouble finding paying students.

What the students sought, above all, was knowledge of the seven liberal arts. Grammar, rhetoric, and logic (or dialectic) belonged to the "beginning" arts, the so-called trivium. Logic, involving the technical analysis of texts as well as the application and manipulation of arguments, was a transitional subject leading to the second, higher part of the liberal arts, the quadrivium. This comprised four areas of study that might today be called theoretical math and science: arithmetic (number theory), geometry, music (theory rather than practice), and astronomy. Of these arts, logic had pride of place in the schools, while masters and students who studied the quadrivium generally did so outside of the classroom.

The goal of twelfth-century scholars was to gather, order, systematize, and clarify all knowledge. That God existed, nearly everyone believed. But scholars like Anselm of Bec were not satisfied by belief alone. Anselm's faith, as he put it, "sought understanding." He emptied his mind of all concepts except that of God and then, using the tools of logic, proved God's very existence in his *Monologion*. Gilbert of Poitiers (*c.*1075-1154) systematized Bible commentaries, helping to create the *Glossa Ordinaria*, the standard compendium of all teachings on the Bible. Peter Abelard (1079-1142), who declared that "nothing can be believed unless it is first understood," drew together conflicting authoritative texts on 156 key subjects in his *Sic et Non* (*Yes and No*), including "That God is one and the contrary" and "That it is permitted to kill men and the contrary." Leaving the propositions unresolved, Abelard urged his students to discover the reasons behind the disagreements. Soon Peter Lombard (*c.*1100-1160) adopted Abelard's method of juxtaposing opposing positions, but he supplied his own reasoned resolutions as well. His *Sententiae* was perhaps the most successful theology textbook of the entire Middle Ages.

One key logical issue for twelfth-century scholars involved the question of "universals": whether a universal—something that can be said of many—is real or simply a linguistic or mental entity. Abelard argued that "things either individually or collectively cannot be called universal, i.e., said to be predicated of many." He was maintaining a position later called "nominalist."[14] The other view was the "realist" position that claimed that things "predicated of many" were universal and real. For example, when we look at diverse individuals of one kind, say Fluffy and Mittens, we say of each of them that they are members of the same species: cat. Realists argued that "cat" was real. Nominalists thought it a mere word.

Later in the twelfth century, scholars found precise tools for this and other logical questions in the works of Aristotle. During Abelard's lifetime, very little of Aristotle's work was available in Europe because it had not been translated from Greek into Latin. By the end of the century, however, that lack had been filled by translators who traveled to Islamic or formerly Islamic cities—Toledo in Spain, Palermo in Sicily—where Aristotle had already been translated into Arabic and carefully commented on by Islamic scholars like Ibn Sina (Avicenna; see p. 150 above) (980-1037) and Ibn Rushd (Averroes) (1126-1198). By the thirteenth century, Aristotle had become the primary philosopher for the scholastics (the scholars of the European medieval universities).

The lofty subjects of the schools had down-to-earth, practical consequences in books for preachers, advice for rulers, manuals for priests, textbooks for students, and guides for living addressed to laypeople. Nor was mastery of the liberal arts the end of everyone's education. Many students went on to study medicine (the great schools for that were at Salerno and Montpellier) or theology (for which Paris was the center). Others studied law; at Bologna, for example, where Gratian worked on canon law, other jurists—such as the so-called Four Doctors—achieved fame by teaching and writing about Roman law. By the mid-twelfth century, scholars had made real progress toward a systematic understanding of Justinian's law codes (see pp. 54-56 of volume 1). The lawyers who emerged from the school at Bologna went on to serve popes, bishops, kings, princes, or communes. Thus the learning of the schools was preached in the churches, consulted in the law courts, and used on the operating tables. It came to unify European culture.

Robert Pullen's life may serve to illustrate the career of a moderately successful schoolman while suggesting some of the practical benefits of the new learning. Born in England, Pullen was sent to school at Laon, in France. Good at his studies, he became a master in turn. Back in England, he was (in the 1130s) the first lecturer in theology at Oxford. But Paris beckoned as the center of theological studies, and as soon as he got a church position in England (and the revenues attached to it), he went off to France. From there, he went to Rome, where his academic training helped him get appointed papal chancellor. He served perfectly capably in this post, meanwhile finding good jobs at the papal curia for some of his students, helping his nephew get a church post (the very one that Pullen had abandoned in England), and obtaining papal privileges for the monastery of yet another of his relatives.

Monastic Splendor and Poverty

That monastery, Sherborne Abbey, was an old-fashioned Benedictine house. There were many others. One that has been excavated particularly fully is Saint-Germain at Auxerre. In the twelfth century (see Fig. 5.1), it boasted a very large church with an elaborate narthex that served as a grand entranceway for liturgical processions. Toward the east of the church, where the altar stood and the monks sang the Offices, stairs led down to a crypt constructed during the Carolingian period. To the north and south were the conventual buildings—the sacristy (which stored liturgical vessels and vestments), the "chapter house" (where *The Benedictine Rule* was read), the common room, refectory (dining hall), kitchens, and cellar. At the center of all was the cloister, entirely enclosed by graceful arcades. Beyond these buildings were undoubtedly others—not yet excavated—for the craftsmen and servants of the monastery, for the ill, for pilgrims and other guests.

The whole purpose of this complex was to allow the monks to carry out a life of arduous and nearly continuous prayer. Every detail of their lives was ordered, every object splendid, every space adorned to render due honor to the Lord of heaven.

The chant mirrored this development. It had expanded enormously since the time of Charlemagne. By the twelfth century, a large repertoire of melodies had

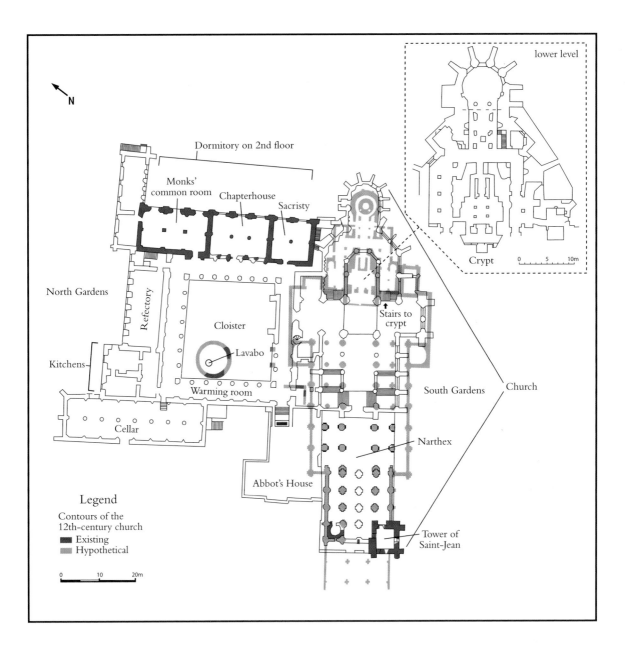

lower level

Crypt

North Gardens

Dormitory on 2nd floor

Monks' common room

Chapterhouse

Sacristy

Refectory

Cloister

Lavabo

Stairs to crypt

Kitchens

Warming room

South Gardens

Church

Cellar

Narthex

Abbot's House

Tower of Saint-Jean

Legend

Contours of the 12th-century church

Existing

Hypothetical

0   10   20m

0   5   10m

grown up, and new methods of musical notation had been elaborated to convey them. Scribes drew staves, sometimes multicolored, to show pitch. In Plate 5.3, a manuscript from the monastery of Saint-Evroult in Normandy, the scribe used a four-line staff (one red, one green, and two others lightly sketched) to indicate the locations of the pitches a-c-e-f.

The architecture and sculpture of twelfth-century churches like Saint-Germain were suited both to showcasing the chant and the honor due to God. The style, called Romanesque, represents the first wave of European monumental architecture. Built of stone, Romanesque churches are echo chambers for the sounds of the chant. Massive, weighty, and dignified, they nevertheless are often enlivened by sculpture, wall paintings, or patterned textures. At Durham Cathedral (built between 1093 and 1133 in the north of England), the stone itself is a warm yellow/pink color, given added zest by piers incised with diamond or zig-zag patterns. (See Plate 5.4.) By contrast, the entire length of the vault of Sant Tomàs de Fluvià, a tiny monastic church in the County of Barcelona, was covered with paintings, a few of which remain today; Plate 5.5 shows the Last Supper. At the pilgrimage church of Vézelay, you see a forest of pillars enlivened by piers whose sculpted capitals are both beautiful and strange (see Plate 5.6). Pisa's famous leaning tower is in fact a Romanesque bell tower; here (Plate 5.7) the decoration is on the exterior, where the bright Italian sun heightens the play of light and shadow.

Santiago de Compostela (built between 1078 and 1124) may serve as an example of a "typical" Romanesque church, though in fact the most typical aspect of that style is its extreme variety. Most of Santiago's exterior was rebuilt in the Baroque period, but the interior is still much as it must have been when twelfth-century pilgrims entered the shrine of Saint James. (See Plate 5.8.) Striking is the "barrel" or "tunnel" vault whose ribs, springing from thin columns attached to the piers, mark the long church

Figure 5.1 (facing page): Saint-Germain of Auxerre (12th cent.)

Plate 5.3: Gloria with Musical Notation, Saint-Evroult (12th cent.). The "Gloria," for which this manuscript page gives both text and music, was a chant of the Mass. Here the usual text of the Gloria has additional tropes (new words and music).

Plate 5.4 (facing page): Durham Cathedral, Interior (1093-1133). Huge and imposing, Durham Cathedral is also inviting and welcoming, with its lively piers, warm colors, and harmonious spaces. Built by Norman bishops, it housed the relics of the Anglo-Saxon Saint Cuthbert; in just such ways did the Normans appropriate the power and prestige of English saints' cults.

Plate 5.5: Sant Tomàs de Fluvià, The Last Supper, Painted Vault (early 12th cent.). Sant Tomàs was one of many monastic and parish churches in the county of Barcelona richly decorated with paintings in the twelfth century. Here Christ is at the Last Supper with his apostles. The depiction closely follows John 13:23 when Jesus announces that one of his disciples will betray him: "Now there was leaning on Jesus's bosom one of his disciples [John] .... [John asked], 'Lord, who is it?' Jesus answered, 'He it is to whom I shall reach bread dipped.' And when he had dipped the bread, he gave it to Judas."

into sections called bays. There are only two levels: the first is formed by the arches that open onto the side aisles of the church; the second is the gallery (or triforium). (Many other Romanesque churches have a third story—a clerestory—of windows.) The plan of Santiago (see Figure 5.2) shows its typical basilica shape with a transept crossing and, at the east end, an aisle (called an "ambulatory") that allows pilgrims to visit the relics housed in the chapels.

Not all medieval people agreed that such opulence pleased or praised God, however. At the end of the eleventh century, the new commercial economy and the profit motive that fueled it led many to reject wealth and to embrace poverty as a key element of religious life. The Carthusian order, founded by Bruno, one-time bishop of Cologne, was such a group. La Grande Chartreuse, the chief house of the order, was built in an Alpine valley, lonely and inaccessible. Each monk took a vow of silence and lived as a hermit in his own small hut. Only occasionally would the monks join the others for prayer in a common oratory. When not engaged in prayer or meditation, the Carthusians copied manuscripts: for them, scribal work was a way to preach God's

word with the hands rather than the mouth. Slowly the Carthusian order grew, but each monastery was limited to only twelve monks, the number of Christ's Apostles.

By contrast, the Cistercians, another new monastic order, expanded rapidly, often by reforming and incorporating existing monasteries. The first Cistercian house was Cîteaux (in Latin, *Cistercium*), founded in 1098 by Robert of Molesme (*c*.1027-1110) and a few other monks seeking a more austere way of life. Austerity they found—and also success. With the arrival of Saint Bernard (*c*.1090-1153), who came to Cîteaux in 1112 along with about thirty friends and relatives, the original center sprouted a small congregation of houses in Burgundy. (Bernard became abbot of one of them, Clairvaux.) By the mid-twelfth century there were more than 300 monasteries—many in France, but also in Italy, Germany, England, Austria, and Spain—following what they took to be the customs of Cîteaux. By the end of the twelfth century, the Cistercians were an order: their member houses adhered to the decisions of a General Chapter; their liturgical practices and internal organization were

Plate 5.7: Leaning Tower (Bell Tower) of Pisa (late 12th cent.). The tower is part of a large cathedral and baptistery complex which, in its layout and design, was meant to imitate—and outshine—the Temple Mount complex at Jerusalem.

standardized. Many nuns, too, as eager as monks to live the life of simplicity and poverty that the Apostles had endured and enjoyed, adopted Cîteaux's customs; some convents later became members of the order.

Although the Cistercians claimed *The Benedictine Rule* as the foundation of their customs, they elaborated a style of life and an aesthetic all their own, largely governed by the goal of simplicity. They even rejected the conceit of dyeing their robes—hence their nickname, the "white monks." White, too, were their houses. Despite regional variations and considerable latitude in interpreting the meaning of "simplicity," Cistercian buildings had a different feel than the great Romanesque churches and Benedictine monasteries of black monks. Foursquare and regular, Cistercian churches and other buildings conformed to a fairly standard plan. (See Figure 5.3.) The churches tended to be small, made of smooth-cut, undecorated stone. Wall and vault

paintings were eschewed, any sculpture was modest at best. Indeed, Saint Bernard wrote a scathing attack on Romanesque sculpture in which, ironically, he admitted its sensuous allure:

> But what can justify that array of grotesques in the cloister where the brothers do their reading? .... What place have obscene monkeys, savage lions, unnatural centaurs, manticores, striped tigers, battling knights or hunters sounding their horns? You can see a head with many bodies and a multi-bodied head.... With such a bewildering array of shapes and forms on show, one would sooner read the sculptures than the books.[15]

The Cistercians had few such diversions, but the simplicity of their buildings and of their clothing also had its beauty. Illuminated by the pure white light that came through clear glass windows, Cistercian churches were luminous, cool, and serene. Plate 5.9 shows the nave of Fontenay Abbey, begun in 1139. There are no wall paintings, no sculpture, no incised pillars. Yet the subtle play of thick piers and thin columns along with the alternation of curved and linear capitals lends the church a sober charm.

True to their emphasis on purity, the Cistercians simplified their communal liturgy, pruning the many additions that had been tacked on in the houses of the black monks. Only the liturgy as prescribed in the *The Benedictine Rule* and one daily Mass were allowed. Even the music for the chant was modified: the Cistercians rigorously suppressed the B flat, even though doing so made the melody discordant, because of their insistence on strict simplicity.

On the other hand, *The Benedictine Rule* did not prevent the Cistercians from creating a new class of monks—the lay brothers—who were illiterate and unable to participate in the liturgy. These men did the necessary labor—field work, stock raising—to support the community at large. Compare Figure 5.3 with Figure 5.1: the Cistercian monastery was in fact a house divided. The eastern half was for the "choir" monks, the western half for the lay brethren. Each half had its own dining room, latrines, and dormitories. The monks were strictly segregated, even in the church, where a screen kept them apart.

Plate 5.8 (facing page): Santiago de Compostela, Interior (1078-1124). Santiago (in the far northwest corner of Spain) was known for its relics of Saint James the Great (*d.*44), apostle and martyr. From the twelfth through fifteenth centuries a major pilgrimage center, the cathedral was built to hold crowds and to usher them, via aisles, from chapel to chapel.

Figure 5.2: A Model Romanesque Church: Santiago de Compostela

Plate 5.9 (facing page): Fontenay Abbey Church, Interior (1139-1147). Compare the bare walls of this Cistercian church with the frescoes of Sant Tomàs de Fluvià (Plate 5.5). How do these different artistic choices reflect different religious sensibilities?

Figure 5.3: Schematic Plan of a Cistercian Monastery

The choir monks dedicated themselves to private prayer and contemplation and to monastic administration. The Cistercian *Charter of Charity* (c.1165), in effect a constitution of the order, provided for a closely monitored network of houses, and each year the Cistercian abbots met to hammer out legislation for all of them. All the houses had large and highly organized farms and grazing lands called "granges," and the monks spent much of their time managing their estates and flocks of sheep, both of which yielded handsome profits by the end of the twelfth century. Clearly part of the agricultural and commercial revolutions of the Middle Ages, the Cistercian order made managerial expertise a part of the monastic life.

Yet the Cistercians also elaborated a spirituality of intense personal emotion. Their writings were filled with talk of love. When we pray, wrote Saint Bernard, "our breast expands .... our interior is filled with an overflowing love."[16] The Cistercians were devoted to the humanity of Christ and to his mother, Mary. While pilgrims continued to stream to the tombs and reliquaries of saints, the Cistercians dedicated all their churches to the Virgin Mary (for whom they had no relics) because for them she signified the model of a loving mother. Indeed, the Cistercians regularly used maternal

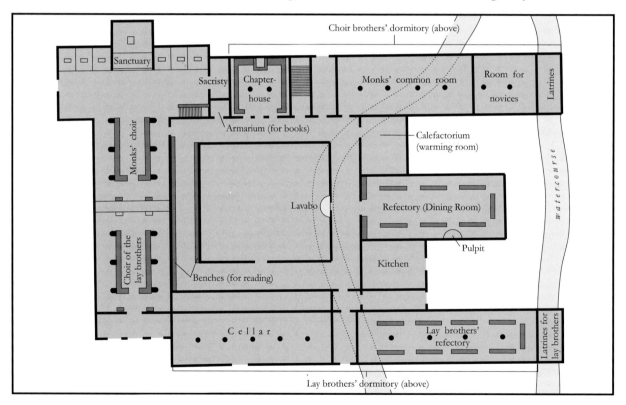

imagery to describe the nurturing care provided to humans by Jesus himself. The Cistercian God was approachable, human, protective, even mothering.

★   ★   ★   ★

In the twelfth century, Europe was coming into its own. Growing population and the profitable organization of the countryside promoted cities, trade, and wealth. Townspeople created new institutions of self-regulation and self-government. Kings and popes found new ways to exert their authority and test its limits. Scholars mastered the knowledge of the past and put it to use in classrooms, royal courts, and papal offices. Monks who fled the world ended up in positions of leadership; the great entrepreneurs of the twelfth century were the Cistercians; and Saint Bernard was the most effective preacher of the Second Crusade.

The power of communities was recognized in the twelfth century: the guilds and communes depended on this recognition. So too did the new theology of the time. In his theological treatise, *Why God Became Man*, Saint Anselm put new emphasis on Christ's humanity: Christ's sacrifice was that of one human being for another. The Cistercians spoke of God's mothering. Historians are in this sense right to speak of the importance of "humanism"—with its emphasis on the dignity of human beings, the splendor of the natural world, and the nobility of reason—in the twelfth century. Yet the stress on the loving bonds that tied Christians together also led to the persecution of others, like Jews and Muslims, who lived outside the Christian community. In the next century European communities would become more ordered, regulated, and incorporated. By the same token, they became even more exclusive.

NOTES

1. *Frederick of Hamburg's Agreement with Colonists from Holland*, in *Reading the Middle Ages: Sources from Europe, Byzantium, and the Islamic World*, ed. Barbara H. Rosenwein (Peterborough, ON, 2006), p.277.

2. *Chronicle of Saint-Bertin*, quoted in *Histoire de la France urbaine*, Vol. 2: *La ville médiévale* (Paris, 1980), p.71, here translated from the French.

3. Henry I, *Privileges for the Citizens of London*, in *Reading the Middle Ages*, p.279.

4. Pope Gregory VII, *Admonition to Henry* in *Power and the Holy in the Age of the Investiture Conflict: A Brief History with Documents*, ed. and trans. Maureen C. Miller (Boston, 2005), p.85.

5. *Roman Lenten Synod* in *The Correspondence of Pope Gregory VII: Selected Letters from the Registrum*, ed. and trans. Ephraim Emerton (New York, 1969), p.91.

6. Donald White, ed., *Medieval History. A Source Book* (Homewood, IL, 1965), pp.351–52.

7. Rabbi Eliezer b. Nathan, *O God, Insolent Men*, in *Reading the Middle Ages*, p.287.

8. Ibn al-Athir, *The First Crusade*, in *Reading the Middle Ages*, p.299.

9. *Anglo-Saxon Chronicle "E,"* quoted in David C. Douglas, *William the Conqueror: The Norman Impact upon England* (Berkeley, 1967), p.348.

10. *Poem of the Cid*, trans. W.S. Merwin (New York, 1959), pp.119–20.

11. Suger, *The Deeds of Louis the Fat*, ed. and trans. Richard C. Cusimano and John Moorhead (Washington, DC, 1992), p.48.

12. Suger, p.107.

13. Helene Wieruszowski, *The Medieval University* (Princeton, 1966), pp.123-24.

14. Abelard, *Glosses on Porphyry*, in *Reading the Middle Ages*, p.314.

15. St. Bernard, *Apologia*, in *Reading the Middle Ages*, p.331.

16. Bernard of Clairvaux, *On the Song of Songs*, Vol. 1, trans. Kilian Walsh, Cistercian Fathers Series, 4 (Kalamazoo, 1977), p.58.

FURTHER READING

Asbridge, Thomas. *The First Crusade: A New History*. Oxford, 2004.

Benson, Robert L., and Giles Constable, eds. *Renaissance and Renewal in the Twelfth Century*. Cambridge, 1982.

Berman, Constance Hoffman. *The Cistercian Evolution: The Invention of a Religious Order in Twelfth-Century Europe*. Philadelphia, 2000.

Blumenthal, Uta-Renate. *The Investiture Controversy: Church and Monarchy from the Ninth to the Twelfth Century*. Philadelphia, 1988.

Harris, Jonathan. *Byzantium and the Crusades*. London, 2003.

Iogna-Prat, Dominique. *Order and Exclusion: Cluny and Christendom Face Heresy, Judaism, and Islam (1000-1150)*. Translated by Graham Robert Edwards. Ithaca, NY, 2002.

Lawson, M.K. *Cnut: The Danes in England in the Early Eleventh Century*. London, 1993.

Little, Lester K. *Religious Poverty and the Profit Economy in Medieval Europe*. Ithaca, NY, 1978.

Mews, Constant J. *Abelard and Heloise*. Oxford, 2005.

Miller, Maureen C. *The Formation of a Medieval Church: Ecclesiastical Change in Verona, 950-1150*. Ithaca, NY, 1993.

Reilly, Bernard F. *The Kingdom of León-Castilla under Queen Urraca, 1109-1126*. Princeton, 1982.

Riley-Smith, Jonathan, ed. *The Oxford History of the Crusades*. Oxford, 1999.

Robinson, Ian S. *Henry IV of Germany*. Cambridge, 2000.

Southern, R.W. *Scholastic Humanism and the Unification of Europe*. Vol. 1: *Foundations*. Oxford, 1995.

Tyerman, Christopher. *God's War: A New History of the Crusades*. Cambridge, MA, 2006.

Weinfurter, Stefan. *The Salian Century: Main Currents in an Age of Transition*. Trans. Barbara M. Bowlus. Philadelphia, 1999.

Winroth, Anders. *The Making of Gratian's Decretum*. Cambridge, 2000.

To test your knowledge of this chapter, please go to
www.rosenweinshorthistory.com
and click "Study Questions."

SIX

INSTITUTIONALIZING ASPIRATIONS (c.1150-c.1250)

The lively developments of early twelfth-century Europe were institutionalized in the next decades. Fluid associations became corporations. Rulers hired salaried officials to staff their administrations. Churchmen defined the nature and limits of religious practice. While the Islamic world largely went its own way, only minimally affected by European developments, Byzantium was carved up by its Christian neighbors.

TWO NON-EUROPEAN HEIRS OF THE ROMAN EMPIRE: THE SEQUEL

Nothing could be more different than the fates of the Islamic world and of Byzantium at the beginning of the thirteenth century. The Muslims remained strong; the Byzantine Empire nearly came to an end.

Islam on the Move

Like grains of sand in an oyster's shell—irritating but also generative—the Christian states of the Levant and Spain helped spark new Islamic principalities, one based in the Maghreb, the other in Syria and Egypt. In the Maghreb, the Almohads (1147-1266), a

Berber group espousing a militant Sunni Islam, combined conquest with a program to "purify" the morals of their fellow Muslims. In al-Andalus their appearance induced some Islamic rulers to seek alliances with the Christian rulers to the north. But other Andalusian rulers joined forces with the Almohads, who replaced the Almoravids as rulers of the whole Islamic far west by 1172. (See Map 6.1.) At war continuously with Christian Spanish rulers, in 1212 they suffered a terrible defeat. For the Christian victors, the battle was known simply by its place name, Las Navas de Tolosa; but for the Almohads, it was known as "The Punishment." It was the beginning of the end of al-Andalus.

Meanwhile, however, in the shadow of the Crusader States, Nur al-Din (*r.*1146-1174), son of Zengi (see p. 197), forged a united Syria. Soon, in the 1150s, he conquered the county of Edessa and cut the principality of Antioch in half. In 1168 he sent his general Shirkuh to Egypt to aid the Fatimid vizier there. But Shirkuh turned against the vizier and took his place. Two months later, when Shirkuh died, his nephew Saladin (*r.*1171-1193) succeeded him, and when the Fatimid caliph died, Saladin simply took over Egypt, ostensibly in the name of Nur al-Din.

Map 6.1: The Almohads before the Battle of Las Navas de Tolosa (1212)

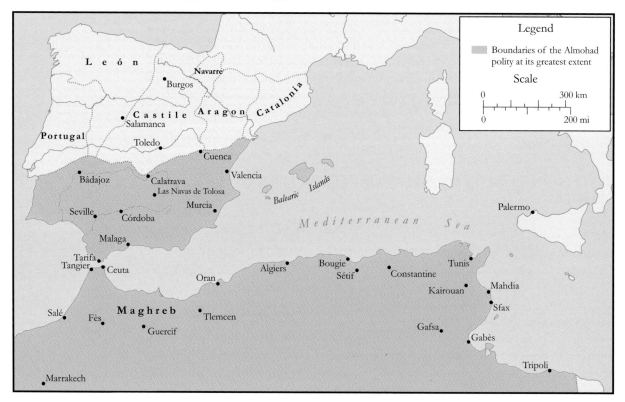

Three years later, when Nur al-Din died, Saladin was ready to take over Syria. By 1183 he was master of Egypt, most of Syria, and part of Iraq. Like the Almohads, Saladin was determined to reform the faith along the Sunni model and to wage *jihad* against the Christian states in his backyard:

> [Saladin] perceived that his gratitude for God's favor towards him, evidenced by his strong grasp on sovereignty, his God-given control over the lands, and the people's willing obedience, could only be demonstrated by his endeavoring to exert himself to the utmost and to strive to fulfill the precept of Jihad.[1]

Thus did ibn Shaddad, a close associate of Saladin's, describe the motivations behind the battle of Hattin in 1187, in which the Kingdom of Jerusalem was taken by Saladin's forces. The Christian army was badly defeated, the Crusader States reduced to a few port cities. For about a half-century thereafter, Saladin's descendants (the Ayyubids) held on to the lands he had conquered. Then the dynasty gave way (as we have often seen happen) to new military leaders. The chief difference this time was that these leaders were uniformly of Turkic slave and ex-slave origins—they were *mamluks*. The Mamluk Sultanate was exceptionally stable, holding on to Egypt and most of Syria until 1517.

The Undoing of Byzantium

In 1204 the leaders of the Fourth Crusade made a "detour" and conquered Constantinople instead. We shall later explore some of the reasons why they did so. But in the context of Byzantine history, the question is not why the Europeans attacked but rather why the Byzantines lost the fight.

Certainly the Byzantines themselves had no idea they were "in decline." Prior to 1204, they had reconquered some of Anatolia. In the capital, the imperial court continued to function; its bureaucracy and machinery of taxation were still in place; and powerful men continued to vie to be emperors—as if there were still power and glory in the position. Yet much had changed from the heyday of the Comneni.

While the economy, largely based on peasant labor, boomed in the twelfth century, this ironically brought the peasants to their knees. Every landowner needed cultivators, but peasants had no way to bargain to improve their lot. Peasants worked for the state on imperial lands. They worked for military men when the emperors took to giving out *pronoiai*— grants of land to soldiers rather than wages in return for military service. Finally, peasants worked for the *dynatoi*, the great landowners who dominated

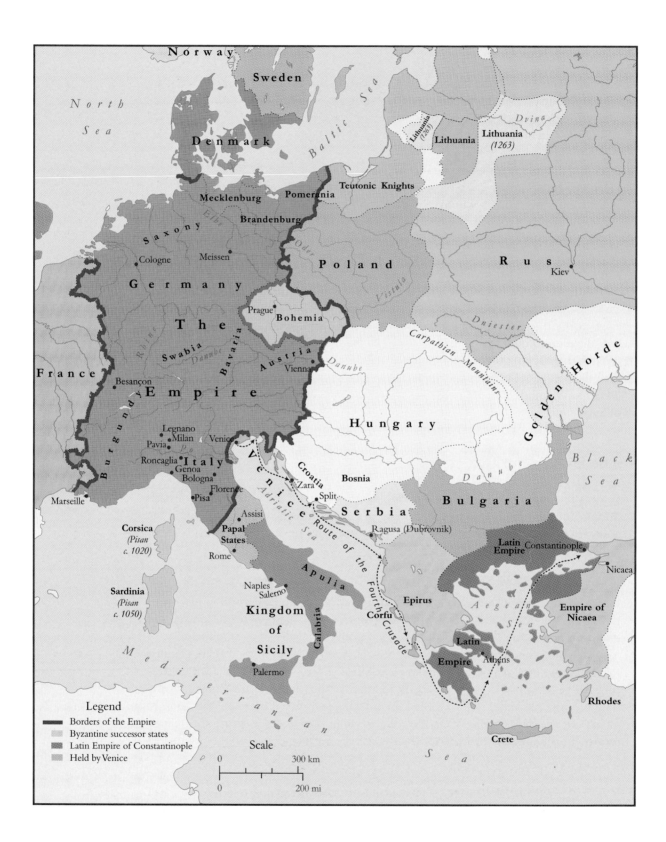

N o r w a y

S w e d e n

*North
Sea*

Baltic Sea

Dvina

D e n m a r k

Lithuania
(1263)

Lithuania

Lithuania
(1263)

Teutonic Knights

Mecklenburg   **Pomerania**

Brandenburg

Elbe

Oder

P o l a n d

R u s

Cologne •
• Meissen

G e r m a n y

Kiev •

Rhine

T h e

Prague •   **Bohemia**

Vistula

Dniester

S w a b i a

B a v a r i a

Danube

Austria

Vienna •

Danube

H u n g a r y

Carpathian Mountains

G o l d e n   H o r d e

F r a n c e

E m p i r e

Legnano •
• Milan   Venice •
Pavia •

Besançon •

B u r g u n d y

Po

I t a l y

Roncaglia •

Genoa •
Bologna •

Marseille •

Florence •
• Pisa

Assisi •

**Papal
States**

Rome •

Croatia

Zara •

Split •

Bosnia

Serbia

Adriatic Sea

Route of the Fourth Crusade

Ragusa (Dubrovnik) •

B u l g a r i a

*Black
Sea*

Danube

**Latin
Empire**

Constantinople •

• Nicaea

Corsica
*(Pisan
c. 1020)*

Sardinia
*(Pisan
c. 1050)*

Naples •
• Salerno

**K i n g d o m
o f
S i c i l y**

A p u l i a

C a l a b r i a

Palermo •

Epirus

Corfu

*Aegean
Sea*

**Empire of
Nicaea**

**Latin
Empire**

Athens •

Rhodes

Mediterranean

Sea

Crete

Legend

— Borders of the Empire
  Byzantine successor states
  Latin Empire of Constantinople
  Held by Venice

Scale

0   300 km

0   200 mi

whole regions. To all they paid taxes and rents. But there were only so many peasants, certainly not enough to cultivate all the land that the elites wanted to bring into production.

Manpower was scarce in every area of the economy. Skilled craftsmen, savvy merchants, and seasoned warriors were needed, but where were they to be found? Sometimes Jews were called upon; more often foreigners took up the work. Whole army contingents were made up of foreigners: Cumans, "Franks" (the Byzantine name for all Europeans), Turks. Forced to fight on numerous fronts, the army was not very effective; by the end of the twelfth century the Byzantines had lost much of the Balkans to what historians call the Second Bulgarian Empire.

Foreigners, mainly Italians, dominated Byzantium's long-distance trade. Italian neighborhoods (complete with homes, factories, churches, and monasteries) crowded the major cities of the empire. At the capital city itself, stretched along the Golden Horn like pearls on a string, were the Venetian Quarter, the Amalfitan Quarter, the Pisan Quarter, and the Genoese Quarter: these were the neighborhoods of the Italian merchants, exempt from imperial taxes and uniformly wealthy. (See Map 4.1 on p. 140.) They were heartily resented by the rest of Constantinople's restive and impoverished population, which needed little prodding to attack and loot the Italian quarters in 1182 and again in 1203, when they could see the crusaders camped right outside their city.

Map 6.2 (facing page): Central Europe, *c.*1250

None of this meant that Europeans had to take over, of course. Yet in 1204, crusader armies breached the walls of Constantinople, encountered relatively little opposition, plundered the city for three days, and finally declared one of their leaders, Baldwin of Flanders, the new emperor. The Venetians gained the city harbor, Crete, and key Greek cities; other crusaders carved out other states. (See Map 6.2.) So did some Byzantines, however, and eventually, in 1261, their successors managed to recapture Constantinople and re-establish their empire until it fell for good in 1453 to the Ottoman Turks.

THE INSTITUTIONALIZATION OF GOVERNMENT IN THE WEST

Some Byzantines thought that the West bested them in 1204 because it had a better "sense of decorum," a better sense of order, than they had.[2] Given the meticulous court protocol and well-oiled bureaucracy at Constantinople, it is hard to see how people there could have viewed the Europeans as better organized. But the Byzantine critics had a point. While their emperors were favoring family members and their *dynatoi* were creating regional dynasties, some Western governments were becoming more impersonal. They were, in effect, in the midst of a new phase of self-definition, codification, and institutionalization.

Law, Authority, and the Written Word in England

One good example is England. The king hardly needed to be present: the government functioned by itself, with its own officials to handle administrative matters and record keeping. The very circumstances of the English king favored the growth of an administrative staff: his frequent travels to and from the Continent meant that officials needed to work in his absence, and his enormous wealth meant that he could afford them.

True, a long period of civil war (1135-1154) between the forces of two female heirs

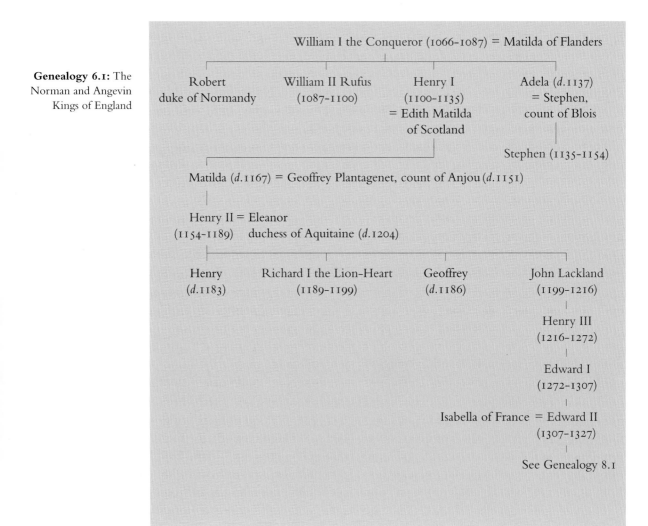

Genealogy 6.1: The Norman and Angevin Kings of England

to the Norman throne (Matilda, daughter of Henry I, and Adela, Henry's sister) threatened royal power. As in Germany during the Investiture Conflict, so in England the barons and high churchmen consolidated their own local lordships during the war; private castles, symbols of their independence, peppered the countryside. But the war ended when Matilda's son, Henry of Anjou, ascended the throne as the first "Angevin" king of England.[3] (See Genealogy 6.1: The Norman and Angevin Kings of England.) Under Henry II (r.1154-1189), the institutions of royal government in England were extended and strengthened.

THE REFORMS OF HENRY II

Henry was count of Anjou, duke of Normandy, and overlord of about half the other counties of northern France. He was also duke of Aquitaine by his marriage to Eleanor, heiress of that vast southern French duchy. As for his power in the British Isles: the princes of Wales swore him homage and fealty; the rulers of Ireland were forced to submit to him; and the king of Scotland was his vassal. Thus Henry exercised sometimes more, sometimes less power over a realm stretching from northern England to the Pyrenees. (See Map 6.3.) For his Continental possessions, he was vassal of the king of France.

Once on the English throne, Henry destroyed or confiscated the private castles built during the civil war and regained the lands that had belonged to the crown. Then he proceeded to extend his power, above all by imposing royal justice. Already the Anglo-Saxon kings had claimed rights in local courts, particularly in capital cases, even though those courts were dominated by powerful men largely independent of royal authority. The Norman kings added to Anglo-Saxon law in the area of land holding. Henry built on these institutions, regularizing, expanding, and systematizing them. The Assize of Clarendon in 1166 recorded that the king

> decreed that inquiry shall be made throughout the several counties and throughout the several hundreds ... whether there be ... any man accused or notoriously suspect of being a robber or murderer or thief.... And let the justices inquire into this among themselves and sheriffs among themselves.[4]

"Throughout the several counties and throughout the several hundreds": these were the districts into which England had long been divided. Henry aimed to apply a *common* law regarding chief crimes—a law applicable throughout England—to all men and women in the land. Moreover, he meant his new system to be habitual and routine. There had always been justices to enforce the law, but under Henry, there were many more of them; they were trained in the law and required to make regular

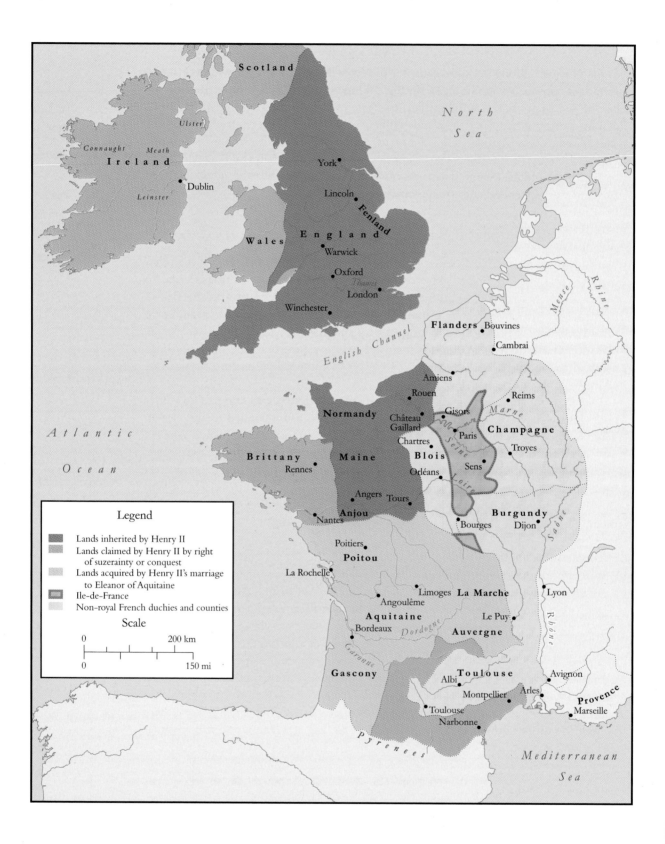

Scotland

North Sea

Ulster

Connaught *Meath*
Ireland
Leinster
• Dublin

York •
Lincoln •
Fenland
Wales
England
Warwick •
Oxford •
Thames
London •
Winchester •

English Channel

Flanders Bouvines •
Cambrai •

Amiens •

Rouen •
Marne
Normandy Château Gisors • Reims •
Gaillard Paris • **Champagne**
Chartres • Troyes •
Brittany **Maine** **Blois** Sens •
Rennes • Orléans •
Seine *Loire*
Angers • Tours • **Burgundy**
Anjou Bourges • Dijon •
Nantes •

Atlantic
Ocean

Poitiers •
Poitou
La Rochelle • *Saône*
Limoges • **La Marche**
Angoulême • Lyon •
Aquitaine Le Puy •
Bordeaux • *Dordogne* **Auvergne**
Garonne **Toulouse**
Gascony Albi • Avignon •
Montpellier • Arles •
Toulouse • **Provence**
Narbonne • Marseille •

Pyrenees

Mediterranean
Sea

Meuse *Rhine*

Rhône

Legend

▨ Lands inherited by Henry II
▨ Lands claimed by Henry II by right
of suzerainty or conquest
▨ Lands acquired by Henry II's marriage
to Eleanor of Aquitaine
▨ Ile-de-France
▨ Non-royal French duchies and counties

Scale

0   200 km
|——|——|——|——|——|
0   150 mi

visitations to each locality, inquiring about crimes and suspected crimes. (They were therefore called "itinerant justices" — from *iter*, Latin for journey. The local hearing that they held was called an eyre, also from *iter*.) The king required twelve representatives of the local knightly class — the middling aristocracy, later on known as the "gentry" — to meet during each eyre and either give the sheriff the names of those suspected of committing crimes in the vicinity or arrest the suspects themselves and hand them over to the royal justices. While convicted members of the knightly class often got off with only a fine, hanging or mutilation were the normal penalties for criminals. Even if acquitted, people "of ill repute" were to "cross the sea," exiled from England.[5]

Henry also exercised new control over cases that we would call "civil," requiring all cases of property ownership to be authorized by a royal writ. Unlike the Angevin reforms of criminal law, this requirement affected only the class of free men and women — a minority. While often glad to have the king's protection, they grumbled at the expense and time required to obtain writs. Consider Richard of Anstey's suit to gain his uncle's property: over the course of five years, he paid out a great deal of money for royal writs; for journeys to line up witnesses and to visit various courts; for the expenses of his clerical staff; and for gifts to numerous officials. Yet it was all worthwhile in the end, for "*at length* by grace of the lord king and by the judgment of his court my uncle's land was adjudged to me."[6]

Map 6.3 (facing page): The Angevin and Capetian Realms in the Late Twelfth Century

The whole system was no doubt originally designed to put things right after the civil war. Although these law-and-order measures were initially expensive for the king — he had to build many new jails, for example — they ultimately served to increase royal income and power. Fines came from condemned criminals and also from any knightly representative who might shirk his duties before the eyre; revenues poured in from the purchase of writs. The exchequer, as the financial bureau of England was called, recorded all the fines paid for judgments and the sums collected for writs. The amounts, entered on parchment leaves sewn together and stored as rolls, became the Receipt Rolls and Pipe Rolls, the first of many such records of the English monarchy and an indication that writing had become a tool to institutionalize royal rule in England.

Perhaps the most important outcome of this expanded legal system was the enhancement of royal power and prestige. The king of England touched (not personally but through men acting in his name) nearly every man and woman in the realm. However, the extent of royal jurisdiction should not be exaggerated. Most petty crimes did not end up in royal courts but rather in more local ones under the jurisdiction of a lord. Thus the case of Hugh Tree came before a manorial court run by officials of the monastery of Bec. They held that he was "in mercy [liable to a fine] for his beasts caught in the lord's garden."[7] He had to pay 6 pence to his lord (in this case the monastery); no money went to the king. This helps explain why manorial lords—barons, knights, bishops, and monasteries like Bec—held on tenaciously to their local prerogatives.

In addition to local courts were those run by and for the clergy. Had Hugh Tree committed murder, he would have come before a royal court. Had he been a homicidal cleric, however, he would have come before a church court, which could be counted on to give him a mild punishment. No wonder that churchmen objected to submitting to the jurisdiction of Henry II's courts. But Henry insisted, and the ensuing contest between the king and his appointed archbishop, Thomas Becket (1118-1170), became the greatest battle between the church and the state in the twelfth century. The conflict over whose courts should have jurisdiction over "criminous clerks"—clerics accused of crimes—simmered for six years, until Henry's henchmen murdered Thomas, unintentionally turning him into a martyr. Although Henry's role in the murder remained ambiguous, public outcry forced him to do public penance for the deed. In the end, the struggle made both institutions stronger, as church and royal courts expanded side-by-side to address the concerns of an increasingly litigious society.

Defining the Role of the English King

Henry II and his sons Richard I the Lion-Heart (r.1189-1199) and John (r.1199-1216) were English kings with an imperial reach. Richard was rarely in England, since half of France was his to subdue (see Map 6.3, paying attention to the areas in various shades of peach). Responding to Saladin's conquest of Jerusalem, Richard went on the abortive Third Crusade (1189-1192), capturing Cyprus on the way and arranging a three-year truce with Saladin before rushing home to reclaim his territory from his brother, John, and the French king, Philip II (r.1180-1223). (His haste did him no good; he was captured by the duke of Austria and released only upon payment of a huge ransom, painfully squeezed out of the English people.)

When Richard died in battle in 1199, John took over. But if he began with an imperial reach, John must have felt a bit like the Byzantine emperor in 1204, for in that very year the king of France, Philip II, confiscated his northern French territories for defying his overlordship. It was a purely military victory, and John set out to win the territories back by gathering money wherever and however he could in order to pay for an abler military force. He forced his barons and many members of the gentry to pay him "scutage"—a tax—in lieu of army service. He extorted money in the form of "aids"—the fees that his barons and other vassals ordinarily paid on rare occasions, such as the knighting of the king's eldest son. He compelled the widows of his barons and other vassals to marry men of his choosing or pay him a hefty fee to remain single. With the wealth pouring in from these effective but unpopular measures, John was able to pay for a navy and hire mercenary troops.

All was to no avail. Philip's forces soundly defeated John's in 1214 at the battle of Bouvines. It was a defining moment, not so much for the Continent (English rule would continue there until the fifteenth century) as for England, where the barons — supported by many members of the gentry and the towns — organized, rebelled, and called the king to account. At Runnymede, just south of London, in June 1215, John was forced to agree to the charter of baronial liberties called Magna Carta, or "Great Charter," so named to distinguish it from a smaller charter issued around the same time concerning royal forests.

Magna Carta was intended to be a conservative document defining the "customary" obligations and rights of the nobility and forbidding the king to break from these without consulting his barons. Beyond this, it maintained that all free men in England had certain customs and rights in common that the king was obliged to uphold. "To no one will we sell, to no one will we refuse or delay right or justice."[8] In this way, Magna Carta documented the subordination of the king to written provisions; it implied that the king was not above the law. Copies of the charter were sent to sheriffs and other officials, to be read aloud in public places. Everyone knew what it said, and later kings continued to issue it — and have it read out — in one form or another. Though not a "constitution," nevertheless Magna Carta was an important step in the institutionalization of the English government.

Spain and France in the Making

Two states — Spain and France — started small and beleaguered but slowly grew to embrace the territory we associate with them today. In Spain, the *reconquista* was the engine driving expansion. Like the king of England, the kings from northern Spain came as conquerors. But unlike England, Christian Spain had numerous kings who competed with one another. By the mid-thirteenth century, Spain had the three-fold political configuration that would last for centuries (compare Map 6.1 on p. 220 with Map 7.5 on p. 276 and Map 8.5 on p. 320): to the east was the kingdom of Aragon-Catalonia; in the middle was Castile; and in the southwest was Portugal.

All of the Spanish kings appointed military religious orders similar to the Templars to form permanent garrisons along their ever-moving frontier with al-Andalus. But how were the kings to deal with formerly Muslim-controlled lands? When he conquered Cuenca in 1177, King Alfonso VIII of Castile (r.1158-1214) established a bishopric and gave the city a detailed set of laws (*fueros*) that became the model for other conquests. Confiding enforcement to local officials, the king issued the *fueros* to codify, as its preface puts it, "judicial institutions in behalf of safeguarding peace and the rights of justice between clergy and laity, between townsmen and peasants, among the needy and the poor."[9] The preface might have added that the laws also regulated relations between local Christians, Muslims, and Jews.

The kingdom of France was smaller and more fragile than Spain; it was lucky that it did not confront an Islamic frontier or competing royal neighbors (though a glance at Map 6.3 shows that it was surrounded by plenty of independent counts and dukes). When Philip II (r.1180-1223) came to the throne at the age of fourteen, his kingdom consisted largely of the Ile-de-France, a dwarf surrounded by giants. Philip seemed an easy target for the ambitions of English King Henry II and the counts of Flanders and Champagne. Philip, however, played them off against one another. Through inheritance he gained a fair portion of the county of Flanders in 1191. Soon his military skills came to the fore as he wrenched Normandy from the king of England in 1204. This was the major conquest of his career, and in its wake he soon forced the lords of Maine, Anjou, and Poitou, once vassals of the king of England, to submit to him. A contemporary chronicler dubbed him Philip Augustus—after the expansionist first Roman emperor—and Philip's seal, used to authenticate his documents, boasted an eagle, the symbol of imperial power.

Philip did more than expand; he integrated his Norman conquest into his kingdom. Norman nobles promised him homage and fealty, while Philip's royal officers went about their business in Normandy—taxing, hearing cases, careful not to tread on local customs, but equally careful to enhance the flow of income into the French king's treasury. Gradually the Normans were brought into a new "French" orbit just beginning to take shape, constructed partly out of the common language of French and partly out of a new notion of the king as ruler of all the people in his territory.

Although there was never a French "common law" to supersede local ones, the French king, like the Spanish and English, succeeded in extending royal power through governmental bureaucracy. After 1194, Philip had all his decrees written down, establishing permanent repositories in which to keep them. Like the Angevin kings of England, Philip relied on members of the lesser nobility—knights and clerics, most of them educated in the city schools—to do the work of government. They served as officers of his court; as *prévôts*, officials who oversaw the king's estates and collected his taxes; and as *baillis* (or, in some places, seneschals) who not only supervised the *prévôts* but also functioned as judges, presiding over courts that met monthly, making the king's power felt locally as never before.

Of Empires and City-States

The empire ruled by the German king was an oddity. Elsewhere, smaller states were the norm. But the German king's empire spanned both Germany and Italy. In its embrace of peoples of contrasting traditions, it was more like Byzantium than like England. The location of the papacy made the empire different as well. Every other state was a safe distance away from the pope; but the empire had the pope in its throat. Tradition, prestige, and political self-respect demanded that the German king also be the emperor: Conrad III (r.1138-1152), though never actually crowned at Rome, nevertheless delighted in calling himself "August Emperor of the Romans" (while demeaning the Byzantine emperor as "King of the Greeks"). But being emperor meant controlling Italy and Rome. The difficulty was not only the papacy, defiantly opposed to another major power in Italy, but also the northern Italian communes, independent city-states in their own right.

THE REVIVAL AND DETERIORATION OF THE EMPIRE

Like the Angevin Henry II of England, Frederick I Barbarossa (r.1152-1190) came to the throne after a long period of bitter civil war between families—the Staufen and the Welfs—spawned in the wake of the Investiture Conflict. Contemporaries hailed him as a reconciler of enemies: he was Staufen on his father's side and Welf on his mother's. (See Genealogy 6.2: Rulers of Germany and Sicily.) Like the English king, Frederick held a kingdom and more. But he lacked Henry's wealth. As a result he was forced to rely on personal loyalties, not salaried civil servants. He could not tear down princely castles as Henry had done. Instead, he conceded the German princes their powers, requiring them in turn to recognize him as the source of those powers, and committing them to certain obligations, such as attending him at court and providing him with troops.

Frederick had to deal with more than the princes; he had to confront the papacy. In 1157, at the Diet of Besançon, Pope Adrian IV sent Frederick a letter that coyly referred to the imperial crown as the pope's *beneficium*—"benefit" or, more ominously, "fief." "A great tumult and uproar arose from the princes of the realm at so insolent a message," wrote Rahewin, a cleric who had access to many of the documents and people involved at the time. "It is said that one of the [papal] ambassadors, as though adding sword to flame, inquired: 'From whom then does he have the empire, if not from our lord the pope?' Because of this remark, anger reached such a pitch that one of [the princes] ... threatened the ambassador with his sword."[10]

Frederick calmed his supporters, but in the wake of this incident, he countered the "holy church" by coining an equally charged term for his empire: *sacrum imperium*—the "sacred empire." In 1165 he exhumed the body of Charlemagne, enclosing the

Henry IV
emperor (1056–1106)

Henry the Black   Henry V   Agnes = Frederick I of Hohenstaufen
duke of Bavaria   emperor (1106–1125)   duke of Swabia

Henry the Proud   Judith = Frederick II   Conrad III
duke of Saxony and Bavaria   duke of Swabia   king (1138–1152)

Henry the Lion   Frederick I Barbarossa
duke of Saxony and Bavaria   emperor (1152–1190)

Otto IV   Henry VI = Constance of Sicily   Philip of Swabia
king (1198–1218)   emperor (1191–1197)   king (1198–1208)
emperor (1209–1218)

Frederick II
king of Sicily (1198–1250)
king of Germany (1212–1250)
emperor (1220–1250)

Manfred
king of Sicily (d.1266)

Constance = Peter III
queen of Sicily (d.1302)   king of Aragon (d.1285)

Genealogy 6.2: Rulers of Germany and Sicily

dead emperor's arm in an ornate reliquary casket (Plate 6.1) and setting the wheels of canonization in motion. (Charlemagne was named a saint by Frederick's anti-pope, Pascal III. See the list of Popes and Antipopes to 1500 on p. 359 to see the many competing popes of Barbarossa's reign.)

Finally, Frederick had to deal with Italy. As emperor, he had claims on the whole peninsula, but he had no hope—or even interest—in controlling the south. By contrast, northern Italy beckoned: added to his own inheritance in Swabia (in southwestern Germany), its rich cities promised to provide him with both a compact power base and the revenues that he needed. (See Map 6.2.)

Taking northern Italy was, however, nothing like, say, conquering Normandy, which was used to ducal rule. The communes of Italy were themselves states (autonomous cities, yes, but each also with a good deal of surrounding land, their *contado*), jealous of their liberties, rivalrous, and fiercely patriotic. Frederick made no concessions to their sensibilities. Emboldened by theories of sovereignty that had been elaborated by the revival of Roman law, he marched into Italy and, at the Diet of Roncaglia (1158), demanded all

> dukedoms, marches, counties, consulates, mints, market tolls, forage taxes, wagon tolls, gate tolls, transit tolls, mills, fisheries, bridges, all the use accruing from running water, and the payment of an annual tax, not only on the land, but also on their own persons.[11]

Meanwhile, Frederick brought the Four Doctors (see p. 204) from Bologna to Roncaglia to hear court cases. He insisted that the conquered cities be governed by his own men, sending in *podestà* (city managers) who were often German-speaking and heavy-handed. No sooner had the *podestà* at Milan taken up his post, for example, than he immediately ordered an inventory of all taxes due the emperor and levied new and demeaning labor duties. He even demanded that the Milanese carry the wood and stones of their plundered city to Pavia, to build new houses there. This was a double humiliation: Milan had been at war with Pavia.

By 1167, most of the cities of northern Italy had joined with Pope Alexander III (1159-1181) to form the Lombard League against Frederick. Defeated at the battle of Legnano in 1176, Frederick agreed to the Peace of Venice the next year and withdrew most of his forces from the region. But his failure in the north led him to try a southern strategy. By marrying his son Henry VI (r.1190-1197) to Constance, heiress of the Kingdom of Sicily, Frederick Barbarossa linked the fate of his dynasty to a well-organized monarchy that commanded dazzling wealth.

As we have seen (p. 181), the Kingdom of Sicily had been created by Normans. In theory, it was held as a fief from the pope, who recognized its boundaries (lapping at the southern edge of the papal states) in 1156 in the treaty of Benevento. Both multilingual and multi-religious, the Kingdom of Sicily embraced Jews, Muslims, Greeks, and Italians. Indeed, the Normans saw themselves as heirs to the Byzantines and Muslims and frequently came close to conquering Byzantium and North Africa. Taking over the Byzantine and Islamic administrative apparatuses already in place in their kingdom, they crafted a highly centralized government, with royal justices circuiting the kingdom and salaried civil servants drawn from the level of knights and townsmen.

Henry and Constance's son Frederick II (1194-1250) tried to unite Sicily, Italy, and

Germany into an imperial unit. He failed: the popes, eager to carve out their own well-ordered state in the center of Italy, could not allow a strong monarch to encircle them. Declaring war on Frederick, the papacy not only excommunicated him several times but also declared him deposed and accused him of heresy, a charge that led to declaring a crusade against him in the 1240s. These were fearsome actions. The king of France urged negotiation and reconciliation, but others saw in Frederick the devil himself. In the words of one chronicler, Frederick was "an evil and accursed man, a schismatic, a heretic, and an epicurean, who 'defiled the whole earth' (Jer.51:25)" because he sowed the seeds of division and discord in the cities of Italy.[12]

This was one potent point of view. There were others, more admiring. Frederick was a poet, a patron of the arts, and the founder of the first state-supported university, which he built at Naples. His administrative reforms in Sicily were comparable to Henry II's in England: he took what he found and made it routine. In the *Constitutions of Melfi* (1231) he made sure that his salaried officials worked according to uniform procedures, required nearly all litigation to be heard by royal courts, regularized commercial privileges, and set up a system of royal taxation. In 1232 he began minting gold coins, a turning point in European currency.

Plate 6.1: Reliquary Casket for Charlemagne's Arm (*c.*1166–1170). Pairing the cult of Charlemagne with that of the Madonna, this reliquary casket, made to hold Charlemagne's arm, depicts Mary and the Child in the center of an arcade. Mother and child are flanked on either side by archangels. Frederick Barbarossa is depicted within the arch on the far left, while his wife, Beatrice, is on the far right, thus associating the reigning rulers with the sainted emperor.

The struggle with the papacy obliged Frederick to grant enormous concessions to the German princes to give himself a free hand. In effect, he allowed the princes to turn their territories into independent states. Until the nineteenth century, Germany was a mosaic, not of city-states like Italy but of principalities. Between 1254 and 1273 the princes, split into factions, kept the German throne empty by electing two different foreigners who spent their time fighting each other. Oddly enough, it was during this low point of the German monarchy that the term "Holy Roman Empire" was coined. In 1273, the princes at last united and elected a German, Rudolf I (r.1273–1291), whose family, the Habsburg, was new to imperial power. Rudolf used the imperial title to help him gain Austria for his family. But he did not try to assert his power in Italy. For the first time, the word "emperor" was freed from its association with Rome.

The Kingdom of Sicily was similarly parceled out. The papacy tried to ensure that the Staufen dynasty would never again rule by calling upon Charles of Anjou, brother of the king of France, to take it over in 1263. Undeterred, Frederick's granddaughter, Constance, married to the King of Aragon (Spain), took the proud title "Queen of Sicily." In 1282, the Sicilian communes revolted against the Angevins in the uprising

known as the "Sicilian Vespers," begging the Aragonese for aid. Bitter war ensued, ending only in 1302, when the Kingdom of Sicily was split: the island became a Spanish outpost, while its mainland portion (southern Italy) remained under Angevin control.

A Hungarian Mini-Empire

Unlike the Kingdom of Sicily, the Kingdom of Hungary reaped the fruits of a period of expansion. In the eleventh century, having solidified their hold along the Danube River (the center of their power), the kings of Hungary moved north and east. In an arc ending at the Carpathian Mountains, they established control over a multi-ethnic population of Germans and Slavs. In the course of the twelfth century, the Hungarian kings turned southward, taking over Croatia and fighting for control over the coastline with the powerful Republic of Venice. They might have dominated the whole eastern Adriatic had not the Kingdom of Serbia re-established itself west of its original site, eager for its own share of seaborne commerce.

The Triumph of the City-States

That Venice was strong enough to rival Hungary in the eastern Adriatic was in part due to the confrontations between popes and emperors in Italy, which weakened both sides. The winners of those bitter wars were not the papacy, not the Angevins, not even the Aragonese, and certainly not the emperors. The winners were the Italian city-states. Republics in the sense that a high percentage of their adult male population participated in their government, they were also highly controlling. For example, to feed themselves, the communes prohibited the export of grain while commanding the peasants in the *contado* to bring a certain amount of grain to the cities by a certain date each year. City governments told the peasants which crops to grow and how many times per year they should plow the land. The state controlled commerce as well. At Venice, exceptional in lacking a *contado* but controlling a vast maritime empire instead, merchant enterprises were state run, using state ships. When Venetians went off to buy cotton in the Levant, they all had to offer the same price, determined by their government back home.

Italian city-state governments outdid England, Sicily, and France in their bureaucracy and efficiency. While other governments were still taxing by "hearths," the communes devised taxes based on a census (*catasto*) of property. Already at Pisa in 1162 taxes were being raised in this way; by the middle of the thirteenth century, almost all the communes had such a system in place. But even efficient methods of taxation did not bring in enough money to support the two main needs of the commune: paying their officials and, above all, waging war. To meet their high military expenses, the communes created state loans, some voluntary, others forced. They were the first in Europe to do so.

CULTURE AND INSTITUTIONS IN TOWN AND COUNTRYSIDE

Organization and accounting were the concerns of lords outside of Italy as well. But no one adopted the persona of the business tycoon; the prevailing ideal was the chivalrous knight. Courts were aristocratic centers, organized not only to enhance but also to highlight the power of lord and lady. Meanwhile, in the cities, guilds constituted a different kind of enclave, shutting out some laborers and women but giving high status to masters. Universities too were a sort of guild. Artistic creativity, urban pride, and episcopal power were together embodied in Gothic cathedrals.

Inventorying the Countryside

Not only kings and communes but great lords everywhere hired literate agents to administer their estates, calculate their profits, draw up accounts, and make marketing decisions. Money financed luxuries, to be sure, but even more importantly it enhanced aristocratic honor, so dependent on personal generosity, patronage, and displays of wealth. In the late twelfth century, when some townsmen could boast fortunes that rivaled the riches of the landed nobility, noble extravagance tended to exceed income. Most aristocrats went into debt.

The nobles' need for money coincided with the interests of the peasantry, whose numbers were expanding. The solution was the extension of farmland. By the middle of the century, isolated and sporadic attempts to bring new land into cultivation had become regular and coordinated. Great lords offered special privileges to peasants who would do the backbreaking work of plowing marginal land. In 1154, for example, the bishop of Meissen (in Germany) proclaimed a new village and called for peasants from Flanders to settle there. Experts in drainage, the colonists received rights to the swampland they reclaimed. They owed only light monetary obligations to the bishop, who nevertheless expected to reap a profit from their tolls and tithes. Similar encouragement came from lords throughout Europe, especially in northern Italy, England, Flanders, and Germany. In Flanders, where land was regularly inundated by seawater, the great monasteries sponsored drainage projects, and canals linking the cities to the agricultural regions let boats ply the waters to virtually every nook and cranny of the region.

Sometimes free peasants acted on their own to clear land and relieve the pressure of overpopulation, as when the small freeholders in England's Fenland region cooperated to build banks and dikes to reclaim the land that led out to the North Sea. Villages were founded on the drained land, and villagers shared responsibility for repairing and maintaining the dikes even as each peasant family farmed its new holding individually.

On old estates, the rise in population strained to its breaking point the manse organization that had developed in Carolingian Europe, where each household was settled on the land that supported it. Now, in the twelfth century, many peasant families might live on what had been, in the ninth century, the manse of one family. Labor services and dues had to be recalculated, and peasants and their lords often turned services and dues into money rents, payable once a year. With this change, peasant men gained more control over their plots — they could sell them, will them to their sons, or even designate a small portion for their daughters. However, for these privileges they had either to pay extra taxes or, like communes, join together to buy their collective liberty for a high price, paid out over many years to their lord. Peasants, like town citizens, gained a new sense of identity and solidarity as they bargained with a lord keen to increase his income at their expense.

The Culture of the Courts

When Henry II and his wife Eleanor came to Aquitaine, they were never alone. Accompanying them were relatives, vassals, officials, priests, knights, probably a doctor or two, and certainly troubadours. These were poets, musicians, and entertainers all in one. They sang love poems in Occitan, the vernacular of southern France. Eleanor's grandfather, Duke William IX of Aquitaine (1071-1126), is counted the first of the troubadours. But there were certainly people singing his kind of poetry in both Arabic and Hebrew in al-Andalus, which, as we have seen, was just at this time regularly coming into contact (mainly violently, to be sure) with the cultures of the north. By Eleanor's day, there were many troubadours, welcomed at major courts as essential personnel. Bernart de Ventadorn (fl.1150-1180) was among them. Here is one of his verses:

Ai Deus! car no sui ironda,	Ah, God! couldn't I be a swallow
que voles per l'aire	and fly through the air
e vengues de noih prionda	and come in the depths of the night
lai dins so repaire?	into her dwelling there?[13]

The rhyme scheme *seems* simple: *ironda* goes with *prionda*, *aire* with *repaire*. But consider that the verse before it (not printed here) has the -*onda* rhyme in the second and fourth lines (rather than the first and third), while the verse after it has -*aire* in the first and third lines (rather than the second and fourth). In fact the scheme is extremely complex and subtle, an essential skill for a poet whose goal was to dazzle his audience with brilliant originality.

In rhyme and meter, troubadour songs resembled Latin liturgical chants of the same region and period. Clearly, lay and religious cultures overlapped. They overlapped in musical terms as well, in the use, for example, of plucking and percussive instruments. Above all, they overlapped in themes: they spoke of love. The monks (as we have seen with the Cistercians, on p. 216) thought about the love between God and mankind; the troubadours thought about erotic love. Yet the two were deliciously entangled. The verse in which Bernart wishes he could be a swallow continues:

> I fear the heart will melt within me
> if this lasts a little longer.
> Lady, for your love
> I join my hands and worship.
> Beautiful body of the colors of youth,
> what suffering you make me bear.[14]

This is playing with religious imagery. Bernart is ready to pray; he is thinking of a youthful body; he is suffering: he could be a worshiper identifying with Christ on the Cross. At the same time, he subverts the religious: he is thinking of his mistress as (he says) he tosses and turns "on the edge of the bed."[15]

Female troubadours (called *trobairitz*) flirted with the same themes. La Comtessa de Dia (*fl.c.*1200?) sang,

> I've been in great anguish
> over a noble soldier I once had,
> and I want everyone to know, for all time,
> that I loved him—too much!
> Now I see I'm betrayed
> because I didn't yield my love to him.
> For that I've suffered greatly,
> both in my bed and fully clad.[16]

As with the *adab* literature of the Islamic world (see p. 114 of volume 1), the ideals of such courtly poetry emphasized refinement, beauty, and wit, all summed up in the word *cortezia*, "courtliness" or "courtesy."

Historians and literary critics used to use the term "courtly love" to emphasize one of the themes of this literature: the poet expressing overwhelming love for a beautiful married noblewoman who is far above him and utterly unattainable. But this was only one of the many aspects of love that the troubadours sang about: some boasted of sexual conquests; others played with the notion of equality between lovers; still others preached that love was the source of virtue. The real theme of these poems was not courtly love; it was the power of women. No wonder Eleanor of Aquitaine and other aristocratic women patronized the troubadours: they enjoyed the image that it gave them of themselves. Nor was this image a delusion. There were many powerful female lords in southern France. They owned property, commanded vassals, led battles, decided disputes, and entered into and broke political alliances as their advantage dictated. Both men and women appreciated troubadour poetry, which recognized and praised women's power even as it eroticized it.

From southern France the lyric love song spread to Italy, northern France, England, and Germany. Here Occitan was a foreign language, so other vernaculars were used: the *minnesinger* (literally, "love singer") sang in German; the *trouvère* sang in the Old French of northern France. In northern France another genre of poetry grew up as well, poking fun at courtliness and its pretensions. This was the *fabliau* (pl. *fabliaux*), which boasted humbler folk as its protagonists.

Some troubadours wrote about war, not love. "I feel a great joy," wrote the poet Bertran de Born (*fl.* 2nd half of 12th c.), "when I see ranged along the field/ knights and horses armed for war."[17] But warfare was more often the subject of another kind of poem, the *chanson de geste*, "song of heroic deeds." Long recited orally, these vernacular poems appeared in written form at about the same time as troubadour poetry and, like them, the *chansons de geste* played with aristocratic codes of behavior, in this case on the battlefield rather than at court.

The *chansons de geste* were responding to social and military transformations. By the end of the twelfth century, nobles and knights had begun to merge into one class, threatened from below by newly rich merchants and from above by newly powerful kings. At the same time, the knights' importance in battle—unhorsing one another with lances and long swords and taking prisoners rather than killing their opponents—was waning in the face of mercenary infantrymen who wielded long hooks and knives that ripped easily through chain mail, killing their enemies outright. A knightly ethos and sense of group solidarity emerged within this changed landscape. Like Bertran de Born, the *chansons de geste* celebrated "knights and horses armed for war." But they also examined the moral issues that confronted knights, taking up the often contradictory values of their society. Should the fealty of a vassal trump loyalty to his family? In *Raoul de Cambrai*, the answer is no, with tragic results. Bernier, faithful vassal of Raoul de Cambrai, discovers that Raoul has burned the town of Origny and Bernier's mother within it. Renouncing his fidelity to Raoul, Bernier cries out, "Raoul, you scoundrel, may God bring disaster on you! I no longer want to be your vassal, and if I can't avenge this outrage, I shan't think myself worth a penny."[18]

The *chansons de geste*, later also called "epics," focused on battle; other long poems, later called "romances," explored relationships between men and women. Enormously popular in the late twelfth and early thirteenth centuries, romances took up such themes as the tragic love between Tristan and Isolde and the virtuous knight's search for the Holy Grail. Above all, romances were woven around the many fictional stories of King Arthur and his court. In one of the earliest, Chrétien de Troyes (c.1150-1190) wrote about the noble and valiant Lancelot, in love with Queen Guinevere, wife of Arthur. Finding a comb bearing some strands of her radiant hair, Lancelot is overcome:

> Never will the eye of man see anything receive such honor as when he
> begins to adore these tresses. A hundred thousand times he raises them to
> his eyes and mouth, to his forehead and face... . Even for Saint Martin
> and Saint James he has no need.[19]

By making Guinevere's hair an object of adoration, a sort of secular relic, Chrétien here not only conveys the depths of Lancelot's feeling but also pokes a bit of fun at his hero. When Guinevere tests Lancelot in the middle of a tournament by sending him a message to do his "worst," the poet evokes a similar mix of humor and loftiness:

> When he heard this, he replied: "Very willingly," like one who is altogeth-
> er hers. Then he rides at another knight as hard as his horse can carry
> him, and misses his thrust which should have struck him. From that time
> till evening he continued to do as badly as possible in accordance with the
> Queen's desire.[20]

It is an odd, funny, and pitiful episode: the greatest of all knights bested at the whim of a lady. Yet this is part of the premise of "chivalry." The word, deriving from the French *cheval* ("horse"), emphasizes above all that the knight was a horseman, a warrior of the most prestigious sort. Perched high in the saddle, his heavy lance couched in his right arm, the knight was an imposing and menacing figure. Chivalry made him gentle, gave his battles a higher meaning, whether for love of a lady or of God. The chivalric hero was constrained by courtesy, fair play, piety, and devotion to an ideal. Did real knights live up to these ideals? They knew perfectly well that they could not and that it would be absurd if they tried to do so in every particular. But they loved playing with the idea. They were the poets' audience, and they liked to think of themselves as fitting into the tales. When William the Marshal, advisor of English kings, died, his biographer wrote of him as a model knight, courteous with the ladies, brave on the battlefield.

Urban Guilds Incorporated

Courtly "codes" were poetic and playful. City codes were drier but no less compelling. In the early thirteenth century, guilds drew up statutes to determine dues, regulate working hours, fix wages, and set standards for materials and products. Sometimes they came into conflict with town government; this happened to some bread-bakers' guilds in Italy, where communes considered bread too important a commodity to be left to its producers. At other times, the communes supported guild efforts to control wages, reinforcing guild regulations with statutes of their own. When great lords rather than communes governed a city, they too tried to control and protect the guilds. King Henry II of England, for example, eagerly gave some guilds in his Norman duchy special privileges so that they would depend on him.

There was nothing democratic about guilds. In the cloth-making business, the merchant guild that imported the raw wool was generally the overseer of the other related guilds—the shearers, weavers, fullers (the workers who beat the cloth to shrink it and make it heavier), and dyers. In Florence, professional guilds of notaries and judges ranked in prestige and power above craft guilds. Within each guild was another kind of hierarchy. Apprentices were at the bottom, journeymen and -women in the middle, and masters at the top. Young boys and occasionally girls were the apprentices; they worked for a master for room and board, learning a trade. An apprenticeship in the felt-hat trade in Paris, for example, lasted seven years. After their apprenticeship, men and women often worked many years as day laborers, hired by a master when he needed extra help. Some men, but almost never women, worked their way up to master status. They were the ones who dominated the offices and set guild policies.

The codification of guild practices and membership tended to work against women, who were slowly being ousted from the world of workers during the late twelfth century. In Flanders, for example, as the manufacture of woolen cloth shifted from rural areas to cities, and from light to heavy looms, women were less involved in cloth production than they had been on traditional manors. Similarly, water- and animal-powered mills took the place of female hand labor grinding grain into flour— and most millers were male. Nevertheless, at Paris guild regulations for the silk fabric makers assumed that the artisans would be women:

No journeywoman maker of silk fabric may be a mistress [the female equivalent of "master"] of the craft until she has practiced it for a year and a day....
No mistress of the craft may weave thread with silk, or foil with silk.... No
mistress or journeywoman of the craft may make a false hem or border.[21]

By contrast, universities were all-male guilds. (The word *universitas* is Latin for
"guild.") Beginning as organizations of masters and students, the term eventually
came to apply to the school itself. At the beginning of the thirteenth century, the
universities regulated student discipline, scholastic proficiency, and housing while
determining the masters' behavior in equal detail. At the University of Paris, for
example, the masters were required to wear long black gowns, follow a particular
order in their lectures, and set the standards by which students could become masters
themselves. The University of Bologna was unique in having two guilds, one of students and one of masters. At Bologna, the students participated in the appointment,
payment, and discipline of the masters.

The University of Bologna was unusual because it was principally a school of law,
where the students were often older men, well along in their careers (often in imperial service) and used to wielding power. At the University of Paris, young students
predominated, drawn by its renown in the liberal arts and theology. The universities
of Salerno (near Naples) and Montpellier (in southern France) specialized in medicine. Oxford, once a sleepy town where students clustered around one or two masters, became a center of royal administration; its university soon developed a reputation for teaching the liberal arts, theology, science, and mathematics.

The curriculum of each university depended on its speciality and its traditions. At
Paris in the early thirteenth century, students spent at least six years studying the liberal arts before gaining the right to teach. If they wanted to specialize in theology,
they attended lectures on the subject for at least another five years. With books both
expensive and hard to find, lectures were the chief method of communication. These
were centered on important texts: the master read an excerpt aloud, delivered his
commentary on it, and disputed any contrary commentaries that rival masters might
have proposed. Students committed the lectures to memory.

Within the larger association of the university, students found more intimate
groups with which to live: "nations," linked to the students' place of origin. At
Bologna, for example, students belonged to one of two nations, the Italians and the
non-Italians. Each nation protected its members, wrote statutes, and elected officers.

Masters and students both were considered part of another group: clerics. This was
an outgrowth of the original, church-related, purposes of the schools, and it had two
important consequences. First, there were no university women. And second, university men were subject to church courts rather than the secular jurisdiction of towns

or lords. Many universities could also boast generous privileges from popes and kings, who valued the services of scholars. The combination of clerical status and special privileges made universities virtually self-governing corporations within the towns. This sometimes led to friction. When the townsmen of Oxford tried to punish a student suspected of killing his mistress, the masters protested by refusing to teach and leaving the city. Such disputes are called "town against gown" struggles because students and masters wore gowns (the distant ancestors of American graduation gowns). But since university towns depended on scholars to patronize local taverns, shops, and hostels, town and gown normally learned to negotiate with one another to their mutual advantage.

Gothic Style

Certainly town and gown agreed on building style: by c.1200, "Gothic" (the term itself comes from the sixteenth century) was the architecture of choice. Beginning as a variant of Romanesque in the Ile-de-France, Gothic style quickly took on an identity of its own. Gothic architects tried to eliminate heavy walls by enlivening them with sculpture or piercing them with glass, creating a soaring feel by using pointed arches. Suger, abbot of Saint-Denis and the promoter of Capetian royal power (see p. 201), was the style's first sponsor. When he rebuilt portions of his church around 1135, he tried to meld royal and ecclesiastical interests and ideals in stone and glass. At the west end of his church, the point where the faithful entered, Suger decorated the portals with figures of Old Testament kings, queens, and patriarchs, signaling the links between the present king and his illustrious predecessors. Rebuilding the interior of the east end of his church as well, Suger used pointed arches and stained glass to let in light, which Suger believed to be God's own "illumination," capable of transporting the worshiper from the "slime of earth" to the "purity of Heaven."

Gothic was an urban architecture, reflecting—in its grand size, jewel-like windows, and bright ornaments—the aspirations, pride, and confidence of rich and powerful merchants, artisans, and bishops. The Gothic cathedral, which could take centuries to complete, was often the religious, social, and commercial focal point of a city. Funds for these buildings might come from the bishop himself, from the canons (priests) who served his cathedral, or from townsmen. Notre Dame of Paris (Plate 6.2) was begun in 1163 by Bishop Maurice de Sully, whose episcopal income from estates, forests, taxes, and Parisian properties gave him plenty of money to finance the tallest church of its day. Under his successors, the edifice took shape with three stories, the upper one filled with stained glass. Bristling on the outside with flying buttresses—the characteristic "look" of a French Gothic church—it gave no hint of the light and calm within. (See Plate 6.3.) But at Mantes-la-Jolie (about 25 miles west of Paris), it was the merchant guild and the Capetian king together—rather than a bishop—who sponsored the building of the new collegiate church.

However financed, Gothic cathedrals were community projects, enlisting the labor and support of a small army of quarrymen, builders, carpenters, and glass cutters. Houses of relics, they attracted pilgrims as well. At Chartres Cathedral, proud home of the Virgin's tunic, crowds thronged the streets, the poor buying small lead figures of the Virgin, the rich purchasing wearable replicas of her tunic.

The technologies that made Gothic churches possible were all known before the twelfth century. The key elements included ribbed vaulting, which could give a sense of precision and order (as at Notre Dame; consider Plate 6.3 again, concentrating on the orderly rhythm of piers and ribs) or of richness and playful inventiveness (as at Lincoln Cathedral in England: see Plate 6.4). Flying buttresses took the weight of the vault off the walls, allowing most of the wall to be cut away and the open spaces filled by glass. (See Figure 6.1.) Pointed arches made the church appear to surge heavenward.

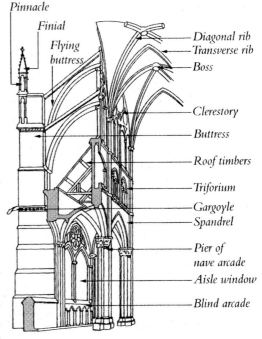

By the mid-thirteenth century, Gothic architecture had spread to most of Europe. Yet the style varied by region, most dramatically in Italy. San Francesco in Assisi is an example of what *Italian* architects meant by a Gothic church. It has high stained glass windows and a pointed, ribbed vault. (See Plate 6.5.) But the focus is not on light and height but on walls, painted decoration, and well-proportioned space. With flying buttresses rare and portal sculpture unobtrusive, Italian Gothic churches convey a spirit of spare and quiet beauty.

Gothic art, both painting and sculpture, echoed and decorated the Gothic church. While Romanesque sculpture played upon a flat surface, Gothic figures were liberated from their background, turning, bending, interacting. At Reims Cathedral the figure of Saint Joseph on the west portal, elegant and graceful, reveals a gentle smile. (See Plate 6.6.) Above his head is carved foliage of striking naturalness. Portals like this were meant to be "read" for their meaning. Joseph is not smiling for nothing; in the original arrangement of the portal he was looking at the figure of a servant while, further to his left, his wife, Mary, presented the baby Jesus in the temple. This was the New Testament story brought to life.

Figure 6.1: Elements of a Gothic Church. This drawing of a section through the nave at Amiens shows the most important features of a Gothic church.

Plate 6.2: Notre Dame of Paris, Exterior (begun 1163). To take the weight of the vault off the walls and open them to glass and light, the architects of Gothic churches such as Notre Dame used flying buttresses, which sprang from the top of the exterior wall. In this photograph they look rather like oars jutting out from the church; see, in particular, the apse (on the viewer's right).

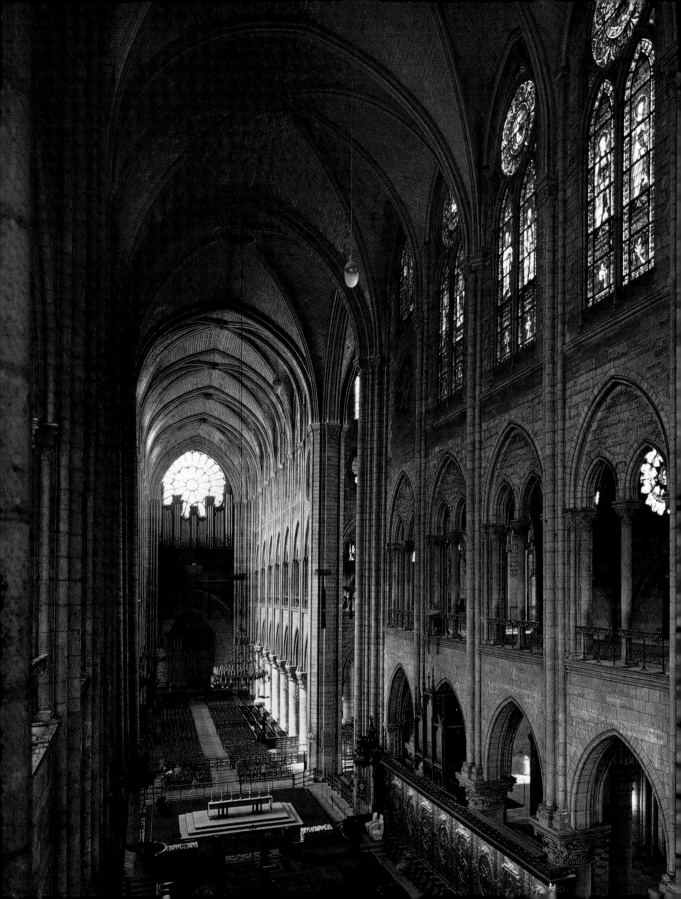

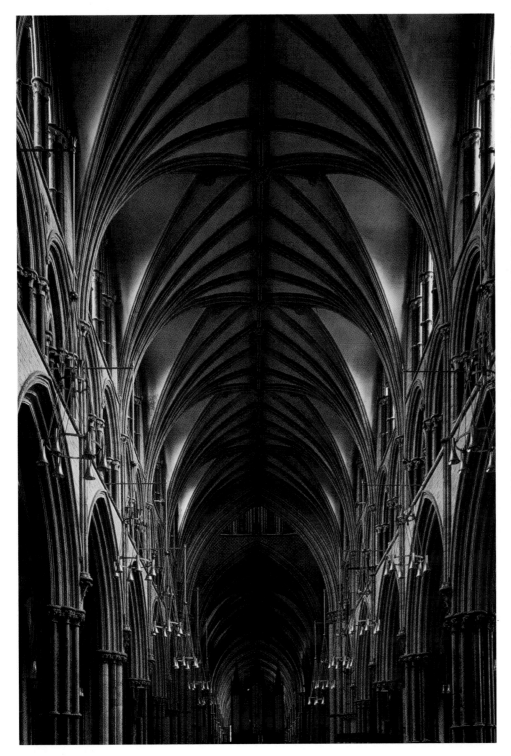

Plate 6.3 (facing page): Notre Dame of Paris, Interior (begun 1163). Compare this interior with that of Santiago in Plate 5.8 (p. 212). Santiago is a typical Romanesque church, with a barrel vault, two stories, and little natural light. By contrast, the Gothic cathedral of Notre Dame (shown here) has an arched vault that soars three stories high, while light from large stained-glass windows suffuses the entire nave.

Plate 6.4: Lincoln Cathedral, Interior (begun *c.*1225). Many English Gothic cathedrals emphasized surface ornament. Here the ribs, which spring from carved moldings on the walls of the nave, are splayed into fans on the vault. Can you find other decorative elements?

Preceeding pages:

Plate 6.5: San Francesco at Assisi (upper church; largely completed by 1239). Influenced by French Gothic, this church of the Franciscan Order in Assisi nevertheless asserts a different aesthetic. Compare it with Notre Dame in Plate 6.3 and Lincoln in Plate 6.4, where the piers and ribs mark off units of space (called "bays"). By contrast, San Francesco presents a unified space. Notre Dame celebrates its soaring height; San Francesco balances its height by its generous width. Unlike French Gothic, Italian Gothic churches gloried in their walls; at San Francesco they were decorated in the 1280s and 1290s with frescoes, the most famous of which illustrated the life and legend of Saint Francis (for whom see below, p. 253).

Plate 6.6: Reims Cathedral, West Portal, Saint Joseph (*c.*1240). Compare Saint Joseph on this Gothic portal with the portrayal of Anger and Lust on the Romanesque capital at Vézelay in Plate 5.6. Forgetting, for the moment, the differences in subject matter, note the change in style: Anger and Lust form—and adhere to—the shape of the capital, but Joseph breaks away from the column behind him and is carved fully in the round.

THE CHURCH IN THE WORLD

Just as the church was taking new interest in the human dimension of Joseph and his wife, so it concerned itself as never before in the lives of ordinary Christians. Under Innocent III (1198-1216)—the first pope to be trained at the city schools and to study both theology and law—the papacy gained a newly grand sense of itself. Innocent thought of himself as ruling in the place of Christ the King; secular kings and emperors existed simply to help the pope, who was the real lawmaker—the maker of laws that would lead to moral reformation. In the thirteenth century, the church sought to define Christianity, embracing some doctrines, rejecting others, and turning against Jews and Muslims with new vigor.

The Fourth Lateran Council (1215)

A council was the traditional method of declaring church law, and this is what Innocent intended when he convened one at his Lateran Palace at Rome in 1215. Presided over by the pope himself, the Fourth Lateran Council produced a comprehensive set of canons—most of them prepared by the pope's committees beforehand—to reform both clergy and laity. In effect it produced a code, in this case one for Christian society as a whole.

For laymen and -women perhaps the most important canons concerned the sacraments. The Fourth Lateran Council required Christians to attend Mass and to confess their sins to a priest at least once a year. Marriage was declared a sacrament, and bishops were assigned jurisdiction over marital disputes. Forbidding secret marriages, the council expected priests to uncover evidence that might impede a marriage. There were many impediments: people were not allowed to marry their cousins, nor anyone related to them by godparentage, nor anyone related to them through a former marriage. Children conceived within clandestine or forbidden marriages were to be considered illegitimate; they could not inherit property from their parents, nor could they become priests.

Like the code of chivalry, the rules of the Fourth Lateran Council about marriage worked better on parchment than in life. Well-to-do London fathers included their bastard children in their wills. On English manors, sons conceived out of wedlock regularly took over their parents' land. The prohibition against secret marriages was only partially successful. Even churchmen had to admit that the consent of both parties made a marriage valid.

The most important sacrament was the Mass, the ritual in which the bread and wine of the Eucharist was transformed into the flesh and blood of Christ. In the twelfth century a newly rigorous explanation of this transformation was promulgated according to which Christ's body and blood were truly present in the bread and wine on the altar. The Fourth Lateran Council not only declared this as church doctrine but also explained it by using a technical term coined by twelfth-century scholars. The bread and wine were "transubstantiated": though the Eucharist continued to *look* like bread and wine, after the consecration during the Mass the bread became the actual body and the wine the real blood of Christ. The council's emphasis on this potent event strengthened the role of the priest, for only he could celebrate this mystery (the transformation of ordinary bread and wine into the flesh of Christ) through which God's grace was transmitted to the faithful.

The Ins and the Outs

As the Fourth Lateran Council provided rules for good Christians, it turned against all others. Some canons singled out Jews and heretics for special punitive treatment; others were directed against Byzantines and Muslims. These laws were of a piece with wider movements. With the development of a papal monarchy that confidently declared a single doctrine and the laws pertaining to it, dissidence was perceived as heresy, non-Christians seen as treacherous.

New Groups within the Fold

The Fourth Lateran Council prohibited the formation of new monastic orders. It recognized that the trickle of new religious groups — the Carthusians is one example — of the early twelfth century had become a torrent by 1215. Only a very few of the more recent movements were accepted into the church, among them the Franciscans, the Beguines, and the Dominicans.

Saint Francis (*c.*1182-1226) had begun a promising career as a cloth merchant at Assisi when he experienced a complete conversion. Clinging to poverty as if, in his words, "she" were his "lady" (thus borrowing the vocabulary of chivalry), he accepted no money, walked without shoes, wore only one coarse tunic, and refused to be confined even in a monastery. He and his followers (called "friars," from the Latin term for "brothers") spent their time preaching, ministering to lepers, and doing manual labor. In time they dispersed, setting up fraternal groups throughout Italy, France, Spain, the Crusader States, and later Germany, England, Scotland, Poland, and elsewhere. Always they were drawn to the cities. Sleeping in "convents" on the outskirts of the towns, the Franciscans became a regular part of urban community life as they preached to crowds and begged their daily bread. Early converts included women: in

1212 the young noblewoman Clare determined to become a Franciscan herself, founding a community of women at San Damiano, a church near Assisi. She meant for the Damianites to follow the rule and lifestyle of the friars. But the church disapproved of the women's worldly activities, and the many sisters following Francis—by 1228 there were at least 24 female communities inspired by him in central and northern Italy—were confined to cloisters under the *Rule* of Saint Benedict. In the course of the thirteenth century the Order of the Sisters of St Francis was joined by a third order, the "Tertiaries," which was made up of laypeople, many of them married. They dedicated themselves to works of charity and to daily church attendance.

The Beguines were still more integral to town life. In the cities of northern France, the Low Countries, and Germany, these women plied the trades of launderers, weavers, and spinners. (Their male counterparts, the "Beghards," were far less numerous). Choosing to live together in informal communities, taking no vows, free to marry if they wished, they dedicated themselves to simplicity and piety. If outwardly ordinary, however, inwardly their religious lives were often emotional and ecstatic, infused with the imagery of love. Mary of Oignies (1177-1213), for example, felt herself to be a pious mother entrusted with the Christ-child, who "nestled between her breasts like a baby.... Sometimes she kissed him as though He were a little child and sometimes she held Him on her lap as if He were a gentle lamb."[22]

Saint Dominic (1170-1221), founder of the Dominican order, was more hardheaded. Reckoning that most preachers failed to counter the sway of heretics in southern France because they came richly clad, on horseback, and followed by a retinue, he and his followers rejected material riches and instead went about on foot, preaching and begging. They soon came to resemble the Franciscans, both organizationally and spiritually; they too were called friars.

DEFINING THE OTHER

The heretics that Dominic confronted were the Albigensians (also called Cathars), one of a number of dualist groups that sprang up in the twelfth century in Italy, the Rhineland, and Languedoc (southern France). Calling themselves Christ's Poor, they preached a world torn between two great forces, one good and the other evil. As the material world was the creation of the devil, they renounced it, rejecting wealth, sex, and meat, and denying the efficacy of the sacraments. Attracting both men and women, these "friends of God" (as they called themselves) believed they were followers of Christ's original message. But the church called them heretics.

The church condemned other, non-dualist movements as heretical not on doctrinal grounds but because these groups allowed their lay members to preach, assuming for themselves the privilege of bishops. At Lyon (in southeastern France) in the 1170s, for example, a rich merchant named Waldo decided to take literally the Gospel message, "If you wish to be perfect, then go and sell everything you have, and give to the poor" (Matt. 19:21). The same message had inspired countless monks and would worry the church far less several decades later, when Saint Francis established his new order. But when Waldo went into the street and gave away his belongings, announcing, "I am not out of my mind, as you think,"[23] he scandalized not only the bystanders but the church as well. Refusing to retire to a monastery, Waldo and his followers, men and women called Waldensians, lived in poverty and went about preaching, quoting the Gospel in the vernacular so that everyone would understand them. But the papacy rejected Waldo's bid to preach freely; and the Waldensians—denounced, excommunicated, and expelled from Lyon—wandered to Languedoc, Italy, northern Spain, and the Mosel valley, just east of France.

EUROPEAN AGGRESSION WITHIN AND WITHOUT

Jews, heretics, Muslims, Byzantines, and pagans: all felt the heavy hand of Christian Europeans newly organized, powerful, and zealous. Meanwhile, even the undeniable Catholicism of Ireland did not prevent its takeover by England.

The Jews

Prohibited from joining guilds, Jews increasingly were forced to take the one job Christians could not have: lending on credit. Even with Christian moneylenders available (for some existed despite official prohibitions), lords borrowed from Jews. Then, relying on dormant anti-Jewish feeling, they sometimes "righteously" attacked their creditors. This happened in 1190 at York, for example, where local nobles orchestrated a brutal attack on the Jews of the city to rid themselves of their debts and the men to whom they owed money. Kings claimed the Jews as their serfs and Jewish property as their own. In England a special royal exchequer of the Jews was created in 1194 to collect unpaid debts due after the death of Jewish creditors. In France, Philip Augustus expelled the Jews from the Ile-de-France in 1182, confiscating their houses, fields, and vineyards for himself. He allowed them to return— minus their property—in 1198.

Attacks against Jews were inspired by more than resentment against Jewish money or desire for power and control. They grew out of the codification of Christian religious doctrine. The newly rigorous definition of the Eucharist as the true body and blood of Christ meant to some that Christ, wounded and bleeding, lay upon the altar. Miracle tales sometimes reported that the Eucharist bled. Reflecting Christian anxieties about real flesh upon the altar, sensational stories, originating in clerical circles but soon widely circulated, told of Jews who secretly sacrificed Christian children in a morbid revisiting of the crucifixion of Jesus. This charge, called "blood libel" by historians, led to massacres of Jews in cities in England, France, Spain, and Germany. In this way, Jews became convenient and vulnerable scapegoats for Christian guilt and anxiety about eating Christ's flesh.

After the Fourth Lateran Council, Jews were easy to spot as well. The council required all Jews to advertise their religion by some outward sign, some special dress. Local rulers enforced this canon with zeal, not so much because they were anxious to humiliate Jews as because they saw the chance to sell exemptions to Jews eager to escape the requirement. Nonetheless, sooner or later Jews almost everywhere had to wear a badge as a sign of their second-class status: in southern France and Spain they had to wear a round badge; in Vienna they were forced to wear pointed hats.

Crusades

Attacks against Jews coincided with newly vigorous crusades. A new kind of crusade was launched against the heretics in southern France; along the Baltic, rulers and crusaders redrew Germany's eastern border; and the Fourth Crusade was rerouted and took Constantinople.

Against the Albigensians in southern France, Innocent III demanded that northern princes take up the sword, invade Languedoc, wrest the land from the heretics, and populate it with orthodox Christians. This Albigensian Crusade (1209-1229) marked the first time the pope offered warriors fighting an enemy within Christian Europe all the spiritual and temporal benefits of a crusade to the Holy Land. In the event, the political ramifications were more notable than the religious results. After twenty years of fighting, leadership of the crusade was taken over in 1229 by the Capetian kings. Southern resistance was broken and Languedoc was brought under the control of the French crown. (On Map 6.3, the area taken over by the French crown corresponds more or less with the region of Toulouse.)

Like Spain's southern boundary, so too Europe's northeast was a moving frontier, driven ever further eastward by crusaders and settlers. By the twelfth century, the peoples living along the Baltic coast—partly pagan, mostly Slavic- or Baltic-speaking—had learned to make a living and even a profit from the inhospitable soil and climate. Through fishing and trading, they supplied the rest of Europe and Russia with slaves, furs, amber, wax, and dried fish. Like the earlier Vikings, they combined commercial competition with outright raiding, so that the Danes and the Saxons (that is, the Germans in Saxony) both benefited and suffered from their presence. It was Saint Bernard (see p. 211) who, preaching the Second Crusade in Germany, urged one to the north as well. Thus began the Northern Crusades, which continued intermittently until the early fifteenth century.

In key raids in the 1160s and 1170s, the king of Denmark and Henry the Lion, the duke of Saxony, worked together to bring much of the region between the Elbe and Oder rivers under their control. They took some of the land outright, leaving the rest in the hands of the Baltic princes, who surrendered, converted, and became their vassals. Churchmen arrived: the Cistercians built their monasteries right up to the banks of the Vistula River, while bishops took over newly declared dioceses. In 1204 the "bishop of Riga"—in fact he had to bring his own Christians with him to his lonely outpost amidst the Livs—founded a military/monastic order called the Sword-Brothers. The monks soon became a branch of the Teutonic Knights, a group originally founded in the Crusader States. They organized crusades, defended newly conquered regions, and launched their own holy wars against the "Northern Saracens." By the end of the thirteenth century, they had brought the lands between Estonia and the Vistula under their sway. (See Map 6.4.) Meanwhile knights, peasants, and townspeople streamed in, colonists of the new frontier. Although less well-known than the crusades to the Levant, the Northern Crusades had more lasting effects, settling the Baltic region with a German-speaking population that brought its western institutions—cities, laws, guilds, universities, castles, manors, vassalage—with it.

Colonization was the unanticipated consequence of the Fourth Crusade as well. Called by Innocent III, who intended it to re-establish the Christian presence in the Holy Land, the crusade was diverted when the organizers overestimated the numbers joining the expedition. The small army mustered was unable to pay for the large fleet of ships that had been fitted out for it by the Venetians. Making the best of adversity, the Venetians convinced the crusaders to "pay" for the ships by attacking Zara (today Zadar), one of the coastal cities that Venice disputed with Hungary. Then, taking up the cause of one claimant to the Byzantine throne, the crusaders turned their sights on Constantinople. We already know the political results. The religious results are more subtle. Europeans disdained the Greeks for their independence from the pope; on the other hand, they considered Constantinople a treasure trove of the most precious of relics, including the True Cross. When, in the course of looting the city, one crusader, the abbot of a German Cistercian monastery, came upon a chest of relics, he "hurriedly and greedily thrust in both hands."[24] There was a long tradition of relic theft in the West; it was considered pious, a sort of holy sacrilege. Thus, when the abbot returned to his ship to show off his booty, the crusaders shouted, "Thanks be to God." In this sense Constantinople was taken so that the saints could get better homes.

Ireland

In 1169 the Irish king of Leinster, Diarmait Mac Murchada (Dermot MacMurrough), enlisted some lords and knights from England to help him first keep, then expand, his kingdom. The English fighters succeeded all too well; when Diarmait died (1171), some of the English decided to stay, claiming Leinster for themselves. The king of England, Henry II, reacted swiftly. Gathering an army, he invaded Ireland in 1171. The lords of the 1169 expedition recognized his overlordship almost immediately, keeping their new territories, but now redefined as fiefs from the king. Most of the native Irish kings submitted in similar manner. The whole of one kingdom, Meath, was given to one of Henry's barons.

Map 6.4: The German Push to the East, Twelfth to Fourteenth Centuries

The English came to stay, and more—they came to put their stamp on the Irish world. It became "English Ireland": England's laws were instituted; its system of counties and courts was put in place; its notions of lordship (in which the great lords parceled out some of their vast lands to lesser lords and knights) prevailed. Small wonder that Gerald of Wales (*d.*1223) could see nothing good in native Irish culture:

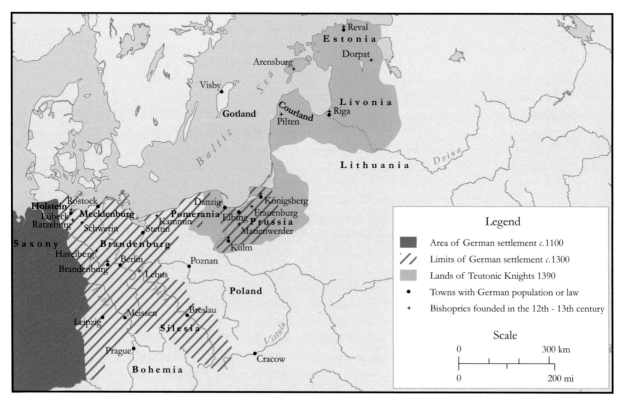

"they are uncultivated," he wrote, "not only in the external appearance of their dress, but also in their flowing hair and beards. All their habits are the habits of barbarians."[25]

★   ★   ★   ★

In the fifty years before and after 1200, Europe, aggressive and determined, pushed against its borders. Whether gaining territory from the Muslims in Spain and Sicily, colonizing the Baltic region and Ireland, or creating a Latin empire at Constantinople, Europeans accommodated the natives only minimally. For the most part, they imposed their institutions and their religion, each defined, formalized, and self-confident.

Self-confidence also led lords and ladies to pay poets to celebrate their achievements and bishops and townspeople to commission architects to erect towering Gothic churches in their midst. Similar certainties lay behind guild statutes, the incorporation of universities, the development of common law, and the Fourth Lateran Council's written definitions of Christian behavior and belief.

An orderly society would require institutions so fearlessly constructed as to be responsive to numerous individual and collective goals. But in the next century, while harmony was the ideal and sometimes the reality, discord was an ever-present threat.

CHAPTER SIX KEY EVENTS

1152-1190	Frederick Barbarossa (king of Germany and emperor)
1154-1189	King Henry II of England
1170	Murder of Thomas Becket
1171	Henry II conquers Ireland
1171-1193	Saladin's rule
1176	Battle of Legnano
1182	Jews expelled from the Ile-de-France
1187	Battle of Hattin
1189-1192	Third Crusade
1192-1250	Frederick II
1198-1216	Pope Innocent III
1204	Fall of Constantinople to Crusaders
1204	Philip II of France takes King John of England's northern French possessions
1212	Battle of Las Navas de Tolosa
1214	Battle of Bouvines
1215	Magna Carta
1215	Fourth Lateran Council
1226	Death of Saint Francis
1273	Election of Rudolf of Habsburg as Holy Roman Emperor

NOTES

1. Ibn Shaddad, *The Rare and Excellent History of Saladin*, in *Reading the Middle Ages: Sources from Europe, Byzantium, and the Islamic World*, ed. Barbara H. Rosenwein (Peterborough, ON, 2006), p.334.

2. *Michael Akominatou tou Choniatou ta sozomena*, ed. Spiro P. Lampros (Athens, 1879-80), 1:183, as quoted in Michael Angold, *The Byzantine Empire: A Political History, 1025-1204*, 2nd ed. (London, 1997), p.314.

3. Henry's father, Geoffrey of Anjou, was nicknamed Plantagenet from the *genêt*, the name of a shrub ("broom" in English) that he liked. Historians sometimes use the sobriquet to refer to the entire dynasty, so Henry II was the first "Plantagenet" as well as the first "Angevin" king of England.

4. *The Assize of Clarendon*, in *Reading the Middle Ages*, p.350.

5. Ibid., p.352.

6. *The Costs of Richard of Anstey's Law Suit*, in *Reading the Middle Ages*, p.354.

7. *Proceedings for the Abbey of Bec*, in *Reading the Middle Ages*, p.361.

8. *Magna Carta*, in *Reading the Middle Ages*, p.381.

9. *The Laws of Cuenca*, in *Reading the Middle Ages*, p.355.

10. *Diet of Besançon*, in *Reading the Middle Ages*, p.376.

11. Otto of Freising and his continuator, Rahewin, *The Deeds of Frederick Barbarossa*, trans. Charles Christopher Mierow with the collaboration of Richard Emery (New York, 1966), p.238, slightly modified.

12. *The Chronicle of Salimbene de Adam*, ed. and trans. Joseph L. Baird, Giuseppe Baglivi and John Robert Kane, Medieval & Renaissance Texts & Studies 40 (Binghamton, NY, 1986), p.5.

13. *Lyrics of the Troubadours and Trouvères: An Anthology and a History*, ed. and trans. Frederick Goldin (New York, 1973), pp.132-33.

14. Ibid., p.133.

15. Ibid.

16. Comtessa de Dia, *I've Been in Great Anguish*, in *Reading the Middle Ages*, p.391.

17. Bertran de Born, *I Love the Joyful Time*, in *Reading the Middle Ages*, p.390.

18. *Raoul de Cambrai*, in *Reading the Middle Ages*, p.388.

19. Chrétien de Troyes, *Arthurian Romances*, trans. W.W. Comfort (New York, 1975), pp.288-89.

20. Ibid., p.341.

21. *Guild Regulations of the Parisian Silk Fabric Makers*, in *Reading the Middle Ages*, pp.362-63.

22. Jacques de Vitry, *The Life of Mary of Oignies*, in *Reading the Middle Ages*, p.408.

23. *Peter Waldo in the Chronicle of Laon*, in *Reading the Middle Ages*, p.404.

24. Gunther of Pairis, *Hystoria Constantinopolitana*, in *The Capture of Constantinople*, ed. and trans. Alfred J. Andrea (Philadelphia, 2007), p.111.

25. Gerald of Wales, *The History and Topography of Ireland* (Harmondsworth, 1982), p.102.

FURTHER READING

Abulafia, David. *Frederick II: A Medieval Emperor*. London, 1988.

Angold, Michael. *The Byzantine Empire, 1025-1204*. 2nd. ed. London, 1997.

Baldwin, John. *The Government of Philip Augustus: Foundations of French Royal Power in the Middle Ages*. Berkeley, 1986.

Bartlett, Robert. *England under the Norman and Angevin Kings, 1075-1225*. Oxford, 2000.

——. *The Making of Europe: Conquest, Colonization and Cultural Change, 950-1350*. Princeton, 1993.

Binski, Paul. *Becket's Crown: Art and Imagination in Gothic England, 1170-1300*. New Haven, 2004.

Bouchard, Constance Brittain. *Strong of Body, Brave and Noble: Chivalry and Society in Medieval France*. Ithaca, NY, 1998.

Cheyette, Fredric L. *Ermengard of Narbonne and the World of the Troubadours*. Ithaca, NY, 2001.

Christiansen, Eric. *The Northern Crusades*. 2nd ed. London, 1997.

Clanchy, Michael T. *England and Its Rulers, 1066-1307*. 3rd ed. 2006.

Cobb, Paul M. *Usama ibn Munqidh: Warrior-Poet of the Ages of Crusades*. Oxford, 2005.

Duggan, Anne. *Thomas Becket*. Oxford, 2005.

Frame, Robin. *The Political Development of the British Isles, 1100-1400*. Oxford, 1990.

Gaunt, Simon, and Sarah Kay, eds. *The Troubadours: An Introduction*. Cambridge, 1999.

Geary, Patrick J. *Furta Sacra: Thefts of Relics in the Central Middle Ages*. Princeton, 1990.

Haverkamp, Alfred. *Medieval Germany, 1056-1273*. Trans. Helga Braun and Richard Mortimer. Oxford, 1988.

Lawrence, C.H. *The Friars: The Impact of the Early Mendicant Movement on Western Society*. London, 1994.

Menocal, Maria Rosa. *The Arabic Role in Medieval Literary History: A Forgotten Heritage*. Philadelphia, 1987.

Möhring, Hannes. *Saladin: The Sultan and His Times, 1138-1193*. Trans. David S. Bachrach. Baltimore, 2008.

Moore, R.I. *The First European Revolution, c. 970-1215*. Oxford, 2000.

——. *The Formation of a Persecuting Society: Power and Deviance in Western Europe, 950-1250*. Oxford, 1987.

Pegg, Mark Gregory. *The Corruption of Angels: The Great Inquisition of 1245-1246*. Princeton, 2001.

Simons, Walter. *Cities of Ladies: Beguine Communities in the Medieval Low Countries, 1200-1565*. Philadelphia, 2001.

Tyerman, Christopher. *God's War: A New History of the Crusades*. Cambridge, MA, 2006.

To test your knowledge of this chapter, please go to
www.rosenweinshorthistory.com
and click "Study Questions."

SEVEN

DISCORDANT HARMONIES
(c.1250-c.1350)

In the shadow of a great Mongol empire that, for about a century, stretched from the East China Sea to the Black Sea and from Moscow to the Himalayas, Europeans were bit players in a great Eurasian system tied together by a combination of sheer force and open trade routes. Taking advantage of the new opportunities for commerce and evangelization offered by the mammoth new empire, Europeans ventured with equal verve into experiments in their own backyards: in government, thought, and expression. Above all, they sought to harmonize disparate groups, ideas, and artistic modes. At the same time, unable to force everything into unified and harmonious wholes and often confronted instead with discord and strife, they tried to purge their society of deviants of every sort.

THE MONGOL HEGEMONY

The Mongols, like the Huns and Seljuks before them, were pastoralists. Occupying the eastern edge of the great steppes that stretch west to the Hungarian plains, they herded horses and sheep while honing their skills as hunters and warriors. Believing in both high deities and slightly lower spirits, the Mongols were also open to other religious ideas, easily assimilating Buddhism, Islam, and even some forms of Christianity. Their empire, in its heyday stretching about 4000 miles from east to west, was the last to be created by the nomads from the steppes.

The Contours of the Mongol Empire

The Mongols formed under the leadership of Chingiz (or Genghis) Khan (*c.*1162–1227). Fusing together various tribes of mixed ethnic origins and traditions, Chingiz created a highly disciplined, orderly, and sophisticated army. Impelled out of Mongolia in part by new climatic conditions that threatened their grasslands, the Mongols were equally inspired by Chingiz's vision of world conquest. All of China came under their rule by 1279; meanwhile, the Mongols were making forays to the west as well. They took Rus in the 1230s, Poland and Hungary in 1241, and might well have continued into the rest of Europe, had not unexpected dynastic disputes and insufficient pasturage for their horses drawn them back east. In the end, the borders of their European dominion rolled back east of the Carpathian Mountains.

Something rather similar happened in the Islamic world, where the Mongols took Seljuk Rum, the major power in the region, by 1243. They then moved on to Baghdad (putting an end to the caliphate there in 1258) and Syria (1259–1260), threatening the fragile crusader states a few miles away. Yet a few months later the Mongols with-

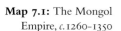

Map 7.1: The Mongol Empire, *c.*1260–1350

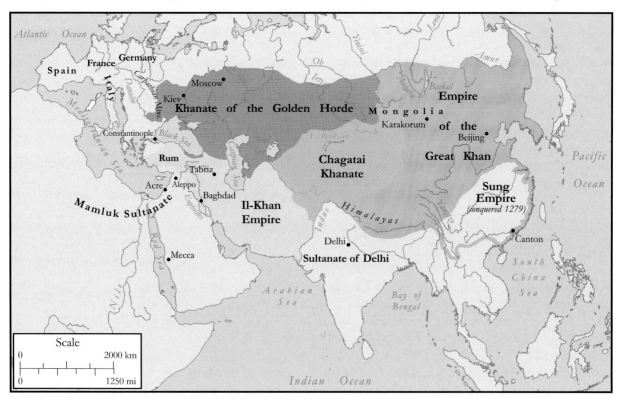

drew their troops from Syria, probably (again) because of inadequate grasslands and dynastic problems. The Mamluks of Egypt took advantage of the moment to conquer Syria themselves. This effectively ended the Mongol push across the Islamic world. It was the Mamluks, not the Mongols, who took Acre in 1291, snuffing out the last bit of the original Crusader States.

By the middle of the thirteenth century, the Mongol empire had taken on the contours of a settled state. (See Map 7.1.) It was divided into four regions, each under the rule of various progeny of Chingiz. The western-most quadrant was dominated by the rulers of Rus, the so-called Golden Horde ("horde" derived from the Turkic word for "court"). Settled along the lower Volga River valley, the Mongols of the Golden Horde combined traditional pastoralism with more settled activities. They founded cities, fostered trade, and gradually gave up their polytheism in favor of Islam. While demanding regular and exactly calculated tribute, troops, and recognition of their overlordship from the indigenous Rus rulers, they nevertheless allowed the Rus princes considerable autonomy. Their policy of religious toleration allowed the Orthodox church to flourish, untaxed, and willing in turn to offer up prayers for the soul of the Mongol khan (ruler). Kiev-based Rus, largely displaced by the Mongols, gave way to the hegemony of northern Rus princes, such as those centered in Lithuania (on the Baltic) and Muscovy, the area around Moscow. As Mongol rule fragmented, in the course of the fifteenth century, Moscow-based Russia emerged.

Mongols and Europeans

Once settled, the Mongols wooed Europe. They sent embassies west, welcomed Christian missionaries, and encouraged European trade. For their part, Europeans initially thought that the Mongols must be Christians; news of Mongol onslaughts in the Islamic world gave ballast to the myth of a lost Christian tribe led by a "Prester John" and his son "King David." Even though Europeans soon learned that the Mongols were not Christians, they dreamed of new triumphs: they imagined, for example, that Orthodox Christians under the Golden Horde would now accept papal protection (and primacy); they flirted with the idea of a Mongol-Christian alliance against the Muslims; and they saw the advent of the "new" pagans as an opportunity to evangelize. Thus in the 1250s the Franciscan William of Rubruck traveled across Asia to convert the Mongols in China; on his way back he met some Dominicans determined to do the same. European missions to the east became a regular feature of the West's contact with the Mongol world.

Such contact was further facilitated by trade. European caravans and ships crisscrossed the Mongol world, bringing silks, spices, ceramics, and copper back from

China, while exporting slaves, furs, and other commodities. (See Map 7.2.) The Genoese, who allied with the Byzantines to overthrow the Latin Empire of Constantinople in 1261, received special trading privileges from both the newly installed Byzantine emperor, Michael VIII Paleologus, and the khans of the Golden Horde. Genoa, which set up a permanent trading post at Caffa (today Feodosiya), on the Black Sea, was followed by Venice, which established its own trade-stations at Tana and Tabriz. These were sites well poised to exploit overland routes. Other European traders and missionaries traveled arduous sea routes, setting sail from the Persian Gulf (controlled by the Mongols) and rounding India before arriving in China. Marco Polo (1254–1324) was the most famous of the travelers to the east only because he left a fascinating travel book:

> [At Kinsai, today Hangzhou] there are ten principal market-places, not to speak of innumerable local ones.... Other streets are occupied by women of the town, ... [who] are to be found throughout the city, attired with great magnificence, heavily perfumed, attended by many handmaids, and

Map 7.2: Mongol-European Trade Routes, *c.*1350

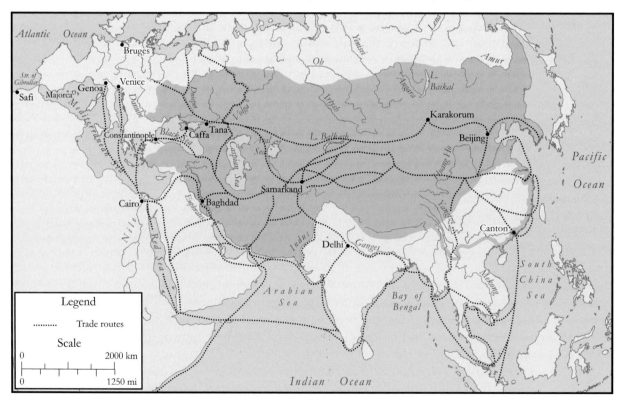

lodged in richly ornamented apartments.... In other streets are established the doctors and astrologers, who also teach reading and writing; and countless other crafts have their allotted places round the squares.[1]

Descriptions such as this fired up new adventurers, eager to seek out the fabulous wealth of the orient. In a sense, the Mongols initiated the search for exotic goods and missionary opportunities that culminated in the European "discovery" of a new world, the Americas.

THE MATURATION OF THE EUROPEAN ECONOMY

The pull of the East on the trade of the great Italian maritime cities was part of a series of shifts in Europe's commercial patterns. Another one, even more important, was towards the Atlantic. At the same time, new roads and bridges within Europe made land trade both possible and profitable. The linkages gave Europeans access to material goods of every sort, but they also heightened social tensions, especially within the cities.

New Routes

The first ships to ply the Atlantic's waters in regular trips were the galleys of Genoese entrepreneurs. By the 1270s they were leaving the Mediterranean via the Strait of Gibraltar, stopping to trade at various ports along the Spanish coast, and then making their way north to England and northern France. (See Map 7.3.) In the western Mediterranean, Majorca, recently conquered by the king of Aragon, sent its own ships to join the Atlantic trade at about the same time. Soon the Venetians began state-sponsored Atlantic expeditions using new-style "great galleys" that held more cargo yet required fewer oarsmen. Eventually, as sailing ships—far more efficient than any sort of galley—were developed by the Genoese and others, the Atlantic passage replaced older overland and river routes between the Mediterranean and Europe's north.

Equally important for commerce were new initiatives in North Africa. As the Almohad Empire collapsed, weak successor states allowed Europeans new elbow room. Genoa had outposts in the major Mediterranean ports of the Maghreb and new ones down the Atlantic coast, as far south as Safi (today in Morocco). Pisa, Genoa's traditional trade rival, was entrenched at Tunis. Catalonia and Majorca, by

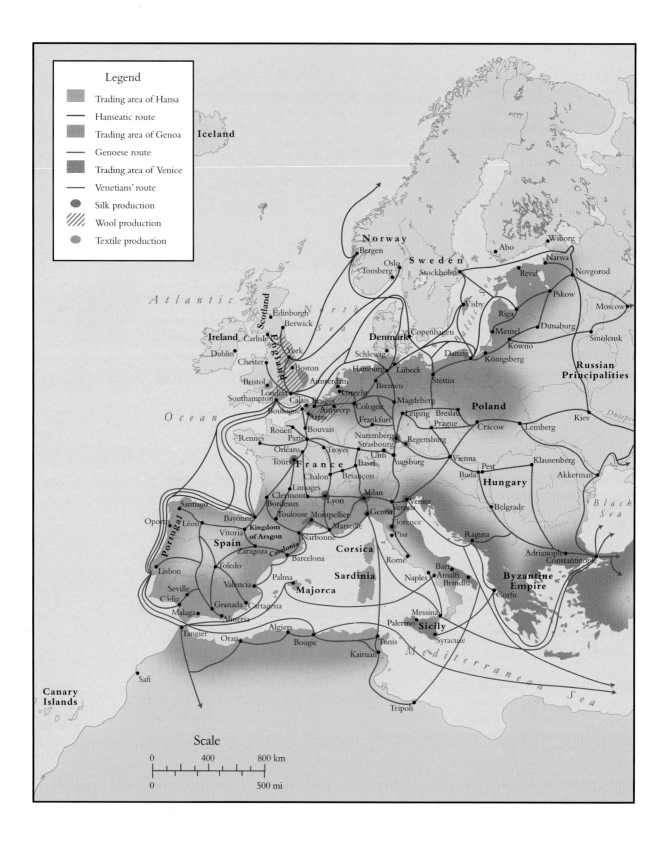

Legend

- Trading area of Hansa
- Hanseatic route
- Trading area of Genoa
- Genoese route
- Trading area of Venice
- Venetians' route
- Silk production
- Wool production
- Textile production

Iceland

Atlantic

Norway
Bergen
Oslo
Tonsberg

Sweden
Stockholm

Abo
Wiborg
Narwa
Novgorod
Reval
Pskow
Visby
Riga
Moscow
Memel
Dunaburg
Smolensk
Kowno
Königsberg
Copenhagen
Danzig

Scotland
Edinburgh
Berwick

Ireland
Dublin
Carlisle
York
Chester
Bristol
Boston
London
Southampton
Calais
Boulogne

England

North Sea

Denmark
Schlewig
Hamburg
Lübeck
Bremen
Stettin
Amsterdam
Utrecht
Bruges
Antwerp
Cologne
Magdeberg
Leipzig
Breslau
Prague
Cracow
Lemberg
Kiev

Poland

Russian Principalities

Ocean

Rouen
Paris
Arras
Bouvais
Rennes
Orléans
Troyes
Tours
France
Chalon
Limoges
Clermont
Bordeaux
Besançon
Lyon
Milan
Venice
Verona
Genoa
Florence
Pisa
Rome

Nuremberg
Strasbourg
Ulm
Basel
Augsburg
Regensburg
Vienna
Pest
Buda
Frankfurt

Hungary
Klausenberg
Akkerman
Belgrade

Dnieper

Black Sea

Ragusa
Adrianople
Constantinople

Byzantine Empire
Corfu

Santiago
Oporto
Léon
Bayonne
Vitoria
Kingdom of Aragon
Narbonne
Zaragoza
Catalonia
Barcelona
Corsica
Sardinia
Majorca
Portugal
Spain
Toledo
Palma
Lisbon
Valencia
Seville
Cádiz
Granada
Cartagena
Malaga
Almeria
Tangier
Oran
Algiers
Bougie
Kairuan
Tripoli
Safi
Canary Islands

Toulouse
Montpellier
Marseille

Naples
Bari
Amalfi
Brindisi
Messina
Palermo
Sicily
Syracuse
Tunis

Mediterranean Sea

Baltic Sea

Scale

| 0 | 400 | 800 km |

| 0 | | 500 mi |

now ruled by the king of Aragon, found their commercial stars rising fast. Catalonia established its own settlements in the port cities of the Maghreb; Majorcans went off to the Canary Islands. Profits were enormous. Besides acting as middlemen, trading goods or commodities from northern Europe, the Italian cities had their own products to sell (Venice had salt and glass products, Pisa had iron) in exchange for African cotton, linen, spices, and, above all, gold. In the mid-thirteenth century, Genoa and Florence were minting coins from gold panned on the upper Niger River, while Venice began minting gold ducats in 1284. The silver standard, which most of Europe had adhered to since the Carolingian age, was giving way to the gold.

At the same time as Genoa, Pisa, Venice, Majorca, and Catalonia were forging trade networks in the south, some cities in the north of Europe were creating their own marketplace in the Baltic Sea region. Built on the back of the Northern Crusades, the Hanseatic League was created by German merchants following in the wake of Christian knights to prosper in cities like Danzig (today Gdansk, in Poland), Riga, and Reval (today Tallinn, in Estonia). Lübeck, founded by the duke of Saxony, formed the Hansa's center. Formalized through legislation, the association of cities agreed that

Map 7.3 (facing page): European Trade Routes, c.1300

> Each city shall ... keep the sea clear of pirates.... Whoever is expelled from one city because of a crime shall not be received in another ... If a lord besieges a city, no one shall aid him in any way to the detriment of the besieged city.[2]

There were no mercantile rivalries here, unlike the competition between Genoa and Pisa in the south. But there was also little glamor. Pitch, tar, lumber, furs, herring: these were the stuff of northern commerce.

The opening of the Atlantic and the commercial uniting of the Baltic were dramatic developments. Elsewhere the pace of commercial life quickened more subtly. By 1200 almost all the cities of pre-industrial Europe were in existence. By 1300 they were connected by a spider's web of roads that brought even small towns of a few thousand inhabitants into wider networks of trade. To be sure, some old trading centers declined: the towns of Champagne, for example, had been centers of major fairs—periodic but intense commercial activity. By the mid-thirteenth century the fairs' chief functions were as financial markets and clearing houses. On the whole, however, urban centers grew and prospered. As the burgeoning population of the countryside fed the cities with immigrants, the population of many cities reached their medieval maximum: in 1300 Venice and London each had perhaps 100,000 inhabitants, Paris an extraordinary 200,000. Many of these people became part of the urban labor force, working as apprentices or servants; but others could not find jobs or became disabled and could not keep them. The indigent and sick posed new challenges for urban communities. To be sure, rich townspeople and princes alike supported the building of new charitable institutions: hospices for the poor, hospitals for the sick, orphanages, refuges for penitent prostitutes. But in big cities the numbers that these could serve were woefully inadequate. Beggars (there were perhaps 20,000 in Paris alone) became a familiar sight, and not all prostitutes could afford to be penitent.

Conflict in the Cities

Map 7.4 (facing page): Piacenza, Late Thirteenth Century

Cities that were part of the most complex trade networks were also the most restive. This was certainly true in Flanders, where the urban population had grown enormously since the twelfth century. Flemish cities depended on England for wool to supply their looms and on the rest of Europe to buy their finished textiles. But Flemish workers were unhappy with their town governments, run by wealthy merchants, the "patricians," whose families had held their positions for generations. When, in the early 1270s, England slapped a trade embargo on Flanders, discontented laborers, now out of work, struck, demanding a role in town government. While most of these rebellions resulted in few political changes, workers had better luck early in the next century, when the king of France and the count of Flanders went to war. The workers (who supported the count) defeated the French forces at the battle of Courtrai in 1302. Thereafter the patricians, who had sided with the king, were at least partly replaced by artisans in the apparatus of Flemish town governments. In the early fourteenth century, Flemish cities had perhaps the most inclusive governments of Europe.

Similar population growth and urban rebellions beset the northern Italian cities. (See Map 7.4 for the ballooning of the walls at Piacenza, a fair measure of its expanding population. Each successive wall meant in large measure the dismantling of the older one.) Italian cities were torn into factions that defined themselves not by loyalties to a king or a count (as in Flanders) but rather by adherence to either the pope or the emperor. "Outsiders," they nevertheless affected inter-urban politics. City factions often fought under the party banners of the Guelfs (papal supporters) or the Ghibellines (imperial supporters), even though for the most part they were waging very local battles. As in the Flemish cities, the late thirteenth century saw a movement by the Italian urban lower classes to participate in city government. The *popolo* ("people") who demanded the changes was in fact made up of many different groups, including crafts and merchant guildsmen, fellow parishioners, and even members of the commune. The *popolo* acted as a sort of alternative commune within the city, a sworn association dedicated to upholding the interests of its members. Armed and militant, the *popolo* demanded a say in matters of government, particularly taxation.

While no city is "typical," the case of Piacenza may serve as an example. Originally

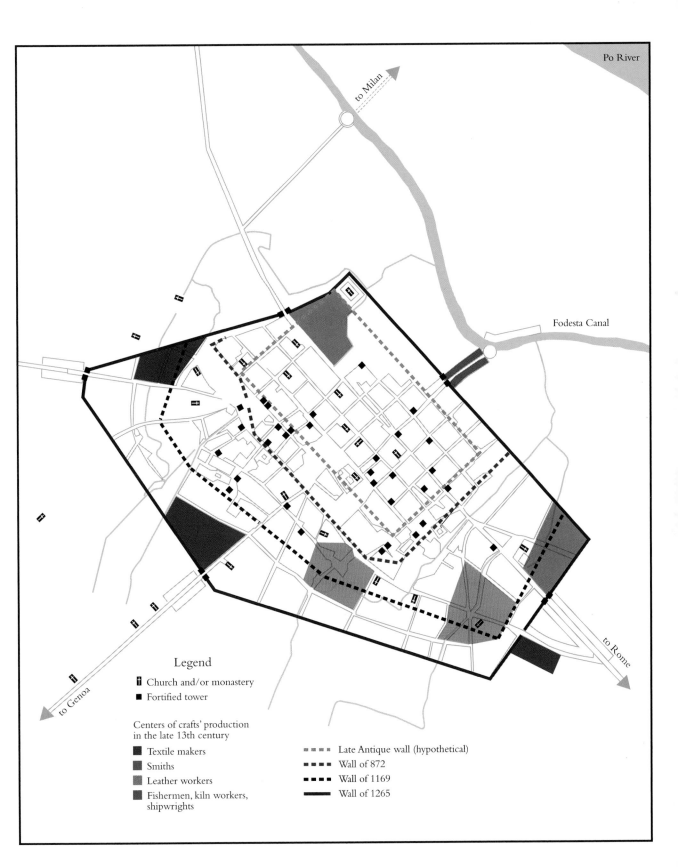

Po River

to Milan

Fodesta Canal

to Genoa

to Rome

Legend

✠ Church and/or monastery

■ Fortified tower

Centers of crafts' production
in the late 13th century

■ Textile makers

■ Smiths

■ Leather workers

■ Fishermen, kiln workers,
  shipwrights

▬ ▬ ▬ Late Antique wall (hypothetical)

▬ ▬ ▬ Wall of 872

▬ ▬ ▬ Wall of 1169

▬▬▬ Wall of 1265

dominated by nobles, the commune of Piacenza granted the *popolo*—led by a charismatic nobleman from the Landi family—a measure of power in 1222, allowing the *popolo* to take over half the governmental offices. A year later the *popolo* and the nobles worked out a plan to share the election of their city's *podestà*, or governing official. Even so, conflict flared up periodically: in 1224, 1231, and again in 1250, when a grain shortage provoked protest:

> In 1250 the common people of Piacenza saw that they were being badly treated regarding foodstuffs: first, because all the corn [grain] that had been sent from Milan, as well as other corn in Piacenza, was being taken to Parma ... [and] second because the Parmesans were touring Piacentine territory buying corn from the threshing floors and fields.... The Parmesans could do this in safety because Matteo da Correggio, a citizen of Parma, was podestà of Piacenza.[3]

In this case, too, members of noble families took the lead in the uprising, but this time the *popolo* of Piacenza divided into factions, each supporting a different competing leader. Eventually one came to the fore—Alberto Scotto, from a family deeply immersed in both commerce and landholding—and in 1291 he took over the city as "rector of the society of merchants and defender of the commune and *popolo*."[4] As ruler and defender of everyone in the city, he was, in effect, a lord, a *signore* (pl. *signori*). Map 7.4 shows some of the features of Piacenza in his day: concentrated centers of craft production, a new wall built in 1265 to enclose most of the population, an impressive number of churches and monasteries, and a generous sprinkling of private towers put up by proud and often warring members of the nobility.

A similar evolution—from commune to the rule of the *popolo* and then to the rule of a *signore*—took place in cities throughout northern Italy and in much of Tuscany as well. It was as if the end of imperial rule in Italy, marked by the fall of Frederick II, ironically brought in its train the creation of local monarchs—the *signori*, who maintained order at the price of repression. By 1300 the commune had almost everywhere given way to the *signoria* (a state ruled by a *signore*), with one family dominating the government.

XENOPHOBIA

Urban discord was fairly successfully defused in Flanders, fairly well silenced in Italy. In neither instance was pluralism valued. Europeans had no interest in hearing multiple voices; rather, they were eager to purge and purify themselves of the pollutants in their midst.

Driving the Jews from the Ile-de-France in the twelfth century (see p. 255) was a dress rehearsal for the expulsions of the thirteenth. In England, the Jews were expelled by local lords and municipalities from various cities in the 1230s and 1240s, at the same time as King Henry III (r. 1216-1272) imposed unusually harsh taxes on them. (For the English kings of this period, see Genealogy 6.1 on p. 224.) By the end of Henry's reign, the Jews were impoverished and their numbers depleted. There were perhaps 3000 Jews in all of England when King Edward I (r. 1272-1307) drew up the *Statute of the Jewry* in 1275, stipulating that they end the one occupation that had been left open to them: moneylending. They were expected to "live by lawful trade and by their labor."[5] But, as the Jews responded in turn, they would be forced to buy and sell at higher prices than Christians, and thus would sell nothing. Fifteen years later Edward expelled them from England entirely.

The story was similar in France. (For the French kings, see Genealogy 8.1 on p. 313.) King Louis IX (r. 1226-1270), later canonized as Saint Louis, reportedly could not bear to look at a Jew and worried that their "poison" might infect his kingdom. In 1242, he presided over the burning of two dozen cartloads of the Talmud (ancient rabbinic commentaries on the Bible), judged at a show-trial in Paris to be insulting to Christians. Actively promoting the conversion and baptism of Jews, Louis offered converts pensions, new names, and an end to special restrictions. His grandson, Philip IV ("The Fair") (r. 1285-1314), gave up on conversion and expelled the Jews from France in 1306. By contrast with England, the French Jewish population had been large; after 1306, perhaps 125,000 French men, women, and children became refugees in the Holy Roman Empire, Spain, and Italy. The few who were later allowed to return were wiped out in popular uprisings in the early 1320s.

Some anti-Jewish movements linked the Jews with lepers. Occupying a profoundly ambivalent place in medieval society, lepers were both revered and despised. Saint Louis used to feed the lepers who came to him, and he supported *leprosaria*, houses to care for them. Saint Francis was praised for ministering to lepers and was admired for kissing them on their hands and mouths. Yet at the same time, lepers were thought tainted by horrible sin; they were made to carry a bell (if they moved about) to alert everyone to their ominous presence; their rights to private property were restricted; and, through rituals of expulsion, they were condemned to live apart from normal people, never "to eat or drink in any company except that of lepers."[6] In the south of France in the 1320s lepers were accused of horrific crimes: of poisoning the wells and streams and of giving Jews consecrated hosts for their wicked rites. Hauled in by local officials, the lepers were tortured, made to confess, then burned.

Only by comparison with lepers does the revulsion against beggars seem mild.

Like leprosy, poverty too was thought to have its social uses. Certainly the mendicants like the Franciscans and Dominicans, who went about begging, were understood to be exercising the highest vocation. And even involuntary beggars were thought (and expected) to pray for the souls of those who gave them alms. Nevertheless the sheer and unprecedented number of idle beggars led to calls for their expulsion:

> If there is a man who has nothing [reads the *Customs of Touraine and Anjou*], and who lives in the town without earning anything, and he likes to go to the tavern, the judge should arrest him and ask what he lives on. And if he understands him to be lying, and that he is debauched [*de mauvaise vie*, literally: of a bad way of life], he should throw him out of the town.[7]

But no group suffered social purging more than heretics. Beginning in the thirteenth century, church inquisitors, aided by secular authorities, worked to search out and extirpate heretics from Christendom. Based in the south of France, the mid-Rhineland, and Italy, the inquisitors began their scrutiny in each district by giving a sermon and calling upon heretics to confess. Then the inquisitors granted a grace period for heretics to come forward. Finally, they called suspected heretics and witnesses to inquests, where they were interrogated:

> Asked if she had seen Guillaume [who was accused of being a heretic] take communion [at Mass] or doing the other things which good and faithful Christians are accustomed to do, [one of Guillaume's neighbors] responded that for the past twelve years she had lived in the village of Ornolac and she had never seen Guillaume take communion.[8]

Often imprisonment, along with torture both physical and mental, was used to extract a confession. Then penalties were assigned. Bernard Gui, an inquisitor in Languedoc from 1308 to 1323, gave out 633 punishments. Nearly half involved imprisonment. A few heretics were required to go on penitential pilgrimages. Forty-one people (6.5 per cent of those punished by Bernard) were burned alive. A large number of (former) heretics were forced to wear crosses sewn to their clothing, rather like Jews, but dishonored by a different marker.

STRENGTHENED MONARCHS AND THEIR ACCOMMODATIONS

The impulse behind "purification" was less hatred than the exercise of power. Expelling the Jews meant confiscating their property and calling in their loans while polishing an image of zealous religiosity. Burning lepers was one way to gain access to the assets of *leprosaria* and claim new forms of hegemony. Imprisonment and burning put heretics' property into the hands of secular authorities. Yet even as kings and other great lords manipulated the institutions and rhetoric of piety and purity for political ends, they learned how to accommodate, mollify, and use—rather than stamp out—new and up-and-coming classes. They came to welcome the broad-based support that representative institutions afforded them.

All across Europe, from Spain to Poland, from England to Hungary, rulers summoned parliaments. Growing out of ad hoc advisory sessions that kings and other rulers held with the most powerful people in their realms, parliaments became solemn and formal assemblies in the thirteenth century, moments when rulers celebrated their power and where the "orders"—clergy, nobles, and commons—assented to their wishes. Eventually parliaments became organs through which groups not ordinarily at court could articulate their interests.

The orders (or "estates") were based on the traditional division of society into those who pray, those who fight, and those who work. Unlike modern classes, defined largely by economic status, medieval orders cut across economic boundaries. The clerics, for example, included humble parish priests as well as archbishops; the commons included wealthy merchants as well as impoverished peasants. That, at least, was the theory. In practice, rulers did not so much command representatives of the orders to come to court as they summoned the most powerful members of their realm, whether clerics, nobles, or important townsmen. Above all they wanted support for their policies and tax demands.

Spanish Cortes

The *cortes* of León-Castile (for this Spanish kingdom, see Map 7.5) were among the earliest representative assemblies called to the king's court and the first to include townsmen. As the *reconquista* pushed southward across the Iberian peninsula, Christian kings called for settlers to occupy the new frontiers. Enriched by plunder, fledgling villages soon burgeoned into major commercial centers. Like the cities of Italy, Spanish towns dominated the countryside. Their leaders—called *caballeros villanos*, or "city horsemen," because they were rich enough to fight on horseback—monopolized municipal offices. In 1188, when King Alfonso IX (*r.*1188-1230) summoned

Iceland

Atlantic

Ocean

North
Sea

Norway

Bergen

Sweden

Baltic Sea

Borga

Reval

Dorpat

Riga

Novgorod

Scotland
Edinburgh

Ireland

Dublin

York

England

Wales

Oxford

Norwich

Cambridge

London Calais

Flanders

Ypres

Bruges
Ghent
Courtrai
Liège

Denmark

Hamburg

Lübeck

Danzig

Vistula

Teutonic Order

Lithuania

Cologne

HOLY

Frankfurt

Poland

Silesia

Rouen

Champagne

Toury
Angers
Paris
Orléans
Bourges

Loire

France

ROMAN

Nuremberg

Regensburg

Bohemia

Augsburg Vienna

Lwów

Dnieper

Khanate of the Golden Horde

Empire

Geneva
Milan

Venice

Buda

Hungary

Dniester

Bordeaux

Gascony

Lyon
Piacenza
Avignon
Genoa

Croatia

Bosnia

Serbia

Bulgaria

Caffa

Black Sea

Santiago
de Compostela

Pamplona

Toulouse

Marseille

Pistoia

Florence

Danube

Trebizond

Burgos

Navarre

Montpellier

Perpignan

Pisa

Papal
States

Ragusa (Dubrovnik)

Constantinople

Rum

Portugal

Saragossa

Aragon-
Catalonia

Barcelona

Corsica
(to Genoa 1284)

Rome

Naples

Kingdom
of Naples

Thessalonika

(subject to
Il-Khan Khanate)

Il-Khan
Khanate

Tagus

Toledo

León-Castile

Lisbon

Córdoba

Granada Granada

Ceuta

Majorca

Sardinia
(to Aragon 1297)

Cagliari

Messina

Palermo

Byzantine Empire

Armenia

Cyprus

Famagusta

Antioch
County
of Tripoli

Beirut
Acre

Kgdm. of
Acre

Sicily
(to Aragon 1282)

Crete

Sea

Marinids

Tlemcen

Bougie

Abdalwahidids

Tunis

Hafsids

Mediterranean

Jerusalem

Damietta

Alexandria

Mamluk Sultanate

Scale

0   400   800 km

0   500 mi

townsmen to the *cortes* for the first time on record, the city *caballeros* served as their representatives, agreeing to Alfonso's plea for military and financial support and for help in consolidating his rule. Once convened at court, these wealthy townsmen joined bishops and noblemen in formally counseling the king and assenting to royal decisions. Beginning with Alfonso X (*r.*1252-1284), Castilian monarchs regularly called on the *cortes* to participate in major political and military decisions and to assent to new taxes to finance them.

Local Solutions in the Empire

In 1356 imperial rule was freed from the papacy but at the same time made dependent on the German princes in the so-called Golden Bull. The princes, who had always had a role in ratifying the king and emperor, were now given the role and title of "electors." When a new emperor was to be chosen, each prince knew in which order his vote would be called, and a majority of votes was needed for election.

Map 7.5 (facing page): Europe, *c.*1280

After the promulgation of the Golden Bull, the royal and imperial level of administration was less important than the local. Yet every local ruler had to deal with the same two classes on the rise: the townsmen (as in Castile and elsewhere) and a group unique to Germany, the ministerials. The ministerials were legally serfs whose services—collecting taxes, administering justice, and fighting wars—were so honorable as to garner them both high status and wealth. By 1300 they had become "nobles" in every way but one: marriage. In the 1270s at Salzburg, for example, the archbishop required his ministerials to swear that they would marry within his lordship or at least get his permission to marry a woman from elsewhere. Apart from this indignity (which itself was not always imposed), the ministerials, like other nobles, profited from German colonization to become enormously wealthy landowners. Some held castles, and many controlled towns. They became counterweights to the territorial princes who, in the wake of the downfall of the Staufen, had expected to rule unopposed. In Lower Bavaria in 1311, for example, when the local duke was strapped for money, the nobles, in tandem with the clergy and the townsmen, granted him his tax but demanded in return recognition of their collective rights. The privilege granted by the duke was a sort of Bavarian Magna Carta. By the middle of the fourteenth century, princes throughout the Holy Roman Empire found themselves negotiating periodically with various noble and urban leagues.

English Parliament

In England, the consultative role of the barons at court had been formalized by the guarantees of Magna Carta. When Henry III (r.1216-1272) was crowned at the age of nine, England was governed for a time by a council consisting of a few barons, professional administrators, and a papal legate. Although not quite "rule by parliament," this council set a precedent for baronial participation in government. But once grown up and firmly in the royal saddle, Henry so alienated barons and commoners alike by his wars, debts, choice of advisers, favoritism, and lax attitude toward reform that the barons threatened rebellion. At Oxford in 1258, they forced Henry to dismiss his foreign advisers (he had favored the Lusignans, from France). He was henceforth to rule with the advice of a Council of Fifteen, chosen jointly by the barons and the king, and to limit the terms of his chief officers. Yet even this government was riven by strife, and civil war erupted in 1264. At the battle of Lewes in the same year, the leader of the baronial opposition, Simon de Montfort (c.1208-1265), routed the king's forces, captured the king, and became England's de facto ruler.

By Simon's day the distribution of wealth and power in England differed from the time of Magna Carta. Well-to-do merchants in the cities could potentially buy out most knights and even some barons many times over. Meanwhile, in the rural areas, the "knights of the shire" as well as some land-holders below them were rising in wealth and standing. These ancestors of the English gentry were politically active: the knights of the shire attended local courts and served as coroners, sheriffs, and justices of the peace, a new office that gradually replaced the sheriff's. The importance of the knights of the shire was clear to Simon de Montfort, who called a parliament in 1264 that included them; when he summoned another parliament in 1265, he added, for the first time ever, representatives of the towns—the "commons." Even though Simon's brief rule ended that very year and Henry's son Edward I (r.1272-1307) became a rallying point for royalists, the idea of representative government in England had emerged, born out of the interplay between royal initiatives and baronial revolts. Under Edward, parliament met fairly regularly, a by-product of the king's urgent need to finance his wars against France, Wales, and Scotland. "We require you," he wrote in one of his summonses to the sheriff of Northamptonshire,

> to cause two knights from [Northamptonshire], two citizens from each city in the same county, and two burgesses from each borough, of those who are especially discreet and capable of laboring, to be elected without delay, and to cause them to come to us [at Westminster].[9]

French Monarchs and the "Estates"

Louis IX, unlike Henry III, was a born reformer. He approached his kingdom as he did himself: with zealous discipline. As an individual, he was (by all accounts) pious, dignified, and courageous. He attended church each day, diluted his wine with water, and cared for the poor and sick (we have already seen his devotion to lepers). Hatred of Jews and heretics followed as a matter of course. Twice Louis went on crusade, dying on the second expedition.

Generalized and applied to the kingdom as a whole, Louis's discipline meant doling out proper justice to all. As the upholder of right in his realm, Louis pronounced judgment on some disputes himself—most famously under an oak tree in the Vincennes forest, near his palace. This personal touch polished Louis's image, but his wide-ranging administrative reforms were more fundamentally important for his rule. Most cases that came before the king were not, in fact, heard by him personally but rather by professional judges in the *Parlement*, a newly specialized branch of the royal court.[10] Louis also created a new sort of official, the *enquêteurs*: like the *missi dominici* of Charlemagne's day, they traveled to the provinces to hear complaints about the abuses of royal administrators. At the same time, Louis made the seneschals and *baillis*, local officials created by Philip Augustus, more accountable to the king by choosing them directly. They called up the royal vassals for military duty, collected the revenues from the royal estates, and acted as local judges. For the administration of the city of Paris, which had been lax and corrupt, Louis found a solution in the joint rule of royal officials and citizens.

There were discordant voices in France, but they were largely muted and unrecognized. Paris may have been governed by a combination of merchants and royalists, but at the level of the royal court, no regular institution spoke for the different orders. This began to change only under Louis's grandson, Philip IV the Fair (r.1285-1314). When Philip challenged the reigning pope, Boniface VIII (1294-1303), over rights and jurisdictions (see below for the issues), he felt the need to explain, justify, and propagandize his position. Summoning representatives of the French estates—clergy, nobles, and townspeople—to Paris in 1302, Philip presented his case in a successful bid for support. In 1308 he called another representative assembly, this time at Tours, to ratify his actions against the Templars—the crusading order that had served as de facto bankers for the Holy Land. Philip had accused the Templars of heresy, arrested their members, and confiscated their wealth. He wanted the estates to applaud him, and he was not disappointed. These assemblies, ancestors of the French Estates General, were convened sporadically until the Revolution of 1789 overturned the monarchy. Yet representative institutions were never fully or regularly integrated into the pre-revolutionary French body politic.

THE CHURCH MILITANT, HUMILIATED, AND REVAMPED

On the surface, the clash between Philip the Fair and Boniface VIII seemed yet one more episode in the ongoing struggle between medieval popes and rulers for power and authority. But by the end of the thirteenth century the tables had turned: the kings had more power than the popes, and the confrontation between Boniface and Philip was one sign of the dawning new principle of national sovereignty.

The Road to Avignon

The issue that first set Philip and Boniface at loggerheads involved the English king Edward I as well: taxation of the clergy. Eager to finance new wars, chiefly against one another but also elsewhere (Edward, for example, conquered Wales and tried, unsuccessfully, to subdue Scotland), both monarchs needed money. When the kings financed their wars by taxing the clergy along with everyone else (as if they were going on crusade), Boniface reacted. In the bull *Clericis Laicos* (1296), he declared that all clerics who paid and all laymen who imposed payments without prior authorization from the pope "shall, by the very act, incur the sentence of excommunication."[11]

Reacting swiftly, the kings soon forced Boniface to back down. But in 1301, testing his jurisdiction in southern France by arresting Bernard Saisset, the bishop of Pamiers, on a charge of treason, Philip precipitated another crisis. Boniface responded with outrage, but we already know (see p. 279) how Philip adroitly rallied public opinion in his favor. After Boniface issued the bull *Unam Sanctam* (1302), which declared that "it is altogether necessary to salvation for every human being to be subject to the Roman Pontiff," Philip's agents invaded Boniface's palace at Anagni (southeast of Rome) to capture the pope, bring him to France, and try him for heresy. Although the citizens of Anagni drove the agents out of town, Philip's power could not be denied. A month later, Boniface died, and the next two popes quickly pardoned Philip and his agents.

The papacy was never quite the same thereafter. In 1309, forced from Rome by civil strife, the popes settled at Avignon, a city technically in the Holy Roman Empire but very close to, and influenced by, France. There they remained until 1378. The Avignon Papacy, largely French, established a sober and efficient organization that took in regular revenues and gave the papacy more say than ever before in the appointment of churchmen and the distribution of church benefices and revenues. Its authority grew: it became the unchallenged judge of sainthood. And the Dominicans and Franciscans became its foot soldiers in the evangelization of the world and the purification of Christendom. These were tasks that required realistic men. When a group of Franciscans objected to their fellows building convents and churches within the cities, they were condemned. The Spirituals, as they were called, cultivated a piety of poverty and apocalypticism, believing that Saint Francis had ushered in a new Age of the Holy Spirit. But the popes, who were the official keepers of Franciscan wealth, advocated the repression of the Spirituals and even had a few burned at the stake.

In some ways, then, the papacy had never been as powerful as it was at Avignon. On the other hand, it was mocked and vilified by contemporaries, especially Italians, whose revenues suffered from the popes' exile from Rome. Francis Petrarch (1304–1374), one of the great literary figures of the day, called the Avignon Papacy the "Babylonian Captivity," referring to 2 Kings 25:11, when the ancient Hebrews were exiled and held captive in Babylonia. Pliant and accommodating to the rulers of Europe, especially the kings of France, the popes were slowly abandoning the idea of leading all of Christendom and were coming to recognize the right of secular states to regulate their internal affairs.

Lay Religiosity

They may have been secular states, but they were peopled by subjects who took their religion very seriously. With the doctrine of transubstantiation (see p. 253), Christianity became a religion of the body: the body of the wafer of the Mass, the body of the communicant who ate it, and equally the body of the believers who celebrated together in the feast of Corpus Christi (the Body of Christ). Eucharistic piety was already widespread in the most urbanized regions of Europe when Juliana of Mont-Cornillon (1193–1258) saw a vision of the full moon with a little defect:

> Then Christ revealed to her that the moon was the present Church, while the breach in the moon symbolized the absence of a feast which he still desired his faithful upon earth to celebrate.... [He asked] that once every year, the institution of the Sacrament of his Body and Blood should be recollected more solemnly and specifically than it was at the Lord's Supper.[12]

Taken up by the papacy and promulgated as a universal feast (whose texts were written by the young scholastic Thomas Aquinas), Corpus Christi was adopted throughout Western Europe. Whole cities created processions for the day. Fraternities dedicated themselves to the Body of Christ, holding their meetings on the feast day, focusing their regular charity on bringing the *viaticum* (or final Eucharist) to the dying. Dramas were elaborated on the theme.

Along with new devotion to the flesh of Christ was devotion to his mother. In the

hands of the Sienese painter Pietro Lorenzetti (*c.*1280/90-1348), for example, Mary's life took on lively detail. In Plate 7.1, an altarpiece depicting the Birth of the Virgin, two servants—one probably the midwife—tenderly wash the infant Mary. Her mother, clearly modeled on the mistress of a well-to-do Italian household, sits up in bed, gazing at the child with dreamy eyes, while, in another room, a little serving boy whispers news of the birth to the expectant father. Both publicly, in feasts dedicated to the major events in Mary's life, and privately, in small and concentrated images made to be contemplated by individual viewers, the Virgin was the focus of intense religious feeling. The ivory carving in Plate 7.2, tiny enough to be held in one hand, was meant to be an aid to private devotion. Books of Hours—small prayer books for laymen and (especially) women—almost always included images of the Virgin for worshippers to contemplate. In Plate 7.3, on the right-hand side, Jeanne d'Evreux, queen of France and the original owner of this Book of Hours, is shown kneeling in prayer within the initial D. This is the first letter of "Domine," "Lord," the opening word of the first prayer of the Office of the Virgin Mary. Above Jeanne is the Annunciation, when Gabriel tells Mary that she will bear the Savior.

That worship could be a private matter was part of wider changes in the ways that people negotiated the afterlife while here on earth. The doctrine of Purgatory, informally believed long before it was declared dogma in 1274, held that the Masses and prayers of the living could shorten the purgative torments that had to be suffered by the souls of the dead. Soon families were endowing special chapels for themselves, private spaces for offering private Masses on behalf of their own members. High churchmen and wealthy laymen insisted that they be buried within the walls of the church rather than outside of it, reminding the living—via their grand tombs and effigies—to pray for them. The effigy of English King Edward II (1307-1327) lies alert: his eyes are open, and an angel guards him at his head

Plate 7.1 (facing page): Pietro Lorenzetti, *Birth of the Virgin* (1342). This painted altarpiece creates an architectural space of real depth in which figures of convincing solidity act and interact; compare them with Saint Joseph in Plate 6.6, p. 251. Note how the ribs and arches of a Gothic church are used here as both decorative and unifying elements.

Plate 7.2: Virgin and Child (1330-1350). Carved in France, this ivory was once painted in color and gilded with gold. Flanked by wings on both sides (each probably containing scenes from the Virgin's life) that could close over the central portion, this portable "box" was a devotional aid suitable for a lay person.

Plate 7.3: Jean Pucelle, *Hours of Jeanne d'Evreux* (*c.*1325-1328). Meant for private devotion, this Book of Hours was lavishly illustrated. Scenes from the life of Christ, the Virgin, and King Louis IX (Jeanne's great-grandfather) contrast with delicate illustrations at the foot of each page. On the left-hand side of the two pages illustrated here is Christ's Betrayal, the moment when Judas brings soldiers and priests to capture Jesus, while Peter cuts off the ear of Malchus, the high priest's slave. This horrific moment is juxtaposed on the right with the promise of the Annunciation. Below, in delicate line-drawings, the frivolity of the world is highlighted: on the left a man on a ram and another on a goat practice jousting with a barrel; on the right, young people play a game of "frog in the middle."

Plate 7.4 (facing page): Tomb and Effigy of Edward II (1330s). From the end of the twelfth century, great laymen and ecclesiastics were remembered with more and more elaborate tombs and effigies. This alabaster effigy of Edward II in the north ambulatory of Gloucester Cathedral was enclosed by a delicate envelope of pinnacles and arches, a shrine fit for a relic.

while a lion rests tamely at his feet. (See Plate 7.4.) This was an awe-inspiring finale for a king who had been deposed by Parliament, imprisoned, and murdered.

THE SCHOLASTIC SYNTHESIS AND ITS FRAYING

Widespread religiosity went hand-in-hand with widespread literacy. In some rural areas, schools for children were attached to monasteries or established in villages. In the south of France, where the church still feared heresy, preachers made sure that they taught children how to read along with the tenets of the faith. In the cities, all merchants and most artisans had some functional literacy: they had to read and write to keep accounts, and, increasingly, they owned religious books for their private devotions. In France, Books of Hours were most fashionable; Psalters were favored in England.

The broad popularity of the friars fed the institutions of higher education. Franciscans and Dominicans now established convents and churches *within* cities; their members attended the universities as students, and many went on to become masters. By the time the other theologians at the University of Paris saw the danger to their independence, the friars were too entrenched to be budged. Besides, the friars—men like Thomas Aquinas (1225-1274) and Bonaventure (1217-1274)—were unarguably the greatest of the scholastics—scholars who mastered the use of logic to summarize and reconcile all knowledge and use it in the service of contemporary society.

Thomas Aquinas's *summae* (sing. *summa*)—long, systematic treatises that attempted to sum up all knowledge—were written to harmonize matters both human and divine. Using the technique of juxtaposing opposite positions, as Abelard had done in his *Sic et Non*, Aquinas (unlike Abelard) carefully explained away or reconciled contradictions, using Aristotelian logic as his tool for analysis and exposition. Aquinas wanted to reconcile faith with reason, to demonstrate the harmony of belief and understanding even though (in his view) faith ultimately surpassed reason in knowing higher truths. Thomas's *Summa against the Gentiles*, for example, written as a guide for missionaries attempting to convert the Muslims, tried to demonstrate the truths of Christian practice and religion through natural reason to the extent possible, taking up questions ranging from the truths of the Christian religion to mundane matters. Are God's truths contrary to reason? Should marriage be between one man and one woman only? Is simple fornication a sin? In the work of Albertus Magnus (*c.*1200-1280), Aquinas's teacher, the topics ranged from biology and physics to theology. In the writings of Saint Bonaventure, for whom Augustine replaced Aristotle as the key philosopher, the topics as such were secondary to an overall vision of the human mind as the recipient of God's beneficent illumination. For Bonaventure, minister general of the Franciscan Order, spirituality was the font of theology. Yet it was the Spiritual Franciscan Peter Olivi (1248-1298) who first defined the very practical word "capital": wealth with the potential to generate more wealth.

The scholastics' teachings were preached to townsmen by the friars as a matter of course. They came as well to permeate the thought of the reclusive contemplatives in the cities of Italy, the Netherlands, and the Rhineland, who absorbed the vocabulary of the schools from their confessors. The Dominican Meister Eckhart (d.1327), who studied at Paris before beginning a career of teaching and preaching in Germany, and who enriched the German language with new words for the abstract ideas of the schools, was himself a contemplative: a mystic who saw union with God as the goal of human life.

These thirteenth-century scholastics united in apparent harmony the secular realm with the sacred. But at the end of the century, fissures began to appear. In the writings of the Franciscan John Duns Scotus (c.1266-1308), for example, the world and God were less compatible. As with Bonaventure, so too with John, human reason could know truth only by divine illumination. But John argued that this illumination came not as a matter of course but only when God chose to intervene. John saw God as willful rather than reasonable; the divine will alone determined whether human reason could soar to knowledge. Further unraveling the knot tying reason and faith together was William of Ockham (c.1285-c.1347), another Franciscan who nevertheless disputed Duns Scotus vigorously. For Ockham, reason was unable to prove the truths of faith; it was apt only for things human and worldly, where, in turn, faith was of no use. Ockham himself turned his attention to the nature of government, arguing the importance of the state for human society. But several of his contemporaries looked at the physical world: Nicole Oresme (c.1320-1382), for example, following Ockham's view that the simplest explanation was the best, proposed that the sun, not the earth, was the center of the heavens.

HARMONY AND DISSONANCE IN WRITING, MUSIC, AND ART

On the whole, writers, musicians, architects, and artists, like scholastics, presented complicated ideas and feelings in harmony. Writers explored the relations between this world and the next; musicians found ways to bridge sacred and secular genres of music; artists used fleshy, natural forms to evoke the divine.

Vernacular Literature

Plate 7.5 (facing page): The Motet *S'Amours* (*c.*1300). Like the composer of *S'Amours*, the artist of this page (painted not long after the music itself was written) weaves together three separate stories. In the S of the word "S'Amours," which is sung by the disconsolate lover (the top voice), the artist presents, by contrast with the text, two very contented lovers petting both animals and each other. To the right of this happy scene is the initial A, the first letter of the word "Au," which is sung by the victorious lover of the middle voice. Again ironically, *this* figure is sad and lonely. By reversing the moods of the two voices with his pictures, is the artist commenting on the fickleness of love? Beneath the "Ecce" of the third voice is a hunting scene, complete with stag, hound, and hawk. The hunt was often used as a metaphor for amorous relations.

In the hands of Dante Alighieri (1265-1321), vernacular poetry expressed the order of the scholastic universe, the ecstatic union of the mystic's quest, and the erotic and emotional life of the troubadour. In his *Commedia*—later known as the *Divine Comedy*—Dante asks a soul in Hell to introduce herself; she begins with her hometown: "The city where I was born lies on that shore where the Po descends."[13] Dante himself was a child of the Arno, the river that flows through Florence. An ardent Florentine patriot and member of the "Whites" party, the faction that opposed papal intervention in Tuscany, he was condemned to death and expelled from the city by the "Blacks" after their victory in 1301. The *Commedia* was written in bitter exile, peopled with Dante's friends, lovers, enemies, and the living and dead whom he admired and reviled. Told in the first person, it presents Dante as a traveler who passes through Hell, Purgatory, and Paradise, a soul seeking and finding God in the blinding light of love. Just as Thomas Aquinas used Aristotle's logic to lead him to important truths, so Dante used the pagan poet Virgil as his guide through Hell and Purgatory. And just as Aquinas believed that faith went beyond reason to even higher truths, so Dante found a new guide, Beatrice, representing earthly love, to lead him through most of Paradise. But only faith in the form of the divine love of the Virgin Mary could bring Dante to the culmination of his journey, the inexpressible and ravishing vision of God.

In other writers, the harmony of heaven and earth was differently expressed. In the anonymous prose *Quest of the Holy Grail* (*c.*1225), the adventures of the knights of King Arthur's Table were turned into a fable to teach the doctrine of transubstantiation and the wonder of the vision of God. In *The Romance of the Rose*, begun by one author (Guillaume de Lorris, a poet in the romantic tradition) and finished by another (Jean de Meun, a poet in the scholastic tradition), a lover seeks the rose, his true love, but is continually thwarted by personifications of love, shame, reason, abstinence, and so on. They present him with arguments for and against love, but in the end, erotic love is embraced in the divine scheme—and the lover plucks the rose.

The Motet

Already by the tenth century, the chant in unison had been joined by a chant of many voices: polyphony. At first voice met voice in improvised harmony, but in the twelfth century polyphony was increasingly composed as well. In the thirteenth century its most characteristic form was the motet. Created at Paris, probably in the milieux of the university and the royal court, the motet harmonized the sacred with the worldly, the Latin language with the vernacular.

Two to four voices joined together in a motet. The most common sort from the second half of the thirteenth century had three voices. The lowest, often taken from a liturgical chant, generally consisted of one or two words, suggesting that it was normally played on an instrument (such as a vielle or lute) rather than sung. The second and third voices had different texts and melodies, sung simultaneously. The form allowed for the mingling of religious and secular motives. Very likely motets were performed by the clerics who formed the entourages of bishops or abbots—or by university students—for their own entertainment and pleasure. In the motet "S'Amours," whose opening music is pictured in Plate 7.5, the top voice complains (in French): "If Love had any power, I, who have served him all my life with a loyal heart, should surely have noticed." By contrast, the middle voice, also singing in French, rejoices in Love's rewards: "At the rebirth of the joyous season, I must begin a song, for true Love, whom I desire to serve, has given me a reason to sing." Meanwhile the lowest voice sings the Latin word "Ecce"—"Look!"[14]

Complementing the motet's complexity was the development of new schemes to indicate rhythm. The most important, that of Franco of Cologne in his *Art of Measurable Song* (c.1260), used different shapes to mark the number of beats each note should be held. (See Figure 7.1; the music in Plate 7.5 uses a similar rhythmic system.) Allowing for great flexibility and inventiveness in composition, Franco's scheme became the basis of modern musical notation.

Figure 7.1: Single Notes and Values of Franconian Notation

Name and shape of note		Value (in beats)	Modern equivalent
Duplex long		6	
Perfect long		3	
Imperfect long		2	
Breve		1	
Semibreve			
Minor + major		$\frac{1}{3} + \frac{2}{3}$	
Three minor		$\frac{1}{3} + \frac{1}{3} + \frac{1}{3}$	

New Currents in Art

Flexibility and inventiveness describe the art of Franco's time as well. It had new patrons to serve: the urban elite. In the Paris of Saint Louis's day, for example, wealthy merchants coveted illuminated law books and romances; rich students prized illustrated Bibles as essential fashion accessories; churchmen wanted beautiful service books; the royal family wanted lavishly illustrated Bibles, Psalters, and Books of Hours; and the nobility aspired to the same books as their sovereigns. The old-fashioned *scriptoria* that had previously produced books, with scribes and artists working in the same place, gave way to specialized workshops, often staffed by laypeople. Some workshops produced the raw materials: the ink, gold leaf, or parchment; others employed scribes to copy the texts; a third kind was set up for the illuminators; and a fourth did nothing but bind the finished books. This was not mass production, however, and the styles of different artists are clear, if subtle. In Plate 7.6, the artist of one workshop has made the apostle John conform to the shape of an S, his body out of joint, yet utterly elegant. But another Parisian artist working at about the same time in a different shop on a different book painted a thinner John, almost ramrod straight, with a flaming head of hair. (See Plate 7.7.)

Meanwhile, in Italy, especially at Pisa, sculptors, also working in shops, were melding the sort of Gothic naturalism exemplified by Saint Joseph of Reims in Plate 6.6 (on p. 251) with the classical style of Roman sculpture we saw on the Roman sarcophagus relief of Meleager in Plate 1.3 (on p. 35 of volume I). By 1250 Pisa was a commercial and artistic hub: it was the port of call for Byzantine artists after 1204, and it was in intense competition with Genoa (as we have seen) for Mediterranean trade. But it was also losing ground, its place soon to be taken by Catalonia. In this highly charged atmosphere, artistic development was rapid. For the Duomo of Siena, for example, Nicola Pisano and his assistants created a pulpit (built 1265-1268) composed of eight panels. The Adoration of the Magi, the panel shown in Plate 7.8, has the same dense crowds as the Meleager sarcophagus. Today all the color is gone, but originally Nicola painted the backgrounds and gilded the hemlines with gold, emphasizing details that brought the event "to life," melding the everyday world of thronging people and animals with the mystery of the divine incarnation.

Within a half-century, the weighty, natural forms of the sculptors found a home in painting as well, above all in the paintings of Giotto (1266-1337). In one of his commissions to decorate the private chapel of the richest man in Padua, for example, Giotto filled the walls with frescoes of scenes from Christ's and the Virgin's lives. (See Plate 7.9.) Throughout, Giotto experimented with the illusion of depth, weight, and volume, his figures expressing unparalleled emotional intensity as they reacted to events in the world-space created by painted frames. In the *Massacre of the Innocents*, depicted in Plate 7.10, Herod gives the order; we see his soldiers carrying it out, mothers resisting and weeping, children piled dead and naked on the ground, and one child, legs akimbo, readied for the final blow. The emotional treatment of the theme was new and revolutionary. But the painting was also traditional, depicting an allegory of spiritual battle, with the bloody powers of the secular state arrayed (on the

maligno positus e. Et scim{us}
q{uonia}m filius dei uenit. et dedit
nob sensu ut cognoscam{us} uer{um}
d{eu}m. z simus in uero filio ei{us}.
Hic e uer{us} d{eu}s. z uita et{er}na. Fi
lioli. custodite uos a simula
cris. amen. Explic epl{a} ioh{a}i{s} i.

[S]Enior Incipit
electe d{omi}ne et na
tis ei{us}
q{uo}s ego diligo
i{n} ueritate. z no{n}
ego solus s; z os q{ui} cognou{er}{un}t
ueritate{m} p{ro}pt{er} ueritate{m} q{ue} p{er}manet
i{n} nob et nobcu{m} erit in eternu{m}.
Sit nobis cu{m} g{rat}ia m{ise}r{icordi}a pax a d{e}o
p{at}re z a x{rist}o ih{es}u filio p{at}ris in ueri
tate z caritate. Gauis{us} su{m}
ualde q{uonia}m inueni de filijs tuis
ambulantes i{n} ueritate. sic{ut} ma{n}
datu{m} accepim{us} a p{at}re. Et nu{n}c rogo
te d{omi}na. no{n} ta{m}q{uam} mandatu{m}
nouu{m} scribens tibi s; q{uo}d habu
im{us} ab initio ut diligam{us}
alterutru{m}. Et hec e caritas. ut
ambulem{us} sec{un}d{u}m mandata ei{us}
hoc e eni{m} mandatu{m} ut que{m}ad
modu{m} audistis ab initio in
eo ambuletis. q{uonia}m multi se
ductores exier{un}t i{n} mundu{m}. qui
no{n} cofitentur ih{es}m xp{istu}m uenisse
i{n} carne. hic e seductor z antixr{istu}s.

uidere uos metipos ne p{er}datis
q{uo}d op{er}ati estis. s; ut m{er}cede{m} ple
na{m} accipiatis. O{mn}is q{ui} rece
dit z no{n} p{er}manet in doctrina xp{ist}i
d{eu}m no{n} h{abe}t. Q{ui} p{er}manet i{n} doc
trina xp{ist}i. hic z filiu{m} z p{atr}em h{abe}t.
Siquis uenit ad uos z hanc
doctrinam n{on} affert. nolite eu{m} re
cipe{re} in domu{m} nec aue ei dix{er}i
tis. Qui eni{m} dicit ei aue. com{m}u
nicat op{er}ib{us} ei{us} malignis. Et
cepoxi nobi{s} ut in die d{omi}ni m{a}i
ih{es}u xp{ist}i no{n} efficiamini. plu
ra h{abe}ns uob scribe{re}. nolui p{er} car
ta{m} z atrame{n}tu{m}. Spero eni{m} me
futuru{m} ad uos. z os ad os loq{ui}
ut gaudiu{m} uestru{m} sit plenu{m}.
Salutat te filij sororis tue e
lecte amen. Explic epl{a} ioh{a}i{s} ij.

[S]Enior gaio carissimo. qu{e}m
ego diligo in
ueritate. k{arissim}e
de om{n}ib{us} ora
ne facio p{ro}sp{er}e te ingredi
z ualere sic{ut} p{ro}sp{er}e agit a{n}i{m}a
tua. Gauis{us} su{m} ualde ue
nientib{us} fr{atr}ib{us} z testimoniu{m}
p{er}hibentib{us} ueritati tue. sic{ut}
tu in ueritate a{m}bulas. Maio
rem hac n{on} habeo g{rati}a{m} z le{titi}a{m}. q{uonia}m
ut audia{m} filios meos in uer{itate}

non h{ab}o g{rati}am que in g{ra}ec codicib{us}

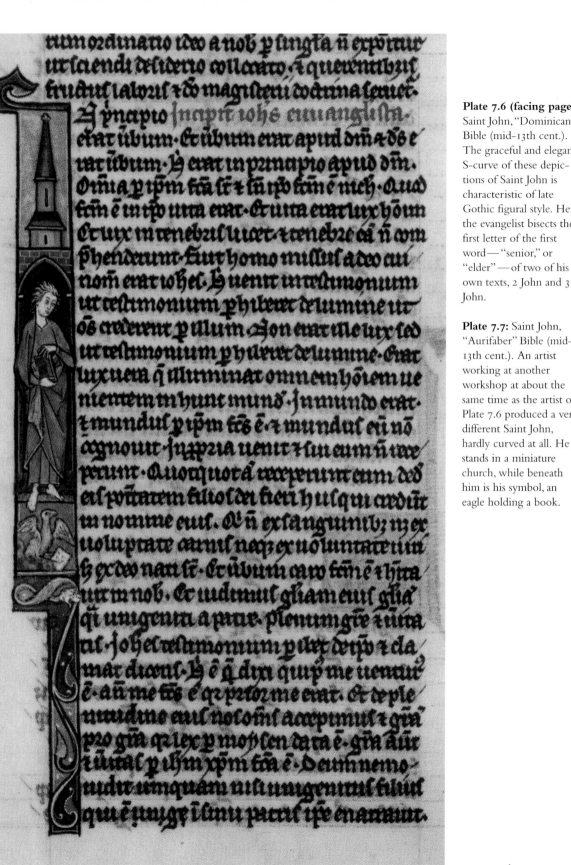

Plate 7.6 (facing page): Saint John, "Dominican" Bible (mid–13th cent.). The graceful and elegant S-curve of these depictions of Saint John is characteristic of late Gothic figural style. Here the evangelist bisects the first letter of the first word—"senior," or "elder"—of two of his own texts, 2 John and 3 John.

Plate 7.7: Saint John, "Aurifaber" Bible (mid–13th cent.). An artist working at another workshop at about the same time as the artist of Plate 7.6 produced a very different Saint John, hardly curved at all. He stands in a miniature church, while beneath him is his symbol, an eagle holding a book.

Plate 7.8: Nicola Pisano, Pulpit (1265-1268). *The Adoration of the Magi*, the scene on this panel of the Siena pulpit, was a very traditional Christian theme (see an early representation on the Franks Casket, Plate 2.7, pp. 94-95 of volume 1), but here the sculptor, Nicola Pisano, has imagined it as a crowd scene and filled it with little details—like the camels— to make it "come to life."

Plate 7.9 (facing page): Giotto, Arena Chapel, Padua (1304-1313). Giotto brought to painting the sensibilities of a sculptor. Just as Nicola Pisano's figures (see Plate 7.8) had depth and roundness, so did Giotto's painted ones. And just as Nicola used telling details to humanize scenes from the Bible, so Giotto's paintings, which covered the walls of the Arena Chapel with the narrative of humanity's redemption through Christ and the Final Judgment, were filled with homey particulars.

left) against the moral authority of the church (on the right) represented by pleading mothers, innocent babes, and a baptistery looming above them all.

Just as Italian art was influenced by northern Gothic style, so in turn the new Italian currents went north. In France, for example, illuminators for the royal court made miniature spaces for figures in the round, creating illusions of depth. Have another look at Jean Pucelle's *Hours of Jeanne d'Evreux* (Plate 7.3 on p. 284). In the picture of Christ's Betrayal on the left-hand side, the old S-shape figures are still favored, but the soldiers who crowd around Christ are as dense and dramatic as Herod's minions in Giotto. On the right-hand page, Mary, surprised by the angel of the Annunciation, sits in a space as deep as Herod's tower in Plate 7.10. Influenced perhaps by the look of sculpted figures such as those on Nicola's Siena pulpit, Pucelle painted in *grisaille*, a bare gray highlighted by light tints of color.

CRISIS

The artistic interest in crowd scenes may have been inspired not only by ancient art but by current living conditions. The cities were swollen with immigrants from the overcrowded countryside. By 1300, the only land left uncleared in France and England was marginal or unworkable with the tools of the day. It is true that farms were producing more than ever before, but families also had more hungry mouths to feed. One plot that had originally supported a single family in England was, by the end of the thirteenth century, divided into twenty tiny parcels for the progeny of the original peasant holder. The last known French *villeneuve* ("new town") was founded in 1246; after that, new settlements ceased.

Consider the village of Toury, about 45 miles south of Paris (Map 7.6). It originally consisted of a few peasant habitations (their houses and gardens) clustered around a central enclosure belonging to the lord, in this case the monastery of Saint-Denis (see p. 201). Nearby, across the main route that led from Paris to Orléans, was a parish church. In 1110 Abbot Suger constructed a well-fortified castle on the site of the enclosure. In the course of the thirteenth century, encouraged both by Saint-Denis's policy of giving out lots in return for rents and by a market granted by the king, the village grew rapidly, expanding to the east, then to the west, and finally (by the fourteenth century) to the north. Meanwhile the lands cultivated by the villagers — once called upon to support only a small number of householders — were divided into more than 5000 parcels, which appear as tiny rectangles on Map 7.7.

In general, population growth seems to have leveled off by the mid-thirteenth century, but the static supply of farmland meant that from that time onward France and England would face sudden and severe grain shortages. Climatic changes

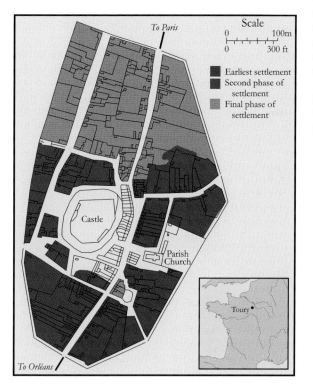

Plate 7.10 (facing page): Giotto, *Massacre of the Innocents*, Arena Chapel (1304–1313). Giotto organized the Arena Chapel paintings like scenes in a comic book, to be read from left to right. The Massacre of the Innocents — illustrating Matt. 2:16–18, where Herod orders the execution of all male children two years old and younger — is at the far right on the south wall; the next scene, in the band underneath, is on the far left. Viewers must make a sort of pilgrimage around the church as they follow the scenes from start to finish.

Map 7.6: The Village of Toury, Fourteenth and Fifteenth Centuries

To Paris

Toury

To Orléans

Scale

0   1 km

0   0.5 mi

Legend

▲ Hamlets

▱ Parcel of land

compounded the demographic situation. In 1309 an extremely wet growing season ruined the grain harvest in southern and western Germany; the towns, where food had to be imported, were hit especially hard.

The so-called Great Famine of 1315-1322 was only the longest and most severe of the cycles of food shortage that afflicted regions as far apart as northern Europe and Constantinople. The region around Paris was struck then, to be sure, and then again in 1328, 1334, and 1340-1341. No sooner had Florence recovered from one famine then it was hit by another: in 1276, 1282, 1286, 1291, 1299, 1302-1303, and 1305. A Flemish chronicler describing the effects of ruined crops in 1315 recalled a scene reminiscent of the piles of babies in Giotto's fresco:

> The people were in such great need that it cannot be expressed. For the cries that were heard from the poor would move a stone, as they lay in the streets with woe and great complaint, swollen with hunger and remaining dead of poverty, so that many were thrown by set numbers, sixty and even more, into a pit.[15]

Map 7.7 (facing page): The Lands of Toury, Fourteenth and Fifteenth Centuries

A whole western European population of vagabonds was created, some of whom may have wandered as far as beyond the Elbe River, to settle in eastern Germany and Poland.

Warfare also took its toll on economic life. To consolidate their rule, princes hired mercenary troops but paid them such poor wages that they plundered the countryside even when they were not fighting. Warring armies had always disrupted farms, ruining the fields as they passed by, but in the thirteenth century burning became a battle tactic, used both to devastate the enemy's territory and to teach the inhabitants a lesson. Here too the cities felt the repercussions. A city's own army could defend its walls against roving troops, but it could not easily stop the flow of refugees who streamed in seeking safety. Lille's population, for example, nearly doubled as a result of the wars between Flanders and France during the first two decades of the thirteenth century. Meanwhile, like other Flemish cities, Lille was obliged to impose new taxes on its population to pay for its huge war debts.

Pressed by war debts, the need for food, and the desire for gain, landlords and town officials alike strove to get more money. Everywhere, customary and other dues were deemed inadequate. In 1315 the king of France offered liberty to all his serfs, mainly to assess a new war tax on all free men. In other parts of France, lords imposed a *taille*, an annual money payment, and many peasants had to go into debt to pay it. Professional moneylenders set up loan offices in the countryside, or wealthy neighbors served as unofficial creditors. Although richer peasants might profit from these developments, the cycle of loan, debt, and repayment left poorer peasants even more impoverished.

In other areas, such as Italy, England, and southern Germany, lords found it useful to give out short-term leases to their peasants. Bypassing the fixed and customary dues whose value decreased as prices rose, these lords simply charged a rent that changed with the market. In Bavaria, for example, the abbot of Baumburg met each year with his peasants to announce new leases and negotiate new rents. In Italy, where peasants had long labored under twenty-five-year leases, landlords and cities introduced a short-term lease; one monastery in Milan doubled its rental income as a result.

To enforce their new taxes and lease arrangements, great lords, both lay and ecclesiastical, installed local agents, eager to collect taxes and to draft young villagers into military service. These officials lived near the villages in fortified houses, well placed to keep an eye on local conditions. They kept account books and computed their profits and their costs. One calculated, for example, that

> You can well have three acres weeded for a penny, and an acre of meadow for fourpence, and an acre of waste meadow for threepence-halfpenny.... And know that five men can well reap and bind two acres a day of each kind of [grain], more or less. And where each takes twopence a day then you must give five-pence an acre....[16]

The remuneration for rural labor was here as finely calculated as a note in Franco's rhythmic scheme.

★   ★   ★   ★

On the western fringe of the Eurasian landmass, Europeans found ways to mesh their institutions of commerce and religion with those of the vast Mongol empire to their east. In many ways medieval Europe reached the zenith of its prosperity, certainly of its population, during the century bisected by 1300. The cities became the centers of culture and wealth. Universities took wing, producing scholasticism, a "scientific revolution" in logical and systematic thought. The friars, among the most prominent of the scholastics, and ministering to an attentive, prosperous, increasingly literate laity, installed themselves right in the center of towns.

Harmony was often achieved through clashes. The synthesis of a scholastic *summa* was possible only when opposite ideas were faced and sorted out. The growth of representative institutions nearly always entailed accommodating the demands of the discontented with the enlightened self-interest of rulers. The great artistic innovations of the day involved reconciling classical with Gothic styles. Poems and musical compositions worked to assimilate the secular order with the divine.

The harmonies were not always sweet, but sweetness need not be a value, in music or in life. More ominous were the attempts to sound single notes: to suppress the voices of the Jews and the heretics, to silence the bells of the lepers. Cities tried to close their gates to beggars. In the next century terrible calamities would construct new arenas for discord and creativity.

CHAPTER SEVEN KEY EVENTS

1188	King Alfonso IX (r.1188–1230) summons townsmen to the cortes
1222	Popolo at Piacenza wins role in government
1225–1274	Thomas Aquinas
1226–1270	King Louis IX (St. Louis) of France
1230s	Mongols conquer Rus
1265	Commons included in English Parliament
1266–1337	Giotto
1279	Mongols conquer China
1284	Gold ducats first minted at Venice
1290	Jews expelled from England
1291	End of the original Crusader States
1302	Battle of Courtrai
1302	Unam Sanctam
1306	Jews expelled from France
1309–1378	Avignon Papacy (Babylonian Captivity)
1315–1322	Great Famine
1321	Death of Dante
1356	Golden Bull promulgated in Germany

NOTES

1. Marco Polo, *The Travels*, in *Reading the Middle Ages: Sources from Europe, Byzantium, and the Islamic World* (Peterborough, ON, 2006), pp.422–23.
2. *Decrees of the [Hanseatic] League*, in *Reading the Middle Ages*, p.430.
3. *The Ghibelline Annals of Piacenza*, in *Reading the Middle Ages*, p.428.
4. Quoted in Trevor Dean, "The Rise of the *Signori*," in *Italy in the Central Middle Ages*, ed. David Abulafia (Oxford, 2004), p.111.

5. *Statute of the Jewry*, in *Reading the Middle Ages*, p.445.

6. *Sarum Manual*, in *Reading the Middle Ages*, pp.443–44.

7. *The* Etablissements de Saint Louis: *Thirteenth-Century Law Texts from Tours, Orléans, and Paris*, trans. F.R.P. Akehurst (Philadelphia, 1996), p.27.

8. Jacques Fournier, *Episcopal Register*, in *Reading the Middle Ages*, pp.435–36.

9. *Summons of Representatives of Shires and Towns to Parliament*, in *Reading the Middle Ages*, p.454.

10. Despite the similarity between the terms *Parlement* and Parliament, both deriving from *parler*, "to talk," the two institutions were different. The first was the central French court of law, the second the English representative institution. It is true that the English Parliament did hear legal cases, but it also discussed foreign affairs, published royal statutes, and (above all) granted taxes to the king.

11. Boniface VIII, *Clericis Laicos*, in *Reading the Middle Ages*, p.455.

12. *The Life of Juliana of Mont-Cornillon*, in *Reading the Middle Ages*, p.480.

13. Dante, *Inferno, Canto 5 (Paolo and Francesca)*, in *Reading the Middle Ages*, p.471.

14. *The Montpellier Codex*, Part IV: *Text and Translations*, trans. Susan Stakel and Joel C. Relihan, in *Recent Researches in the Music of the Middle Ages and Early Renaissance* 8 (Madison, 1985), p.81.

15. Quoted in David Nicholas, *Medieval Flanders* (Harlow, 1992), p.207.

16. "Walter of Henley's Husbandry," excerpted in Georges Duby, *Rural Economy and Country Life in the Medieval West*, trans. Cynthia Postan (rpt. Philadelphia, 1998), p.388.

FURTHER READING

Abulafia, David, ed. *Italy in the Central Middle Ages*. Short Oxford History of Italy. Oxford, 2004.

Binski, Paul. *Medieval Death: Ritual and Representation*. Ithaca, NY, 1996.

Camille, Michael. *Gothic Art: Glorious Visions*. New York, 1996.

Epstein, Steven A. *Genoa and the Genoese, 958-1528*. Chapel Hill, 1996.

Farmer, Sharon. *Surviving Poverty in Medieval Paris: Gender, Ideology, and the Daily Lives of the Poor*. Ithaca, NY, 2002.

Given, James B. *Inquisition and Medieval Society: Power, Discipline, and Resistance in Languedoc*. Ithaca, NY, 1997.

Glick, Leonard B. *Abraham's Heirs: Jews and Christians in Medieval Europe*. Syracuse, NY, 1999.

Jackson, Peter. *The Mongols and the West, 1221-1410*. Harlow, 2005.

Jones, P.J. *The Italian City-State: From Commune to Signoria*. Oxford, 1997.

Jordan, William Chester. *The French Monarchy and the Jews: From Philip Augustus to the Last Capetians*. Philadelphia, 1989.

——. *The Great Famine: Northern Europe in the Early Fourteenth Century*. Princeton, 1996.

Martin, Janet. *Medieval Russia, 980-1584*. Cambridge, 1995.

Mundill, Robin R. *England's Jewish Solution: Experiment and Expulsion, 1262-1290*. Cambridge, 1998.

Nirenberg, David. *Communities of Violence: Persecution of Minorities in the Middle Ages*. Princeton, 1996.

O'Callaghan, Joseph F. *The Cortes of Castile-León, 1188-1350*. Philadelphia, 1989.

Pegg, Mark Gregory. *The Corruption of Angels: The Great Inquisition of 1245-1246*. Princeton, 2001.

Rubin, Miri. *Corpus Christi: The Eucharist in Late Medieval Culture*. Cambridge, 1991.

Strayer, Joseph R. *The Reign of Philip the Fair*. Princeton, 1980.

White, John. *Art and Architecture in Italy, 1250-1400*. 3rd ed., New Haven, 1993.

◆I◆I◆I◆I◆I◆I◆I◆I◆I◆

To test your knowledge of this chapter, please go to
www.rosenweinshorthistory.com
and click "Study Questions."

EIGHT

CATASTROPHE AND CREATIVITY
(*c*.1350-*c*.1500)

Struck by a plague that carried off from a fifth to a half of its population, shaken by Ottoman Turks who conquered Constantinople and moved into the Balkans, buffeted by internal wars that threatened the very foundations of its political life, Europe shuddered. Soon, however, it shrugged and forged ahead. Those who survived war and disease enjoyed a higher standard of living than before; new-style political entities gained powers that the old had never had; and new-rigged sailing ships, manned by hopeful adventurers and financed by rich patrons, plied the seas east- and westwards. By 1500, Europe was poised to conquer the globe.

CRISES AND CONSOLIDATIONS

In the 1340s, the first pandemic since the Plague of Justinian (see pp. 64-66 of volume 1) made swift inroads into Europe even while France and England were waging a long and debilitating Hundred Years' War. Popular revolts and insurrections, the bitter harvest of war and economic contraction, rocked both town and countryside. Meanwhile a schism within the church—setting first two, then three popes against one another—shattered all illusions of harmony within Christendom. At the same time, however, smaller units gained apparent cohesion under new-style princes.

The Black Death

The Black Death (1346-1353), so named by later historians looking back on the disease, was likely caused by *Yersinia pestis*, the bacterium of the plague. (Some historians dispute this.) Its symptoms, as an eye witness reported, included "tumorous outgrowths at the roots of thighs and arms and simultaneously bleeding ulcerations, which, sometimes the same day, carried the infected rapidly out of this present life."[1]

The disease probably spread from China, arriving in the West along well-worn trade routes with the Mongols. Caffa, the Genoese trading post on the northern shore of the Black Sea, was hit in 1347. From there the plague traveled to Europe and the Middle East, quickly striking Constantinople and Cairo and soon leaving the port cities for the hinterlands. In early 1348 the citizens of Pisa and Genoa, fierce rivals on the seas, were being felled without distinction by disease. Early spring of the same year saw the Black Death at Florence; two months later it had hit Dorset in England. Dormant during the winter, it revived the next spring to infect French ports and countryside, moving on swiftly to Germany. By 1351 it was at Moscow, where it stopped for a time, only to recur in ten- to twelve-year cycles throughout the fourteenth century. (Only the attack of 1346-1353 is called the Black Death.) The disease continued to strike, though at longer intervals, until the eighteenth century.

The effect on Europe's population was immediate and devastating. Famines had already weakened many people's resistance to disease. At Paris, by no means the city hardest hit, about half the population died, mainly children and poor people. In eastern Normandy, perhaps 70 to 80 per cent of the population succumbed. At Bologna, even the most robust—men able to bear arms—were reduced by 35 per cent in the course of 1348. Demographic recovery across Europe began only in the second half of the fifteenth century.

Deaths, especially of the poor, led to acute labor shortages in both town and country. Already in 1351, King Edward III of England issued the Statute of Laborers, forbidding workers to take pay higher than pre-plague wages and fining employers who offered more. Similar laws were promulgated—and flouted—elsewhere. In the countryside, landlords needed to keep their profits up even as their workforce was decimated. They were forced to strike bargains with enterprising peasants, furnishing them, for example, with oxen and seed; or they turned their land to new uses, such as pasturage. In the cities, the guilds and other professions recruited new men, survivors of the plague. Able to marry and set up households at younger ages, these *nouveaux riches* helped reconstitute the population. Although many widows were now potentially the heads of households, deeply rooted customs tended to push them either into new marriages (in northern Europe) or (in southern Europe) into the house of some male relative, whether brother, son, or son-in-law.

Plate 8.1 (facing page): Woodcut from *Der Ackermann aus Böhmen* (*c.*1462). In this book, Death and a plowman (the "Ackermann") argue before God, the plowman accusing Death of injustice. (Death wins in the end.) The dialogue was published with a series of woodcuts by the first printer of illustrated books, Albrecht Pfister (*d.c.*1470). Color tints were then added by hand.

The plague affected both desires and sentiments. Upward mobility in town and country meant changes in consumption patterns, as formerly impoverished groups found new wealth. They chose silk clothing over wool, beer over water. In Italy, where a certain theoretical equality within the communes had restrained consumer spending, cities passed newly toughened laws to restrict finery. In Florence in 1349, for example, a year after the plague first struck there, the town crier roamed the city shouting out new or renewed prohibitions: clothes could not be adorned with gold or silver; capes could not be lined with fur; the wicks of funeral candles had to be made of cotton; women could wear no more than two rings, only one of which could be set with a precious stone; and so on. As always, such sumptuary legislation affected women more than men.

At around the same time, death became an obsession and a cult. There was a newly intense interest in the macabre. The dead were depicted not as in life but as gruesome corpses. Death itself was personified, skeletal and ugly. Plate 8.1 is one of a series of woodcuts made *c*.1462 by an anonymous artist for a poem written by Johannes von Saaz at the beginning of the century. Here death is both literally a grim reaper, cutting down his victims with a scythe, and an archer, ready to shoot two careless young men. Later, in the artistic and literary genre known as the Dance of Death, life itself became a dance with death, as men and women from every class were escorted—sooner or later—to the grave by ghastly skeletons. Blaming their own sins for the plague, penitent pilgrims, occasionally bearing whips to flagellate themselves, crowded the roads. Some fed the rumor that Jews had caused the plague by poisoning the wells, an idea that spread from southern France and northern Spain (where, as we have seen, similar charges had already been leveled in 1320) to Switzerland, Strasbourg, and throughout Germany. At Strasbourg more than 900 Jews were burned in 1349, right in their own cemetery.

Upheavals of War

"And westward, look! Under the Martian Gate," wrote the English poet Geoffrey Chaucer (*c*.1340-1400) in *The Canterbury Tales*, continuing,

> Arcita and his hundred knights await,
> And now, under a banner of red, march on.
> And at the self-same moment Palamon
> Enters by Venus' Gate and takes his place
> Under a banner of white, with cheerful face.
> You had not found, though you had searched the earth,
> Two companies so equal in their worth.[2]

Chaucer's association of war with "cheer" and "valor" was a central conceit of chivalry, giving a rosy tint to the increasingly "total" wars that engulfed even civilian populations in the fourteenth and fifteenth centuries. In the East, the Ottoman Turks took the Byzantine Empire by storm; in the West, England and France fought a bitter Hundred Years' War. Dynastic feuds and princely encroachments marked a tumultuous period in which the map of Europe was remade.

THE OTTOMAN EMPIRE

The establishment of a new Islamic empire—the Ottoman—just south of the Danube River, marked an astonishing transformation of Europe's southeast. (See Map 8.1.) A glance back at Map 7.5 on p. 276 shows no hint of what was to come: in the interstices between Mongol-ruled Rum and the Byzantine Empire, Turkish tribal leaders were carving out ephemeral principalities for themselves. At the beginning of the fourteenth century, Osman (r.1299-1326), after whom the Ottomans were named, took the lead. (See the list of Ottoman Emirs and Sultans on p. 364.) About 150 years

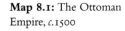

Map 8.1: The Ottoman Empire, c.1500

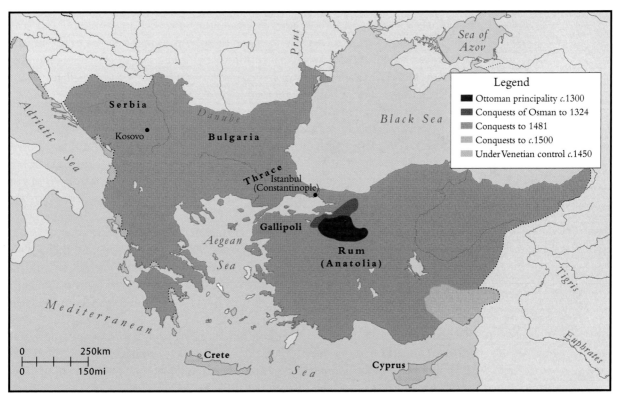

later the chronicler Ashikpashazade, looking back on Osman's achievements, stressed his wisdom, his cunning, and, above all, his legitimacy by right of jihad: "What does the sultan [the last Seljuk ruler of Rum] have to do with it?" the chronicler has Osman ask those who want the sultan's permission before appointing a religious leader. "It is true that the sultan endowed me with this banner. But it is I who carried the banner into battle with the infidels!"[3]

Attracting other Turkish princes to fight alongside him, Osman carved out a principality in Byzantium's backyard. But rather than unite in the face of these developments, rival factions within the Byzantine state tried to take advantage of the Ottomans. It was as ally to one claimant for the Byzantine throne that Ottoman troops arrived in Gallipoli in 1354. They remained long after their welcome had run out. In the 1360s they took Thrace and then, under the energetic leadership of Bayezid I (r.1389-1402), they conquered much of the Balkans, taking Serbia (at the battle of Kosovo) in 1389 and Bulgaria in 1393.

Map 8.2 (facing page):
The First Phase of the Hundred Years' War, 1337-1360

To the east, the Ottoman advance was aided by the weakening of Mongol power, which began in China with the overthrow of the khanate there. To be sure, the Ottomans were halted by Timur the Lame (Tamerlane) (1336-1405), a warrior leader from the region of Samarkand, who saw himself as restoring the Mongol Empire. But with Timur's death, the Ottomans slowly regained their hold, in part because of the superiority of their elite troops, the janissaries, professional soldiers of slave origin. Adopting the new military hardware of the west—cannons and muskets—the Ottomans retook Anatolia and the Balkans. Under Mehmed II the Conqueror (r.1444-1446, 1451-1481), their cannons accomplished what former sieges had never done, breaching the thick walls of Constantinople in 1453 and bringing the Byzantine Empire to an end.

The new Ottoman state had come to stay. Its rise was due to its military power and the weakness of its neighbors. But its longevity—it did not begin to decline until the late seventeenth century—was due to more complicated factors. Building on a theory of absolutism that echoed similar ideas in the Christian West, the Ottoman rulers acted as the sole guarantors of law and order; they considered even the leaders of the mosques to be their functionaries, soldiers without arms. Prospering from taxes imposed on their relatively well-to-do peasantry, the new rulers spent their money on roads to ease troop transport and a navy powerful enough to oust the Italians from their eastern Mediterranean outposts. Eliminating all signs of rebellion (which meant, for example, brutally putting down Serb and Albanian revolts), the Ottomans created a new world power.

The new state eventually changed Europe's orientation. Europeans could—and did—continue to trade in the Mediterranean with the Ottomans. But on the whole they preferred to treat them as a barrier to the Orient. Not long after the fall of Constantinople, as we shall see, the first transatlantic voyages began.

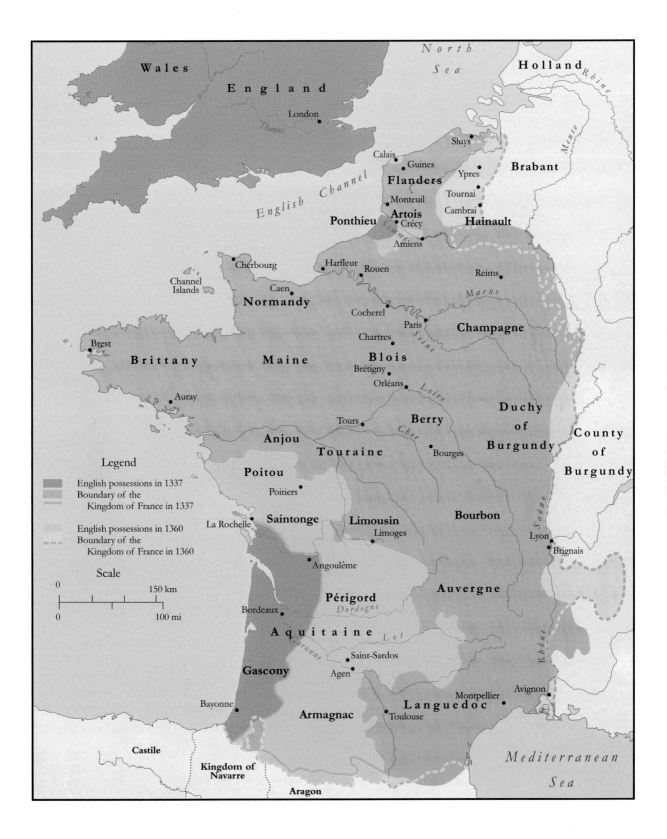

Wales

England

North Sea

Holland

Rhine

London

Thames

Sluys

Calais

Guines

Ypres

Brabant

Flanders

Meuse

Monteuil

Tournai

Artois

Cambrai

Hainault

Ponthieu

Crécy

English Channel

Amiens

Somme

Cherbourg

Harfleur

Rouen

Reims

Channel
Islands

Caen

Normandy

Marne

Cocherel

Paris

Champagne

Brest

Chartres

Seine

Brittany

Maine

Blois

Brétigny

Auray

Orléans

Loire

Duchy
of
Burgundy

County
of
Burgundy

Anjou

Berry

Touraine

Tours

Cher

Bourges

Poitou

Legend

English possessions in 1337
Boundary of the
Kingdom of France in 1337

Poitiers

Limousin

Bourbon

Saintonge

Limoges

La Rochelle

Saône

English possessions in 1360
Boundary of the
Kingdom of France in 1360

Lyon

Brignais

Scale

Angoulême

Auvergne

0   150 km

Périgord

0   100 mi

Dordogne

Bordeaux

Lot

Aquitaine

Garonne

Gascony

Saint-Sardos

Rhône

Agen

Avignon

Bayonne

Armagnac

Languedoc

Montpellier

Toulouse

Castile

*Mediterranean
Sea*

Kingdom of
Navarre

Aragon

Although in the seventeenth century English rulers would set their sights on the Americas and the Indies, between 1350 and 1500, they were still preoccupied with older claims. The Hundred Years' War (in fact fought sporadically over more than a century, from 1337 to 1453) was the English king's bid to become ruler of France. Beyond this dynastic dispute were England's long-standing claims to Continental lands, many of which had been confiscated by Philip II of France and the rest by Philip VI in 1337. (See Map 8.2, paying particular attention to English possessions in 1337.) Beyond that were Flemish-English economic relations, to which English prosperity and taxes were tied. Ultimately, the war was not so much between England and France as between two conceptions of France: one, a centralized monarchy, the other, an association of territories ruled by counts and dukes.

Genealogy 8.1 (facing page): Kings of France and England and the Dukes of Burgundy during the Hundred Years' War

As son of Isabella, last living child of the French king Philip the Fair, Edward III of England was in line for the French throne when Charles IV died in 1328. The French nobles awarded it, instead, to Philip VI, the first Valois king of France. (See Genealogy 8.1: Kings of France and England and the Dukes of Burgundy during the Hundred Years' War.) Edward's claims led to the first phase of the Hundred Years' War. Looking back on it, the chronicler Froissart tried to depict knightly fighters as its gallant protagonists:

> As soon as Lord Walter de Manny discovered ... that a formal declaration of war had been made ... he gathered together 40 lances [each lance being a knight, a servant, and two horses], good companions from Hainaut and England ... [because] he had vowed in England in the hearing of ladies and lords that, "If war breaks out between my lord the king of England and Philip of Valois who calls himself king of France, I will be the first to arm myself and capture a castle or town in the kingdom of France."[4]

In fact knights like Walter de Manny and his men were outmoded; the real heroes of the war were the longbowmen—non-knightly fighters who, by wielding a new-style bow and arrows that flew far and penetrated deeply, gave English troops the clear advantage. By 1360, the size of English possessions in southern France was approximately what it had been in the twelfth century. (Look at Map 8.2 again, this time considering "English Possessions in 1360," and compare it with Map 6.3 on p. 226.)

English successes were nevertheless short-lived. Harrying the border of Aquitaine, French forces chipped away at it in the course of the 1380s. Meanwhile, sentiments for peace were gaining strength in both England and France; a treaty to put an end to the fighting for a generation was drawn up in 1396. Yet the "generation" was hardly

Louis IX (Saint Louis)
king of France (1226-1270)

Philip III
king of France (1270-1285)

Philip IV the Fair
(1285-1314)

Charles of Valois
(d.1325)

Louis X
(1314-1316)

Philip V
(1316-1322)

Charles IV
(1322-1328)

Isabella
= Edward II
king of England
(1307-1327)

Philip VI
king of France
(1328-1350)

John I
(1316)

(daughters)

(daughters)

Edward III
king of England
(1327-1377)

John II
king of France
(1350-1364)

Edward
the Black Prince

Lionel
duke of Clarence

John of Gaunt
duke of Lancaster

Edmund
duke of York

Charles V
king of France
(1364-1380)

Philip the Bold
duke of Burgundy
(1364-1404)

Richard II
king of England
(1377-1399)
= Isabel

Henry IV
king of England
(1399-1413)

Charles VI
king of France
(1380-1422)

John the Fearless
duke of Burgundy
(1404-1419)

Henry V =
king of England
(1413-1422)

(1) Catherine (2) = Owain
Tudor

Isabel
= Richard II
king of England

Charles VII
king of France
(1422-1461)

Philip the Good
duke of Burgundy
(1419-1467)

Henry VI
king of England
(1422-1461)

Louis XI
king of France
(1461-1483)

Charles the Bold
duke of Burgundy
(1467-1477)

See Genealogy 8.2

See Genealogy 8.2

Charles VIII
king of France
(1483-1498)

Mary of Burgundy
(1477-1482)
= Maximillian of
Habsburg

grown when Henry V (r.1413-1422) came to the throne and revived England's Continental claims. Demanding nearly all of the land that the Angevins had held in the twelfth century, he struck France in 1415 in a concerted effort to conquer both cities and countryside. Soon Normandy was Henry's, and, determined to keep it, he forced all who refused him loyalty into exile, confiscating their lands and handing the property over to his own followers. (See Map 8.3.)

Map 8.3 (facing page):
English and Burgundian
Hegemony in France,
c.1430

Henry's plans were aided by a new regional power: Burgundy. A marvel of shrewd marriage alliances, canny purchases, and outright military conquests, the Duchy of Burgundy forged by Philip the Bold (r.1364-1404) was a cluster of principalities with one center at Dijon (the traditional Burgundy) and another at Lille, in the north (the traditional Flanders). The only unity in these disparate regions was provided by the dukes themselves, who traveled tirelessly from one end of their duchy to the other, participating in elaborate ceremonies—lavish entry processions into cities, wedding and birth festivities, funerals—and commissioning art and music that both celebrated and justified their power. (See Map 8.4.)

Like the kings of France, Philip the Bold was a Valois, but his grandson, Philip the Good (r.1419-1467), decided to link his destiny with England, long the major trading partner of Flanders. Thus, with the support of the Burgundians, the English easily marched into Paris, inadvertently helped by the French king, Charles VI (r.1380-1422), whose frequent bouts of insanity created a vacuum at the top of France's leadership. The Treaty of Troyes (1420) made Henry V the heir to the throne of France.

Had Henry lived, he might have made good his claim. But he died in 1422, leaving behind an infant son to take the crown of France under the regency of the duke of Bedford. Meanwhile, with Charles VI dead the same year, Charles VII, the French "dauphin," or crown prince, was disheartened by defeats. Only in 1429 did his mood change; Jeanne d'Arc (Joan of Arc), a sixteen-year-old peasant girl from Domrémy (part of a small enclave in northern France still loyal to the dauphin), arrived at Chinon, where Charles was holed up, to convince him and his theologians that she had been divinely sent to defeat the English. As she wrote in an audacious letter to the English commanders, "The Maid [as she called herself] has come on behalf of God to reclaim the blood royal. She is ready to make peace, if you [the English] are willing to settle with her by evacuating France."⁵

In effect, Jeanne inherited the moral capital that had been earned by the Beguines and other women mystics. When the English forces laid siege to Orléans (the prelude to their moving into southern France—see Map 8.3), Jeanne not only wrote the letter to the English quoted above but was allowed to join the French army. Its "miraculous" defeat of the English at Orléans (1429) turned the tide. "Oh! What an honor for the feminine sex!" wrote the poet Christine de Pisan (1364-c.1430), continuing,

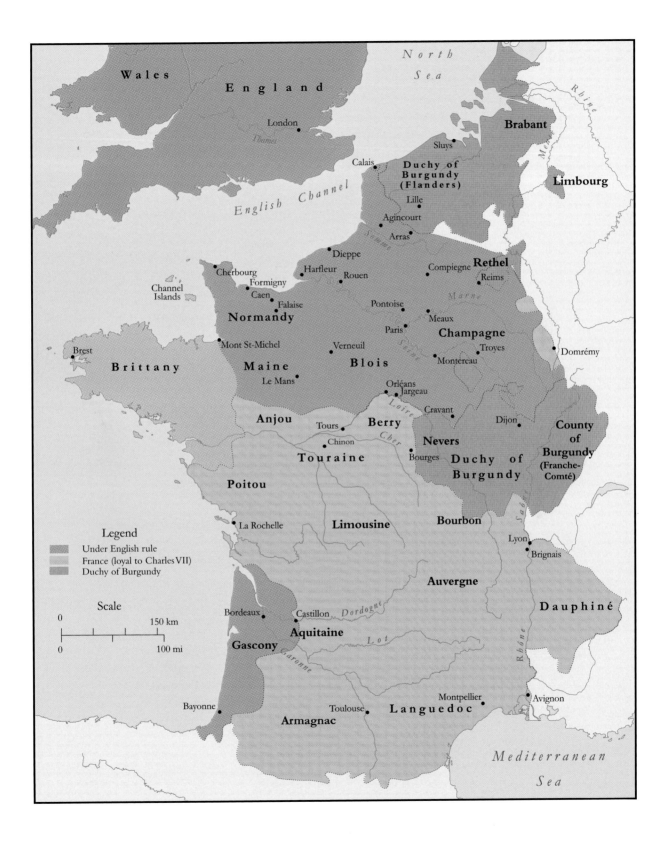

Wales

England

London

North Sea

Brabant

Rhine

Sluys

Calais

Duchy of Burgundy (Flanders)

Limbourg

English Channel

Lille

Agincourt

Arras

Somme

Dieppe

Harfleur

Rouen

Compiègne

Rethel

Reims

Cherbourg

Formigny

Caen

Falaise

Channel Islands

Normandy

Pontoise

Marne

Meaux

Champagne

Paris

Seine

Troyes

Domrémy

Mont St-Michel

Verneuil

Montereau

Brest

Maine

Blois

Le Mans

Brittany

Orléans

Jargeau

Cravant

Dijon

Anjou

Tours

Berry

Loire

Nevers

County of Burgundy (Franche-Comté)

Chinon

Cher

Bourges

Touraine

Duchy of Burgundy

Poitou

La Rochelle

Limousine

Bourbon

Saône

Lyon

Brignais

Legend

Under English rule

France (loyal to Charles VII)

Duchy of Burgundy

Auvergne

Dauphiné

Scale

0   150 km

0   100 mi

Bordeaux

Castillon

Dordogne

Aquitaine

Lot

Gascony

Garonne

Rhône

Montpellier

Avignon

Bayonne

Toulouse

Languedoc

Armagnac

Mediterranean Sea

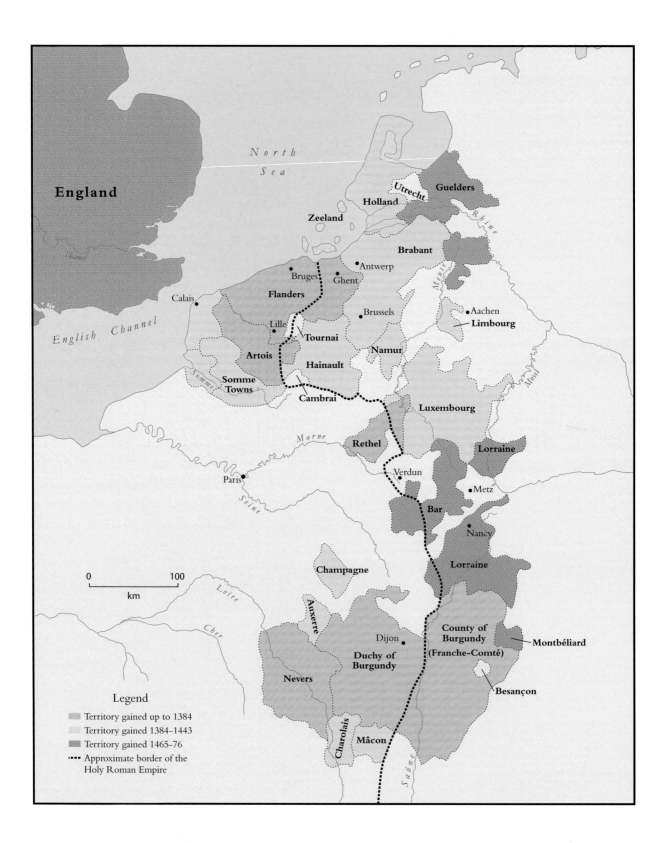

England

North Sea

Utrecht

Holland

Guelders

Zeeland

Rhine

Brabant

•Antwerp

Bruges•

Ghent.

Calais•

Flanders

Brussels

Meuse

Aachen•

Limbourg

English Channel

Lille•

Tournai

Artois

Hainault

Namur

Moselle

Somme

Somme
Towns

Cambrai

Luxembourg

Marne

Rethel

Lorraine

Metz•

Paris•

•Verdun

Seine

Bar

Nancy•

Champagne

Lorraine

Loire

0   100

km

Auxerre

Cher

Dijon•

County of
Burgundy
(Franche-Comté)

Montbéliard•

Duchy of
Burgundy

Nevers

•Besançon

Legend

Charolais

Mâcon

Saône

Territory gained up to 1384

Territory gained 1384–1443

Territory gained 1465–76

Approximate border of the
Holy Roman Empire

It is obvious that God loves it
That all those vile people,
Who had laid the whole kingdom to waste—
By a woman this realm is now made safe and sound,
Something more than five thousand men could not have done—
And those traitors purged forever![6]

Soon thereafter Jeanne led Charles to Reims, deep in English territory, where he was anointed king. Captured by Burgundians in league with the English in 1430, Jeanne was ransomed by the English and tried as a heretic the following year. Found guilty, she was famously burned, eventually becoming a symbol of martyrdom as well as triumphant French resistance. In fact it took many more years, indeed until 1453, for the French to win the war. One reason for the French triumph was their systematic use of gunpowder-fired artillery: in one fifteen-month period around 1450, the French relied heavily on guns and cannons to capture more than seventy English strongholds. Diplomatic relations helped the French as well: after 1435, the duke of Burgundy abandoned the English and supported the French, at least in lukewarm fashion.

Map 8.4 (facing page): The Duchy of Burgundy, 1363-1477

The Hundred Years' War devastated France in the short run. During battles, armies destroyed cities and harried the countryside, breaking the morale of the population. Even when not officially "at war," bands of soldiers—"Free Companies" of mercenaries that hired themselves out to the highest bidder, whether in France, Spain, or Italy—roved the countryside, living off the gains of pillage. Nevertheless, soon after 1453, France began a long and steady recovery. Merchants invested in commerce, peasants tilled the soil, and the king exercised more power than ever before. A standing army was created, trained, billeted, and supplied with weapons, including the new "fiery" artillery, all under royal command.

Burgundy, so brilliantly created a century earlier, fell apart even more quickly: Charles the Bold's expansionist policies led to the formation of a coalition against him, and he died fighting just outside the city of Nancy in 1477. His daughter, Mary, his only heir, tried to stave off French control by quickly marrying Maximilian of Habsburg. This was only partly successful: while she brought the County of Burgundy and most of the Low Countries to the Holy Roman Empire, the French kings were able to absorb the southern portions of the duchy of Burgundy as well as the Somme Towns in the north. Soon (in 1494) France was leading an expedition into Italy, claiming the crown of Naples.

In England, the Hundred Years' War brought about a similar political transformation. Initially France's victory affected mainly the topmost rank of the royal house itself. The progeny of Edward III formed two rival camps, York and Lancaster (named after some of their lands in northern England). (See Genealogy 8.2: York and Lancastrian

[Tudor] Kings.) Already in 1399, unhappy with Richard II, who had dared to disinherit him, the Lancastrian Henry had engineered the king's deposition and taken the royal scepter himself as Henry IV. But when his grandson Henry VI lost the war to France, the Yorkists quickly took advantage of the fact. A series of dynastic wars—later dubbed the "Wars of the Roses" after the white rose badge of the Yorkists and the red of the Lancastrians—was fought from 1455-1487. In 1461, Edward of York deposed Henry, becoming Edward IV. Upon his death in 1483 there was further intrigue as his brother, Richard III, seized the eleven-year-old Edward V and his brother, packing them off to the Tower of London, where they were soon murdered. Two years later, Richard himself was dead on the fields of Bosworth, and Henry VII, the first Tudor king, was on the throne.

Genealogy 8.2: York and Lancastrian (Tudor) Kings

YORKIST DYNASTY · LANCASTRIAN (TUDOR) DYNASTY

Edward III
(1327-1377)

Edward
the Black Prince
(d.1376)

Lionel
duke of Clarence
(d.1368)

John of Gaunt
duke of Lancaster
(d.1399)

Richard II
(1377-1399)

Henry IV
(1399-1413)

Henry V = (1) Catherine (2) = Owain
king of England   Tudor
(1413-1422)

Richard III
(1483-1485)

Edward IV
(1461-1483)

Henry VI
(1422-1461)

Henry VII
(1485-1509)

Edward V
(1483)

| direct descendant
= married to
⋮ indirect descendant

All of this would later be grist for Shakespeare's historical dramas, but at the time it was more the stuff of tragedy, as whole noble lines were killed off, Yorkist lands were confiscated for the crown, and people caught in the middle longed for a strong king who would keep the peace. When the dust settled, the Tudors were far more powerful than previous English kings had been.

Princes, Knights, and Citizens

The Hundred Years' War, the Wars of the Roses, and other, more local wars of the fifteenth century brought to the fore a kind of super-prince: mighty kings (as in England, Scotland, and France), dukes (as in Burgundy), and *signori* (in Italy). All were supported by mercenary troops and up-to-date weaponry, putting knights and nobles in the shade. Yet the end of chivalry was paradoxically the height of the chivalric fantasy. We have already seen how delighted Froissart was by Walter de Manny's chivalric vow. Heraldry, a system of symbols that distinguished each knight by the sign on his shield, came into full flower around the same time. Originally meant to advertise the fighter and his heroic deeds on the battlefield, it soon came to symbolize his family, decorating both homes and tombs. Kings and other great lords founded and promoted chivalric orders with fantastic names—the Order of the Garter, the Order of the Golden Buckle, the Order of the Golden Fleece. All had mainly social and honorific functions, sponsoring knightly tournaments and convivial feasts precisely when knightly jousts and communal occasions were no longer useful for war.

While super-princes were the norm, there were some exceptions. In the mountainous terrain of the alpine passes, a coalition of members of urban and rural communes along with some lesser nobles promised to aid one another against the Habsburg emperors. Taking advantage of rivalries within the Holy Roman Empire, the Swiss Confederation created *c.*1500 a militant state of its own. Structured as a league, power was in the hands of urban citizenry and members of peasant communes. The nobility gradually disappeared as new elites from town and countryside took over. Unlike the great European powers in its "republican" organization, Switzerland nevertheless conveniently served as a reservoir of mercenary troops for its princely neighbors.

Venice maintained its own republicanism via a different set of compromises. It was dominated by a Great Council, from whose membership many of the officers of the state were elected, including the "doge," a life-long position. Between 1297 and 1324 the size of the Council grew dramatically: to its membership of 210 in 1296, more than a thousand new names were added by 1340. At the same time, however, the Council was gradually closed off to all but certain families, which were in this way turned into a hereditary aristocracy. Accepting this fact constituted the compromise

Scale

0 — 500 km

0 — 300 mi

Boundary of the
Holy Roman Empire

NORWAY   **SWEDEN**
Bergen
Oslo
Stockholm

Scotland   *North Sea*

Denmark
Copenhagen
Baltic Sea

Königsberg
(Kaliningrad)
Danzig
(Gdansk)

Ireland
Dublin

Lancaster
York

England
London

Lübeck
Hamburg
Bremen

Poland
Cracow

Vistula

Atlantic Ocean

Cassel   Ghent
Flanders   **Brabant**
(Burgundy)   *(Burgundy)*
Tournai
Arras   **Luxembourg**
(Burgundy)

Cologne
Mainz

Holy Roman Empire

Prague
Bohemia
Tabor

Normandy
Paris
Seine

Brittany
Orléans
Loire

Vienna

Danube

Hungary

Poitiers
Bourges

Burgundy   **Franche-Comté**
(Burgundy)

Swiss Confederation
Constance

F r a n c e

Bordeaux

Rep. of Venice

Duchy of Milan   Bergamo
Milan   Verona   Venice
Lodi   Mantua   Padua
Genoa

Gascony
Avignon
Provence
(French in 1486)
Marseilles

Languedoc

Rep. of Genoa

Rep. of Florence
Rimini
Pisa   Florence
Siena   Urbino
Papal States
Rome

Republic of Adriatic Venice

Adriatic Sea

Bosnia
(Ottoman in 1463)

Serbia *(Ottoman in 1459)*

Herzegovina
(Ottoman in 1465)

Albania
(Ottoman in 1479)

Navarre
Aragon
Catalonia
Barcelona

Corsica
(Genoa)

Sardinia

Kingdom of Naples
Naples

Portugal
Lisbon

C a s t i l e
Córdoba
Duero
Tagus
Guandiana
Guadalquiver
Granada
G r a n a d a

Valencia
K i n g d o m   o f   A r a g o n
Ebro

Majorca

Cagliari

Palermo
Sicily

Mediterranean Sea

(Portuguese in 1471)

of the lower classes. Its counterpart by the ruling families was to suppress (in large measure) their private interests in favor of the general welfare of the city. That welfare depended mainly on the sea for both necessities and wealth. Only at the end of the fourteenth century did the Venetians begin to expand within Italy itself, becoming a major land power in the region (see Map 8.5). But as it gobbled up Bergamo and Verona, Venice collided with the interests of Milan. Wars between the two city-states ended only with the Peace of Lodi in 1454. Soon the three other major Italian powers—Florence, the papacy, and Naples—joined Venice and Milan in the Italic League, which kept the status quo in Italy for forty years, until the French invasion of 1494.

Revolts in Town and Country

Map 8.5 (facing page): Western Europe, *c.*1450

While power at the top was consolidating, discontent seethed from below. Throughout the fourteenth century popular uprisings across Europe gave vent to discontent. The "popular" component of these revolts should not be exaggerated, as many were led by petty knights or wealthy burghers. But they also involved large masses of people, some of whom were very poor indeed. At times articulating universal principles, these revolts were often deeply rooted as well in local grievances.

Long accustomed to a measure of self-government in periodic assemblies that reaffirmed the customs of the region, the peasants of Flanders reacted boldly when the count's officials began to try to collect new taxes. Between 1323 and 1328, Flemish peasants drove out the officials and their noble allies, redistributing the lands that they confiscated. The peasants set up an army, established courts, collected taxes, and effectively governed themselves. The cities of Flanders, initially small, independent pockets outside of the peasants' jurisdiction, soon followed suit, with the less wealthy citizens taking over city government. It took the combined forces of the rulers of France and Navarre plus a papal declaration of crusade to crush the peasants at the battle of Cassel in 1328.

Anti-French and anti-tax activities soon resumed in Flanders, however, this time at Ghent, where the weavers had been excluded from city government since 1320. When England prepared for the opening of the Hundred Years' War, it cut off wool exports to Flanders, putting the weavers (who depended on English wool) out of work. At Ghent the weavers took the hint and rallied to the English cause. Led by Jacob van Artevelde, himself a landowner but now spokesman for the rebels, the weavers overturned the city government. By 1339, Artevelde's supporters dominated not only Ghent but also much of northern Flanders. A year later, he was welcoming the English king Edward III to Flanders as king of France. Although Artevelde was assassinated in 1345 by weavers who thought he had betrayed their cause, the tensions that brought him to the fore continued. The local issues that pitted weavers against the other classes in the city were exacerbated by the ongoing hostility between England and France. Like a world war, the Hundred Years' War engulfed its bystanders.

In France, uprisings in the mid-fourteenth century signaled further strains of the war. At the disastrous battle of Poitiers (1356), King John II of France was captured and taken prisoner. The Estates General, which prior to the battle had agreed to heavy taxes to counter the English, met in the wake of Poitiers to allot blame and reform the government. When the new regent (the ruler in John's absence) stalled in instituting the reforms, Étienne Marcel, head of the merchants of Paris, led a plot to murder some royal councilors and take control of Paris. But the presence of some Free Company troops in Paris led to disorder there, and some of Marcel's erstwhile supporters blamed him for the riots, assassinating him in 1358.

Meanwhile, outside Paris, the Free Companies harried the countryside. In 1358 a peasant movement formed to resist them. Called the Jacquerie by dismissive chroniclers (probably after their derisive name for its leader, Jacques Bonhomme—Jack Goodfellow), it soon turned into an uprising against the nobility, failures as knights (in the eyes of the peasants) because of their loss at Poitiers and their inability to defend the rural peace. The revolt was depicted in sensationally gory detail: "Those evil men," wrote Froissart, "pillaged and burned everything and violated and killed all the ladies and girls without mercy, like mad dogs."[7] Perhaps. But the repression of the Jacquerie was at least equally brutal and, in most places, quicker.

More permanent in their consequences were peasant movements in England; Wat Tyler's Rebellion of 1381 is the most famous. During this revolt, groups of "commons" (in this case mainly country folk from south-east England) converged on London to demand an end to serfdom: "And they required that for the future no man should be in serfdom, nor make any manner of homage or suit to any lord, but should give a rent of 4 pennies an acre for his land."[8] Most immediately, the revolt was a response to a poll tax of one shilling per person, the third fiscal imposition in four years passed by Parliament to recoup the expenses of war. More profoundly, it was a clash between new expectations of freedom (in the wake of the Black Death, labor was worth much more) and old obligations of servitude. The egalitarian chant of the rebels signaled a growing sense of their own power:

When Adam delved [dug] and Eve span [spun],
Who then was the gentleman?

Although Tyler, the leader of the revolt, was soon killed and the rest of the commons dispersed, the death knell of serfdom in England had in fact been sounded, as the rebels went home to bargain with their landlords for new-style leases.

In the decades just before this in a number of Italian cities, cloth workers chafed under regimes that gave them no say in government. At Florence in 1378, matters came to a head as a coalition of wool workers (most of whom were barred from any guild), small businessmen, and some disaffected guild members challenged the ruling elites. The *ciompi* (wool-carders) rebellion, as the movement was called, succeeded briefly in taking over the Florentine government and permitting some new guilds to form there. But the movement soon splintered, and, strapped for money, it resorted to forced loans, an expedient that backfired. By 1382, the old elite was back in power, determined not to let the lower classes rise again; in the next century, the Florentine republic gave way to rule by a powerful family of bankers, the Medici.

Economic Contraction

While the Black Death was good for the silk trade, and the Hundred Years' War stimulated the manufacture of arms and armor, in other spheres economic contraction was the norm. After 1340, with the disintegration of the Mongol Empire, easy trade relations between Europe and the Far East were destroyed. Within Europe, rulers' war machines were fueled by new taxes and loans—some of them forced. At times, rulers paid back the loans; often they did not. The great import-export houses, which loaned money as part of their banking activities, found themselves advancing too much to rulers all too willing to default. In the 1340s the four largest firms went bankrupt, producing, in domino effect, the bankruptcies of hundreds more.

War did more than gobble up capital. Where armies raged, production stopped. Even in intervals of peace, Free Companies attacked not only the countryside but also merchants on the roads. To ensure its grain supply, Florence was obliged to supply guards all along the route from Bologna. Merchants began investing in insurance policies, not only against losses due to weather but also against robbers and pirates.

Meanwhile, the plague dislocated normal economic patterns. Urban rents fell as houses went begging for tenants, while wages rose as employers sought to attract scarce labor. In the countryside, whole swaths of land lay uncultivated. The monastery of Saint-Denis, so rich and powerful under Abbot Suger in the twelfth century, lost more than half its income from land between 1340 and 1403. As the population fell and the demand for grain decreased, the Baltic region—chief supplier of rye to the rest of Europe—suffered badly; by the fifteenth century, some villages had disappeared.

Yet, as always, the bad luck of some meant the prosperity of others. While Tuscany lost its economic edge, cities in northern Italy and southern Germany gained new muscle, manufacturing armor and fustian (a popular textile made of cotton and flax) and distributing their products across Europe. The whole center of economic growth was in fact shifting northwards, from the Mediterranean to the European heartlands. There was one unfortunate exception: the fourteenth century saw the burgeoning of the slave trade in southern Europe. Girls, mainly from the Mongol world but also sometimes Greeks or Slavs (and therefore Christians), were herded onto ships; those who survived the harrowing trip across the Mediterranean were sold on the open market in cities such as Genoa, Florence, and Pisa. They were high-prestige purchases, domestic "servants" with the allure of the Orient.

THE CHURCH DIVIDED

The fourteenth and fifteenth centuries saw deep divisions within the church. Popes fought over who had the right to the papacy, and ordinary Catholics disputed about that as well as the very nature of the church itself.

The Great Schism

Between 1378 and 1409, rival popes—one line based in Avignon, the other in Rome—claimed to rule as vicar of Christ; from 1409 to 1417, a third line based in Bologna joined them. (See the list of Popes and Antipopes to 1500 on p. 362.) The popes at each venue excommunicated the others, surrounded themselves with their own college of cardinals, and commanded loyal followers. The Great Schism (1378-1417)—as this period of popes and antipopes is called—was both a spiritual and a political crisis.

Exacerbating political tensions, the schism fed the Hundred Years' War: France supported the pope at Avignon, England the pope at Rome. In some regions the schism polarized individual communities: for example, around 1400 at Tournai, on the border of France and Flanders, two rival bishops, each representing a different pope, fought over the diocese. Portugal, more adaptable and further from the fray, simply changed its allegiance four times.

The crisis began with the best of intentions. Stung by criticism of the Avignon papacy, Pope Gregory XI (r.1370-1378) left Avignon to return to Rome in 1377. When he died a year later, the cardinals elected an Italian as Urban VI (1378-1389). Soon finding Urban high-handed, however, the French cardinals thought better of what they had done. At Anagni, declaring Urban's election invalid and calling on him to resign, they elected Clement VII, who installed himself at Avignon. The papal monarchy was now split. The group that went to Avignon depended largely on French resources to support it; the group at Rome survived by establishing a *signoria*, complete with mercenary troops (*condottieri*) to collect its taxes and fight its wars. Thus, Urban's successor, Boniface IX (1389-1404), reconquered the papal states and set up governors (many of them his family members) to rule them. Desperate for more revenues, the popes turned all their prerogatives into sources of income. Boniface, for example, put church benefices on the open market and commercialized "indulgences"—acts of piety (such as viewing a relic or attending a special church feast) for which people were promised release from Purgatory for a specific number of days. Now money payments were declared equivalent to performing the acts. Many people willingly made such purchases; others were outraged that Heaven was for sale.

Solutions to end the schism eventually coalesced around the idea of a council. The "conciliarists"—those who advocated the convening of a council that would have authority over even the pope—included both university men and princes anxious to flex their muscles over the church. At the Council of Pisa (1409), which neither of the popes attended, the delegates deposed them both and elected a new man. But the two deposed popes refused to budge: there were now *three* popes, one at Avignon, one at Rome, and a third at Bologna. The successor of the newest one, John XXIII, turned to the emperor to arrange for another council.

The Council of Constance (1414-1418) met to resolve the papal crisis as well as to institute church reforms. In the first task it succeeded, deposing the three rivals and electing Martin V as pope. In the second, it was less successful, for it did not end the fragmentation of the church. National, even nationalist, churches had begun to form, independent of and sometimes in opposition to papal leadership. Meanwhile the conciliar movement continued, developing an influential theory that held that church authority in the final instance resided in a corporate body (whether representing prelates or more broadly the community of the faithful) rather than the pope.

POPULAR RELIGIOUS MOVEMENTS IN ENGLAND AND BOHEMIA

In England, the radical Oxford-trained theologian John Wyclif (*c.*1330-1384), influenced in part by William of Ockham (see p. 287), argued for a very small sphere of action for the church. In his view, the state alone should concern itself with temporal things, the pope's decrees should be limited to what was already in the Gospels, the laity should be allowed to read and interpret the Bible for itself, and the church should stop promulgating the absurd notion of transubstantiation. At first the darling of the king and other powerful men in England (who were glad to hear arguments on behalf of an expanded place for secular rule), Wyclif appealed as well (and more enduringly) to the gentry and literate urban classes. Derisively called "Lollards" (idlers) by the church and persecuted as heretics, the followers of Wyclif were largely, though not completely, suppressed in the course of the fifteenth century.

Considerably more successful were the Bohemian disciples of Wyclif. In Bohemia, part of the Holy Roman Empire but long used to its own monarchy (see Map 8.5), the disparities between rich and poor helped create conditions for a new vision of society in which religious and national feeling played equal parts. There were at least three inequities in Bohemia: the Germans held a disproportionate share of its wealth and power, even though Czechs constituted the majority of the population; the church owned almost a third of the land; and the nobility dominated the countryside and considered itself the upholder of the common good. In the hands of Jan Hus (c.1370–1415), the writings of Wyclif were transformed into a call for a reformed church and laity. All were to live in accordance with the laws of God, and the laity could disobey clerics who were more interested in pomp than the salvation of souls. Hus translated parts of the Bible into Czech while encouraging German translations as well. Furthering their vision of equality within the church, Hus's followers demanded that all the faithful be offered not just the bread but also the consecrated wine at Mass. (This was later called Utraquism, from the Latin *sub utraque specie*— communion "in both kinds.") In these ways, the Hussites gave shape to their vision of the church as the community of believers — women and the poor included. Hus's friend Jerome of Prague identified the whole reform movement with the good of the Bohemian nation itself, taking over the traditional claim of the nobility.

Burned as a heretic at the Council of Constance, Hus nevertheless inspired a movement that transformed the Bohemian church. The Hussites soon disagreed about demands and methods (the most radical, the Taborites, set up a sort of government in exile in southern Bohemia, pooling their resources while awaiting the Second Coming), but most found willing protectors among the Bohemian nobility. In the struggle between these groups and imperial troops — backed by a papal declaration of crusade in Bohemia — a peculiarly Bohemian church was created, with its own special liturgy for the Mass.

Churches under Royal Leadership: France and Spain

"National" churches did not need popular revolts to spark them. Indeed, in France and Spain they were forged in the crucible of growing royal power. In the Pragmatic Sanction of Bourges (1438), Charles VII surveyed the various failings of the church in France and declared himself the guarantor of its reform. Popes were no longer to appoint French prelates nor grant benefices to churchmen; these matters now came under the jurisdiction of the king.

Similar rights were claimed by the crown in Spain about a half-century later, when the marriage of Ferdinand (r.1479–1516) and Isabella (r.1474–1504) — dubbed the

"Catholic Monarchs" by the pope—united Aragon and Castile. In their hands, Catholicism became an instrument of militant royal sovereignty. King and queen launched an offensive against the Muslims in Granada (conquering the last bit in 1492) and determined to purge the *conversos* (Christians of Jewish heritage) in their midst.

Like the war against the Muslims, the persecution of the *conversos* in Spain had deep roots. The relatively peaceful co-existence of Christians and Jews in most of Spain during the twelfth and thirteenth centuries had ended in the fourteenth. Virulent anti-Jewish pogroms in 1391 led many Spanish Jews to convert to Christianity. But the subsequent successes of the *conversos*—some of whom obtained civil and church offices or married into the nobility—stirred resentment among the "Old Christians." Harnessing popular resentments, the Catholic Monarchs set up their own version of the Inquisition in 1478. Under the friar-inquisitor Tomás Torquemada (1420-1498), wholesale torture and public executions became the norm for disposing of "crypto-Jews." When, in 1492, the monarchs demanded that all remaining Jews convert or leave the country, many chose exile over *conversos* status. Soon the newly "purified" church of Spain was extended to the New World as well, where papal concessions gave the kings control over church benefices and appointments.

DEFINING STYLES

Everywhere, in fact, kings and other rulers were intervening in church affairs, wresting military force from the nobility, and imposing lucrative taxes to be gathered by their zealous and efficient salaried agents. All of this was largely masked, however, behind brilliant courts that employed every possible means to burnish the image of the prince.

Renaissance Italy

In 1416, taking a break from their jobs at the Council of Constance, three young Italians went off on a "rescue mission." One of them, Cincius Romanus (*d.*1445) described the escapade to one of his Latin teachers back in Italy:

> In Germany there are many monasteries with libraries full of Latin books. This aroused the hope in me that some of the works of Cicero, Varro, Livy, and other great men of learning, which seem to have completely vanished, might come to light, if a careful search were instituted. A few days ago, [we] went by agreement to the town of St. Gall. As soon as we

went into the library [of the monastery there], we found *Jason's Argonauticon*, written by C. Valerius Flaccus in verse that is both splendid and dignified and not far removed from poetic majesty. Then we found some discussions in prose of a number of Cicero's orations.... In fact we have copies of all these books. But when we carefully inspected the nearby tower of the church of St. Gall in which countless books were kept like captives and the library neglected and infested with dust, worms, soot, and all the things associated with the destruction of books, we all burst into tears.[9]

Plate 8.2 (facing page): Donatello, *David Standing on the Head of Goliath* (c.1430-1440). David is here portrayed neither as an Old Testament king nor as the author of the psalms, but rather as a beautiful boy.

Cicero, Varro, Livy: these provided the models of Latin and the rules of expression that Cincius and his friends admired. To them the monks of St. Gall were "barbarians" for not wholeheartedly valuing ancient Latin rhetoric, prose, and poetry over all other writings. In the course of the fourteenth century Italian intellectuals turned away from the evolved Latin of their contemporaries to find models in the ancients. Already in 1333 the young Francis Petrarch (1304-1374) traveled through the Low Countries looking for manuscripts of the ancient authors; he discovered Cicero's *Pro Archia*, a paean to poetry, and carefully copied it out.

Petrarch's taste for ancient eloquence and his ability to write in a new, elegant, "classical" style (whether in Latin or in the vernacular) made him a star. But he was not alone, as Cincius' letter proves; he was simply one of the more famous exemplars of a new group calling themselves "humanists." There had been humanists before: we have seen Saint Anselm's emphasis on Christ's saving humanity, Saint Bernard's evocation of human religious emotion, and Thomas Aquinas's confidence in human reason to scale the heights of truth (see pp. 216 and 286). But the new humanists were more self-conscious about their calling, and they tied it to the cultivation of classical literature.

As Cincius' case also shows, if the humanists' passion was antiquity, their services were demanded with equal ardor by ecclesiastical and secular princes. Cincius served Pope John XXIII. Petrarch was similarly employed by princes: for several years, for example, he worked for the Visconti family, the rulers of Milan. As Italian artists associated themselves with humanists, working in tandem with them, they too became part of the movement.

Historians have come to give the name Renaissance to this era of artists and humanists. But the Renaissance was not so much a period as a program. It made the language and art of the ancient past the model for the present; it privileged classical books as "must" reading for an eager and literate elite; and it promoted old, sometimes crumbling, and formerly little-appreciated classical art, sculpture, and architecture as inspiring models for Italian artists and builders. Meanwhile, it downgraded the immediate past — the last thousand years! — as a barbarous "Middle" Age. Above all, the Renaissance gave city communes and wealthy princes alike a new repertory of symbols and styles, drawn from a resonant and heroic past, with which to associate their present power.

At Florence, for example, where the Medici family held sway in the fifteenth century behind a facade of communal republicanism, the sculptor Donatello (*c*.1386-1466) cast a bronze figure of David (see Plate 8.2) to stand in the courtyard of the Medici palace. It was accompanied by a Latin inscription, "Behold, a boy overcame the great tyrant. Conquer, O citizens."[10] The appeal to the Florentines to overcome the enemy (very likely Milan) subtly associated the Medici family with the liberty of the citizenry while disparaging the dukes of Milan as tyrants. Donatello's *David* is strikingly young, self-absorbed—and utterly nude apart from his hat and boots. The first bronze nude cast since antiquity, it combines Christian iconography (David here evokes Christ trampling the serpent) with classical grace (compare David's easy pose with that of the equally triumphant Theseus the Minotaur-slayer in Plate 1.2 on p. 34 of volume 1).

Corporate sponsors also patronized the new-style artists and architects. The Florentine Silk Guild paid the architect Filippo Brunelleschi (1377-1446) to build a Foundling Hospital, a home for abandoned children. The building broke radically from the soaring Gothic style to emphasize calm regularity and low horizontal steadiness (see Plate 8.3). Soon the Opera del Duomo, which was responsible for the upkeep of Florence's cathedral, called on Brunelleschi to provide a dome for Florence's unfinished Gothic cathedral, "vast enough to cover the entire Tuscan population with its shadow," as his admirer Alberti put it.[11]

The Renaissance flourished in many Italian cities besides Florence, among them Rome, Urbino, Mantua, Venice, Milan, and Perugia. At Perugia, for example, the artist Raphael (1483-1520) was commissioned by a noblewoman, Atalanta Baglioni, to paint an altarpiece for her private chapel to commemorate the death of her son. In the *Entombment of Christ* (see Plate 8.4), Raphael joined religious with family feeling, portraying (as the artist's biographer Vasari [*d*.1574] put it) "the grief as they lay him [Christ] to rest felt by the nearest and dearest relations of some much loved person, who had sustained the happiness, dignity and well-being of a whole family."[12]

At Milan, Duke Ludovico il Moro (*r*.1480-1499) gave Leonardo da Vinci (1452-1519) a number of commissions, including painting the *Last Supper* (see Plate 8.5) on one of the walls of the dining hall of a Dominican convent *c*.1497. Here Leonardo demonstrated his mastery of the

Plate 8.3: Brunelleschi, Foundling Hospital (begun 1421). Among the many aspects of antiquity revived by Renaissance artists and architects was the idea of public space. Brunelleschi's portico for the Foundling Hospital formed the eastern side of a piazza (public square). On the north was the church of Santissima Annunziata (just a bit of which is visible in this photograph). Annunziata means "Annunciation," a reference to the Angel Gabriel's announcement to Mary that she would bear the Savior. The entire piazza was, then, devoted to the twin notions of fertility and children.

relatively new science of linear perspective: the hall sheltering Christ and his disciples seems to recede as its walls approach a vanishing point. On the opposite side of the hall, Leonardo added a fresco (now nearly obliterated) of his patron, Ludovico, his wife, and their two children kneeling before an image of the Crucifixion.

These were religious themes, but Ludovico sponsored classical ones as well, some woven into the very fabric of courtly life. At one of his banquets in 1491, for example, boiled fish were presented under covers consisting "of a model of the Colosseum lavishly decorated with gold and mottoes," while a dessert arrived under "ornate lids in gold, in the Royal manner, depicting Rome triumphant with an ox, who together vow never to part, and this represents justice, temperance and great friendship, and many verses testifying to this are recited."[13] No doubt many humanists in Ludovico's employ were kept busy writing the verses.

The Ottoman Court

Some of Ludovico's dinner presentations acted out a different preoccupation — the power of the new Ottoman state. When a whole roasted capon was brought in for each guest, it was accompanied by a little drama:

A bull is presented by Indians and brought in by slaves of the Sultan in a most elaborately decorated procession of gold and silver with two little moors who sing very elaborately and an ambassador with an interpreter, who translates the words of the embassy.[14]

Here the Ottoman sultan was depicted as the lackey of Duke Ludovico, in a pageant that was meant to be very exotic and in need of "translation" (even though Ludovico himself was dubbed "il Moro," the Moor, because of his swarthy complexion). But imagine that the real sultan—the Ottoman ruler—held his own banquet at the same time: at *his* dinner, the lackey would be an *Italian*, and the sultan would have understood his language. For the Ottomans considered the Renaissance court to be their own as well. They had taken Byzantium, purified it of its infidel past (turning its churches into mosques), and reordered it along fittingly traditional lines. Although in popular speech Constantinople became Istanbul (meaning "the city"), its official name remained "Qustantiniyya"—the City of Constantine. The Ottoman sultans claimed the glory of Byzantium for themselves.

Thus Mehmed II continued to negotiate with Genoese traders, while he "borrowed" Gentile Bellini (*c.*1429-1507) from Venice to be his own court artist. In 1479, he posed for his portrait (see Plate 8.6), only a few decades after the genre of portrait painting itself had been "invented" in Europe. On the walls of his splendid Topkapi palace, he displayed tapestries from Burgundy portraying the deeds of Alexander the Great, each no doubt something like the tapestry illustrated in Plate 8.7 below. Just as a statue of David gave glory to the Medici family, so Alexander burnished the image of the sultan. The tapestries were themselves trophies of war: a failed Burgundian crusade against the Ottomans in 1396 had ended in the capture of Duke John the Fearless; his ransom was the Alexander tapestries.

Learning as well as art was key to the sultans' notions of power. Mehmed and his successors staffed their cities with men well schooled in Islamic administration and culture and set up *madrasas* to teach the young. For himself, Mehmed commissioned a copy of Homer's *Iliad* in Greek, epic poetry in Italian, and other literary works by Turkish, Persian, and European writers. His zeal for scholarship was on a lesser scale but not very different in kind from that of the Florentine ruler Cosimo de' Medici (1389-1464), who in the mid-fifteenth century took over the nearly one thousand volumes of ancient Greek and Latin texts that had been collected with painstaking care by the humanist Niccolò Niccoli (1364-1437). Open to all, the Medici library became the model for princely bibliophiles throughout Italy and elsewhere. Calls for further crusades against the infidel Turks (in 1455 and 1459, for example) were in this sense "family disputes," attempts to contest the East's right to common notions of power and legitimacy.

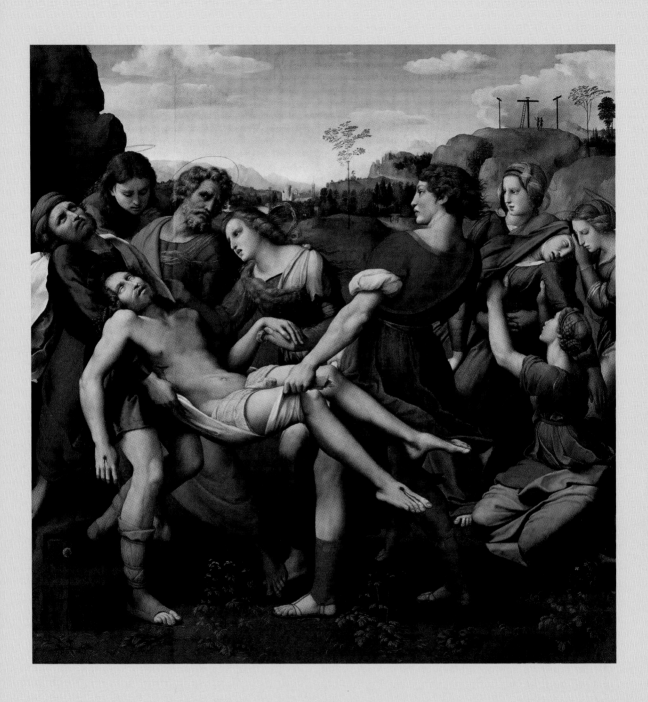

SEEING THE MIDDLE AGES

Plate 8.4 (facing page):
Raphael, *Entombment of Christ* (1507)

Raphael's *Entombment*, the central panel of an altarpiece, is not so much about Christ's entombment as it is about carrying Christ to his tomb. Reading it from right to left, as the artist intended, we see first Christ's mother, the Virgin, her face white as a sheet, swooning into the arms of the three Maries (Holy Women mentioned in the Gospels). The next scene shows two men straining to carry Christ to his tomb, which is indicated by the cave-like opening on the left. Mary Magdalene, one of the Maries, rushes in, hair cascading, to lift Christ's head and hand. In Italy, it was unusual for a narrative such as this to be portrayed on the main panel of an altarpiece. What did Raphael have in mind?

In the first place he had in mind his patron, the noblewoman Atalanta Baglioni. The matriarch of an important Perugian family, she had seen it torn apart by violence. The Perugian chronicler Francesco Matarazzo told the story. Atalanta's son, Grifonetto, had joined a plot to kill all the important men of the family so that "he would become the first of all the family."[1] After a murderous night, he and the others took over the city, but his mother, Atalanta, moved out of his home and "cursed him."[2] Meanwhile, those who had survived the massacre gathered their forces and attacked the city, eventually confronting Grifonetto and stabbing him. As he lay dying, his mother rushed to his side and told her son to "forgive all those who had brought him to his death," thus upholding the honor of the family as "a prudent woman."[3] A few years later, however, when she commissioned the altarpiece from Raphael, a mother's prudence was less important than her grief. The altar itself was meant to serve as the backdrop for commemorative masses on behalf of the soul of Grifonetto and, ultimately, for Atalanta herself, who would have been connected by viewers to the grieving Virgin.

Meleager Sarcophagus, detail (2nd cent.).

Raphael also had in mind the ancient depiction of a group of mourners bearing the body of Meleager on the sarcophagus in Plate 1.3 on p. 35 of volume 1. (See the detail at left.) The relief was well known during the Renaissance. Alberti, an architect and writer of influential guides to painting and sculpture in the 1430s and 1440s, even recommended it as a model for artists interested in showing movement:

They praise a "historia" [a story told through visual means] in Rome, in which the dead Meleager is being carried away, because those who are bearing the burden appear to be distressed and to strain with every limb, while in the dead man there is no member that does not seem completely lifeless; they all hang loose; hands, fingers, neck, all droop inertly down, all combine together to represent death. This is the most difficult thing of all to do.[4]

Atalanta herself was closely connected to the story of Meleager, since her name was the same as that of the woman to whom, according to the Greek myth, Meleager awarded a boar's hide, thus beginning the cycle that would bring about his death. In this way, Atalanta's personal story was assimilated to both a Christian and an ancient narrative in Raphael's altarpiece.

For Raphael, the meaning of the *Entombment* was still more complex. The bearded figure of Joseph of Arimathea, for example, was modeled on an unfinished statue of Saint Matthew by Michelangelo. Finally, the very theme of the altarpiece was probably inspired by Northern Renaissance art (see pp. 334–40 below), such as *The Carrying of Christ to the Tomb* by Rogier van der Weyden or a member of his workshop.

The Workshop of Rogier van der Weyden,
The Carrying of Christ to the Tomb (c.1460–1470).

Further Reading

Chapman, Hugo, Tom Henry, and Carol Plazzotta. *Raphael: From Urbino to Rome*. London, 2004.

Cooper, Donal. "Raphael's Altar-Pieces in S. Francesco al Prato, Perugia: Patronage, Setting and Function." *The Burlington Magazine* 143 (2001): 554–61.

Notes
1. Francesco Matarazzo, *Chronicles of the City of Perugia, 1492–1503*, trans. Edward Strachan Morgan (London, 1905), p.110.
2. Ibid., p.128.
3. Ibid., p.138.
4. Giorgio Vasari, *The Lives of the Artists*, ed. and trans. George Bull (Baltimore, 1965), p.75.

Plate 8.5: Leonardo da Vinci, *Last Supper* (*c.*1497). Leonardo first made his reputation with this painting, which evokes the precise moment when Christ said to his feasting apostles, "One of you is about to betray me." All the apostles react with horror and surprise, but the guilty Judas recoils, his face in shadows. Compare this depiction with the same moment in the Romanesque vault painting of Plate 5.5 on p. 209.

The Northern Renaissance

Northern Europe shared the same notions, but here the symbols of authority and piety were even more eclectic. Burgundy — an hourglass with its top in Flanders, its bottom just above the Alps — embraced nearly all the possibilities. Although Gothic style persisted in northern Europe, especially in architecture, the Greco-Roman world also beckoned. Ancient themes — especially the deeds of heroes, whether real or mythical — were depicted on tapestries that provided lustrous backdrops for rulers of every stripe. The dukes of Burgundy traveled from one end of their dominions to the other with such tapestries in tow. Weavings lined their tents during war and their boats during voyages. In 1459 Philip the Good bought a series of fine tapestries — woven in silk spiced with gold and silver threads — depicting the *History of Alexander the Great* (see Plate 8.7). Reading this tapestry from left to right, we see a city besieged, the trumpeters, archers, and artillery-men and soldiers reflecting the realities of fifteenth-century warfare. At the center, Alexander rises to the sky in a decorated metal cage lifted by four winged griffons. The weaving was the perfect stage setting for the performance of ducal power. No wonder European rulers — from English

Plate 8.6: Gentile Bellini, *Portrait of Mehmed II* (1479). Mehmed, like other Renaissance princes, hired Renaissance artists to give him luster. In the 1460s he tried to obtain the services of the Rimini artist and architect Matteo de' Pasti, but his plans were foiled by Venice, which wanted no rivals at Constantinople. The Venetians sent their own Gentile Bellini instead, who celebrated the sultan's power with this portrait.

Plate 8.7: *History of Alexander the Great,* Tapestry (*c*.1459). To the right of the depiction of his ascent into the air, Alexander appears surrounded by his courtiers. Next he explores the underwater world: seated in a glass bell, he is encircled by sea creatures. Below, now returned to land, Alexander and his men fight dragons and monsters, one of whom is pierced by the hero's sword. Alexander's adventures were recounted in vernacular romances; the text that probably directly inspired this tapestry was *The Book of the Conquests and Deeds of Alexander the Great* by Jean Wauquelin (*d*.1452), a copy of which was owned by the duke of Burgundy.

Plate 8.8: Rogier van der Weyden, *Columba Altarpiece* (1450s). Depicting three standard scenes from Christ's childhood—the Annunciation, the Adoration of the Magi, and the Presentation in the Temple—the *Columba Altarpiece* subtly introduces new themes alongside the old. For example, Christ's death is suggested by the crucifix above Mary in the central panel, while the present time (the fifteenth century) is suggested by the cityscape in the background, which probably represents Cologne, the native city of the man who commissioned the altar and the proud home of the relics of the Magi.

kings to Italian *signori* (and on to Ottoman sultans)—all wanted tapestries from Burgundy for *their* palaces.

At the same time, dukes and other northern European patrons favored a new style of art that emphasized devotion, sentiment, and immediacy. (This style would later be one of the inspirations for Raphael's *Entombment* in Plate 8.4.) Painted in oil-based pigments, capable of showing the finest details and the subtlest shading, Netherlandish art was valued above all for its true-to-life expressivity. In the *Columba Altarpiece* by Rogier van der Weyden—likely commissioned by Johann Dasse, a wealthy merchant from Cologne (Germany)—the donor himself is depicted, hat in hand (to the left), humbly witnessing the visit of the Magi. (See the central panel of Plate 8.8.) Time itself is compressed in this picture, as the immediacy of the painting—its here-and-now presence—belies the historical reality: no merchant of the fifteenth century could possibly have been at the scene.

The emphasis on the natural details of the moment was equally striking in secular paintings from the Netherlands. In *Man in a Red Turban* (see Plate 8.9) by Jan van Eyck (*c*.1390-1441), we even see the stubble of the man's beard. Yet this entirely secular theme—a man in stylish red headgear (evidence of the Turkish allure)—is infused with a quiet inner light that endows its subject with a kind of otherworldliness.

Both the Italian and Northern Renaissances cultivated music and musicians, above all for the aura that they gave rulers, princes, and great churchmen. In Italy, Isabella d'Este (1474-1539), marchesa of Mantua, employed her own musicians—singers, woodwind and string players, percussionists, and keyboard players—while her husband had his own band. In Burgundy the duke had a fine private chapel and musicians, singers, and composers to staff it. In England wealthy patrons founded colleges—Eton (founded by King Henry VI in 1440-1441) was one—where choirs offered up prayers in honor of the Virgin. Motets continued to be composed and sung, but now polyphonic music for larger groups became common as well. In the hands of a composer like John Dunstable (*c*.1385-1453), who probably worked for the duke of Bedford, regent for Henry VI in France during the Hundred Years' War, dissonance was smoothed out. In the compositions of Dunstable and his followers, old juxtapositions of independent lines were replaced by harmonious chords that moved together even as they changed. As Martin le Franc put it in *Le Champion des dames* (1441-1442), "marvelous pleasantness makes their song joyous and notable."[15] Working within the old modal categories, composers made their mark with music newly sonorous and smooth.

Plate 8.9 (facing page): Jan van Eyck, *Man in a Red Turban* (1433). Compare this head with that of the idealized Theseus (Plate 1.2 on p. 34 of volume 1), the somber Saint Mark (Plate 3.8 on p. 132 of volume 1), the jovial Saint Joseph, (Plate 6.6 on p. 251) and the insouciant David (Plate 8.2 on p. 329). Only van Eyck paints his anonymous subject without idealizing or beautifying him; the man's worth and dignity derive only (but importantly) from his individuality.

NEW HORIZONS

Experiment and play within old traditions were thus the major trends of the period. They can be seen in explorations of interiority, in creative inventions, even in the conquest of the globe. Yet their consequences may fairly be said to have ushered in a new era.

Interiority

Donatello's David, dependent on no one for his quiet satisfaction, and van Eyck's red-turbaned man, glowing from within, are similar in their self-involved interiority. David's self-centeredness is that of the hero; van Eyck's man's is that of any ordinary creature of God, the artist's statement about the holiness of nature.

These two styles of interiority were mirrored in religious life and expression. Saint Catherine of Siena (1347-1380) was a woman in the heroic mold. A reformer with a message, she was one of the first in a long line of women (Jeanne d'Arc is another example) to intervene on the public stage because of her private agonies. Chosen by God in distinct words to be his intermediary in the Great Schism, she wrote (or rather dictated) nearly 400 letters to the great leaders of the day, working ceaselessly to bring the pope back to Rome and urging crusade as the best way to purge and revivify the church.

In the Low Countries, northern Germany, and the Rhineland, the *devotio moderna* (the "new devotion") movement, to the contrary, found purgation and renewal in individual reading and contemplation rather than on the public stage. Founded *c.*1380 by Gerhard Groote (1340-1384), the Brethren of the Common Life lived in male or female communities that focused on education, the copying of manuscripts, material simplicity, and individual faith. The Brethren were not quite humanists and not quite mystics, but they drew from both for a religious program that depended very little on the hierarchy or ceremonies of the church. Their style of piety would later be associated with Protestant groups.

Inventions

The enormous demand for books—whether by ordinary lay people, adherents of the *devotio moderna*, or humanists eager for the classics—made printed books a welcome addition to the repertory of available texts, though manuscripts were neither quickly nor easily displaced. The printing press, however obvious in thought, marked a great practical breakthrough: it depended on a new technique to mold metal type. This was first achieved by Johann Gutenberg at Mainz (in Germany) around 1450. The next trick was to get the raw materials that were needed to ensure ongoing production. Paper required water mills and a steady supply of rag (pulp made of cloth); the metal for the type had to be mined and shaped; an ink had to be found that would adhere to metal letters as well as spread evenly on paper.

By 1500 many European cities had publishing houses, with access to the materials that they needed and sufficient clientele to earn a profit. Highly competitive, the presses advertised their wares. They turned out not only religious and classical books but whatever the public demanded. Martin Luther (*c.*1483-1546) may not in fact have nailed his 95 Theses to the door of the church at Wittenberg in 1517, but he certainly allowed them to be printed and distributed in both Latin and German. Challenging prevailing church teachings and practice, the Theses ushered in the Protestant Reformation. The printing press was a powerful instrument of mass communication.

More specialized yet no less decisive for the future were new developments in navigation. Portolan maps, which charted the shape of the Mediterranean coast through accurate measurements from point to point, were used as practical tools by sailors plying the waters. When, at the end of the fifteenth century, Portuguese adventurers made their way down the coast of Africa, they used the same system. But navigating the Atlantic depended on more than maps; it required methods for exploiting the powerful ocean wind systems. New ship designs—the light caravel, the heavy galleon—featured the rigging and sails needed to harness the wind.

Voyages

As we have seen (p. 267), already in the thirteenth century merchants and missionaries from Genoa and Majorca were making forays into the Atlantic. In the fifteenth century the initiative that would eventually take Europeans around the Cape of Good Hope in one direction and to the Americas in the other came from the Portuguese royal house. The enticements were gold and slaves as well as honor and glory. Under King João I (*r.*1385-1433) and his successors, Portugal extended its rule to the Muslim port of Ceuta and a few other nearby cities. (See Map 8.6.) More importantly, João's son Prince Henry "the Navigator" (1394-1460) sponsored expeditions—mainly by Genoese sailors—to explore the African coast: in the mid-1450s they reached the Cape Verde Islands and penetrated inland via the Senegal and Gambia rivers. A generation later, Portuguese explorers were working their way far past the equator; in 1487 Bartholomeu Dias (*c.*1450-1500) sighted the Cape of Good Hope, and at the end of the century Vasco da Gama (*c.*1460-1524) went around Africa and sailed all the way to Calicut (today Kozhikode) in India. In his account of the voyage he made no secret of his methods: when he needed water, he landed on an island and bombarded the inhabitants, taking "as much water as we wanted."[16]

Da Gama's cavalier treatment of the natives was symptomatic of a more profound development: European colonialism. Already in the 1440s, Henry was portioning out the uninhabited islands of Madeira and the Azores to those of his followers who promised to find peasants to settle them. The Azores remained a grain producer, but, with financing by the Genoese, Madeira began to grow cane sugar. The product took Europe by storm. Demand was so high that a few decades later, when few European settlers could be found to work sugar plantations on the Cape Verde Islands, the Genoese Antonio da Noli, discoverer and governor of the islands, brought in African slaves instead. Cape Verde was a microcosm of later European colonialism, which depended on just such slave labor.

Portugal's successes and pretensions roused the hostility and rivalry of Castile. Ferdinand and Isabella's determination to conquer the Canary Islands was in part their "answer" to Portugal's Cape Verde. When, in 1492, they half-heartedly sponsored the

Map 8.6: Long-distance Sea Voyages of the Fifteenth Century

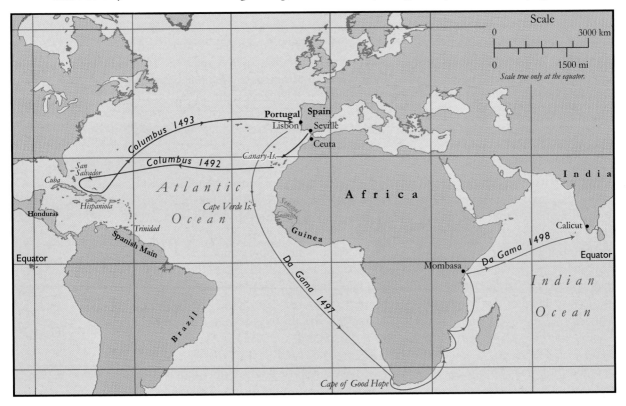

Genoese Christopher Columbus (1451-1506) on a westward voyage across the Atlantic, they knew that they were playing Portugal's game.

Although the conquistadores confronted a New World, they did so with the expectations and categories of the Old. When the Spaniard Hernán Cortés (1485-1547) began his conquest of Mexico, he boasted in a letter home that he had reprimanded one of the native chiefs for thinking that Mutezuma, the Aztec emperor who ruled much of Mexico at the time, was worthy of allegiance:

> I replied by telling him of the great power of Your Majesty [Emperor Charles V, who was also king of Spain] and of the many other princes, greater than Mutezuma, who were Your Highness's vassals and considered it no small favor to be so; Mutezuma also would become one, as would all the natives of these lands. I therefore asked him to become one, for if he did it would be greatly to his honor and advantage, but if, on the other hand, he refused to obey, he would be punished.[17]

The old values lived on.

★   ★   ★   ★

Between the years 1350 and 1500, a series of catastrophes struck Europe. The Black Death felled at least a fifth of the population of Europe. The Hundred Years' War wreaked havoc when archers shot and cannons roared; it loosed armies of freebooters in both town and country during its interstices of peace. The Ottomans conquered Byzantium, took over the Balkans, and threatened Austria and Hungary. The church splintered as first the Great Schism and then national churches tore at the loyalties of churchmen and laity alike.

Yet these catastrophes were confronted, if not always overcome, with both energy and inventiveness. In England, peasants loosed the bonds of serfdom; in Portugal and Spain, adventurers discovered gold and land via the high seas; and everywhere bibliophiles and artists discovered wisdom and beauty in the classical past while princes flexed the muscles of sovereignty. History books normally divide this period into two parts, the crises going into a chapter on the Middle Ages, the creativity saved for a chapter on the Renaissance. But the two happened together, witness to Europe's aggressive resilience. Indeed, in the next century it would parcel out the globe.

*c.*1299–1324	Rule of Osman, founder of Ottomans
1304–1374	Francis Petrarch
*c.*1330–1384	John Wyclif
1337–1453	Hundred Years' War
*c.*1340–1400	Geoffrey Chaucer
1346–1353	Black Death
1351	Statute of Laborers in England
1358	Jacquerie in France
1364–*c.*1430	Christine de Pisan
*c.*1370–1415	Jan Hus
1378	Ciompi revolt in Florence
1378–1417	Great Schism of the papacy
1381	Wat Tyler's Rebellion
*c.*1390–1441	Jan van Eyck
1414–1418	Council of Constance
1429	Jeanne d'Arc leads French army to victory at Orléans
1438	Pragmatic Sanction of Bourges
1444–1446, 1451–1481	Rule of Mehmed II the Conqueror, Ottoman sultan
*c.*1450	Gutenberg invents the printing press
1452–1519	Leonardo da Vinci
1453	Ottoman conquest of Constantinople; end of Byzantine Empire
1454	Peace of Lodi in Northern Italy
1455–1487	Wars of the Roses
1477	Battle of Nancy; end of the Burgundian state
1492	Conquest of Granada; expulsion of Jews from Spain; first trans-Atlantic voyage of Columbus

NOTES

1. Nicephorus Gregoras, *Roman History*, in *Reading the Middle Ages: Sources from Europe, Byzantium, and the Islamic World* (Peterborough, ON, 2006), p.484.

2. Geoffrey Chaucer, *The Canterbury Tales*, trans. Nevill Coghill (Harmondsworth, 1977), p.88.

3. Ashikpashazade, *Osman Comes to Power*, in *Reading the Middle Ages*, p.494.

4. Froissart, *Chronicles*, in *Reading the Middle Ages*, p.512.

5. Jeanne d'Arc, *Letter to the English*, in *Reading the Middle Ages*, p.518.

6. Christine de Pisan, *The Tale of Joan of Arc*, quoted in Nadia Margolis, "The Mission of Joan of Arc," in *Medieval Hagiography: An Anthology*, ed. Thomas Head (New York, 2000), p.822.

7. Froissart, *Chronicles*, ed. and trans. Geoffrey Brereton (Harmondsworth, 1968), p.151.

8. *Wat Tyler's Rebellion*, in *Reading the Middle Ages*, p.523.

9. Cincius Romanus, *Letter to His Most Learned Teacher Franciscus de Fiana*, in *Reading the Middle Ages*, pp.536–37.

10. Quoted in Evelyn Welch, *Art and Society in Italy, 1350-1500* (Oxford, 1997), p.211.

11. Leon Battista Alberti, *On Painting and On Sculpture*, ed. and trans. Cecil Grayson (London: Phaidon Press, 1972), p.32.

12. Giorgio Vasari, *The Lives of the Artists*, ed. and trans. George Bull (Baltimore, 1965), p.290.

13. "A Sforza Banquet Menu (1491)," in *The Renaissance in Europe: An Anthology*, ed. Peter Elmer, Nick Webb, and Roberta Wood (New Haven, 2000), pp.172-75.

14. "A Sforza Banquet Menu," p.173.

15. Quoted in Gustave Reese, *Music in the Renaissance*, rev. ed. (New York, 1959), p.13; translated by Charles Brauner.

16. *A Journal of the First Voyage of Vasco da Gama, 1497-1499*, ed. and trans. E.G. Ravenstein (rpt. New York, 1963), p.30.

17. Hernán Cortés, *The Second Letter*, in *Reading the Middle Ages*, p.558.

FURTHER READING

Aberth, John. *From the Brink of the Apocalypse: Confronting Famine, War, Plague, and Death in the Later Middle Ages*. New York, 2001.

Belozerskaya, Marina. *Rethinking the Renaissance: Burgundian Arts across Europe*. Cambridge, 2002.

Benedictow, Ole J. *The Black Death, 1346-1353: The Complete History*. Woodbridge, Suffolk, 2004.

Blockmans, Wim, and Walter Prevenier. *The Promised Lands: The Low Countries under Burgundian Rule, 1369-1530*. Trans. Elizabeth Fackelman. Ed. Edward Peters. Philadelphia, 1999.

Blumenfeld-Kosinski, Renate. *Poets, Saints, and Visionaries of the Great Schism, 1378-1417*. University Park, 2006.

Cohn, Samuel K., Jr., *The Black Death Transformed: Disease and Culture in Early Renaissance Europe*. London, 2002.

——. *Lust for Liberty: The Politics of Social Revolt in Medieval Europe, 1200-1425*. Cambridge, MA, 2006.

Curry, Ann. *The Hundred Years' War, 1337-1453*. Oxford, 2002.

Fernández-Armesto, Felipe. *Pathfinders: A Global History of Exploration*. New York, 2006.

Goffman, Daniel. *The Ottoman Empire and Early Modern Europe*. Cambridge, 2002.

Hudson, Anne. *The Premature Reformation: Wycliffite Texts and Lollard History*. Oxford, 1988.

Imber, Colin. *The Ottoman Empire, 1300-1650: The Structure of Power*. New York, 2002.

Jardine, Lisa, and Jerry Brotton. *Global Interests: Renaissance Art between East and West*. Ithaca, NY, 2000.

Keen, Maurice. *Chivalry*. New Haven, 1984.

Johnson, Geraldine A. *Renaissance Art: A Very Short Introduction*. Oxford, 2005.

Klassen, John Martin. *The Nobility and the Making of the Hussite Revolution*. New York, 1978.

McKitterick, David. *Print, Manuscript and the Search for Order, 1450-1830*. Cambridge, 2003.

Parker, Geoffrey. *The Cambridge History of Warfare*. Cambridge, 2005.

Wheeler, Bonnie, and Charles Wood, eds. *Fresh Verdicts on Joan of Arc*. New York, 1996.

◆▸◆▸◆▸◆▸◆▸◆▸◆

**To test your knowledge of this chapter, please go to
www.rosenweinshorthistory.com
and click "Study Questions."**

EPILOGUE

Cortéz may have used the old vocabulary of vassalage when speaking of his conquests in the Americas, but clearly the *reality* was so changed that we are right to see the years around 1500 as the turning point between the Middle Ages and a new phase of history. The Middle Ages began when the Roman provinces came into their own. They ended as those provinces—now vastly expanded, rich, and powerful, now "Europe," in fact—became in turn a new imperial power, its tentacles in the New World, Asia, and Africa. In the next centuries, as Europeans conquered most of the world, they (as the Romans had once done) exported themselves, their values, cultures, diseases, inventions, and institutions, while importing, usually without meaning to, many of the people, ideas, and institutions of the groups they conquered. In another phase, one not yet ended, former European colonies—at least some of them—have become, in turn, the center of a new-style empire involving economic, cultural, and (occasionally) military hegemony. It remains to be seen if this empire, too, will eventually be overtaken by its peripheries.

Does anything now remain of the Middle Ages? Without doubt. Bits and pieces of the past are clearly embedded in the present: universities, parliaments, ideas about God and human nature, the papacy, Gothic churches. We cling to some of these bits with ferocious passion, while repudiating others and allowing still more to float in and out of our unquestioned assumptions. Many things that originated in the Middle Ages are now so transformed that only their names are still medieval. And beyond that? Beyond that, "persistence" is the wrong question. The past need not be replayed because it is "us" but rather because it is "not us," and therefore endlessly fascinating.

GLOSSARY

aids In England, this refers to payments made by vassals to their lords on important occasions.

The Annunciation See Virgin Mary (below).

antiking A king elected illegally.

antipope A pope elected illegally.

Book of Hours A prayer book for lay devotion, meant to be read eight times a day either at home or in church. It normally contained the church calendar; a lesson from each of the gospels; prayers and other readings in honor of the Virgin Mary (see below) based on simplified versions of the Divine Office (see Office below); the penitential psalms; the Office of the Dead; and prayers to saints. Some were lavishly illustrated, and even humble ones were usually decorated.

bull An official document issued by the papacy. The word derives from *bulla*, the lead impression of the pope's seal that was affixed to the document to validate it.

canon law The laws of the church. These were at first hammered out as need arose at various regional church councils and in rules issued by great bishops, particularly the pope. Early collections of canon law were incomplete and sometimes contradictory. Beginning in the ninth century, commentators began to organize and systematize them. The most famous of these treatises was the mid-twelfth-century *Decretum* of Gratian, which, although not an official code, became the basis of canon law training in the schools.

cathedral The principal church of a bishop or archbishop.

church To the Roman Catholics of the Middle Ages, this had two related meanings. It signified in the first place the eternal institution created by Christ, composed of the whole body of Christian believers, and served on earth by Christ's ministers—priests, bishops, the pope. Related to the eternal church were individual, local churches (parish churches, cathedrals, collegiate churches, chapels) where the daily liturgy was carried out and the faithful received the sacraments.

cleric A man in church orders.

collegiate church A church for priests living in common according to a rule.

The Crucifixion The execution of Jesus by hanging on a cross (*crux* in Latin). The scene, described in some detail in the Gospels, was often depicted in art; and free-standing crucifixes (crosses with the figure of Jesus on them) were often placed upon church altars.

dogma   The authoritative truth of the church.

empire   Refers in the first instance to the Roman Empire. Byzantium considered itself the continuation of that empire. In the West, there were several successor empires, all ruled by men who took the title "emperor": there was the empire of Charlemagne, which included more or less what later became France, Italy, and Germany; it was followed in the tenth century (from the time of Otto I on) by the empire held (after a crowning at Rome) by the German kings. This could be complicated: a ruler like Henry IV was king of Germany in 1056 at the age of five; he took the real reins of power in 1066; but he was not crowned emperor until 1084. Nevertheless, he *acted* as an emperor long before that. That "German" empire, which lasted until the thirteenth century, included Germany and (at least in theory) northern Italy. Later "German" empires, such at that of the Habsburgs, did not include Italy. Some historians call all of these successor empires of Rome the "Holy Roman Empire," but in fact that term was not used until 1254. The Holy Roman Empire, which had nothing to do with Rome, ended in 1806. By extension, the term empire can refer to other large realms, often gained through conquest, such as the Mongol Empire or the Ottoman Empire.

episcopal   As used for the Middle Ages, this is the equivalent of "bishop's." An "episcopal church" is the bishop's church; an "episcopal appointment" is the appointment of a bishop; "episcopal power" is the power wielded by a bishop.

excommunication   An act or pronouncement that cuts someone off from participation in the sacraments of the church and thus from the means of salvation.

gentry   By the end of the Middle Ages, English landlords consisted of two groups, lords and gentry. The gentry were below the lords; knights, squires, and gentlemen were all considered gentry. Even though the term comes from the Late Middle Ages, it is often used by historians as a rough and ready category for the lesser English nobility from the twelfth century onward.

The Flagellation   The scene in the Gospels (Matt. 27:26 and Mk. 15:15) where Christ is scourged by his executioners prior to his Crucifixion (see above). The scene was frequently depicted by artists.

fresco A form of painting using pigments on wet plaster, frequently employed on the walls of churches.

grisaille Painting in monochrome grays highlighted with color tints.

Guelfs and Ghibellines Guelf was the Italian for Welf (the dynasty that competed for the German throne against the Staufen), while Ghibelline referred to Waiblingen (the name of an important Staufen castle). In the various conflicts between the popes and the Staufen emperors, the "Guelfs" were the factions within the Italian city-states that supported the papacy, while the "Ghibellines" supported the emperor. More generally, however, the names became epithets for various inter- and intra-city political factions that had little or no connection to papal/imperial issues.

illumination The term used for paintings in medieval manuscripts. These might range from simple decorations of capital letters to full-page compositions. An "illuminated" manuscript is one containing illuminations.

layman/ laywoman/laity Men and women not in church orders, not ordained. In the early Middle Ages it was possible to be a monk and a layperson at the same time. But by the Carolingian period, most monks were priests, and, although nuns were not, they were not considered part of the laity because they had taken vows to the church.

Levant The lands that border the eastern shore of the Mediterranean; the Holy Land.

liturgy The formal worship of the church, which included prayers, readings, and significant gestures at fixed times appropriate to the season. While often referring to the Mass (see below), it may equally be used to describe the Offices (see below).

The Madonna See Virgin Mary (below).

Maghreb A region of northwest Africa embracing the Atlas Mountains and the coastline of Morocco, Algeria, and Tunisia.

Mass The central ceremony of Christian worship; it includes prayers and readings from the Bible and culminates in the consecration of bread and wine as the body and blood of Christ, offered to believers in the sacrament of the "Eucharist," or "Holy Communion."

New Testament This work, a compilation of the second century, contains the four Gospels (accounts of the life of Christ) by Matthew, Mark, Luke, and John; the Acts of the Apostles; various letters, mainly from Saints Paul, Peter, and John to fledgling Christian communities; and the Apocalypse. It is distinguished from the "Old Testament" (see below).

Office
In the context of monastic life, the day and night were punctuated by eight periods in which the monks gathered to recite a precise set of prayers. Each set was called an "Office," and the cycle as a whole was called the "Divine Office." Special rites and ceremonies might also be called offices, such as the "Office of the Dead."

Old Testament
The writings of the Hebrew Bible that were accepted as authentic by Christians, though reinterpreted by them as prefiguring the coming of Christ; they were thus seen as the precursor of the "New Testament" (see above), which fulfilled and perfected them.

Presentation in the Temple
An event in the life of Christ and his mother. See The Virgin below.

referendary
A high Merovingian administrative official responsible for overseeing the issuing of royal documents.

relief
This has two separate meanings. In connection with medieval English government, the "relief" refers to money paid upon inheriting a fief. In the history of sculpture, however, "relief" refers to figures or other forms that project from a flat background. "Low relief" means that the forms project rather little, while "high relief" refers to forms that may be so three-dimensional as to threaten to break away from the flat surface.

sacraments
The rites of the church that (in its view) Jesus instituted to confer sanctifying grace. With the sacraments, one achieved salvation. Cut off from the sacraments (by anathema, excommunication, or interdict), one was damned.

scriptorium
(*pl.* scriptoria) The room of the monastery where parchment was prepared and texts were copied, illuminated, and bound.

summa
(*pl.* summae) A compendium or summary. A term favored by scholastics to title their comprehensive syntheses.

The Virgin/
The Virgin Mary/
The Blessed Virgin/
The Madonna
The Gospels of Matthew (1:18-23) and Luke (1:27-35) assert that Christ was conceived by the Holy Spirit (rather than by a man) and born of Mary, a virgin. Already in the fourth century the Church Fathers stressed the virginity of Mary, which guaranteed the holiness of Christ. In the fifth century, at the Council of Chalcedon (451), Mary's perpetual (eternal) virginity was declared. Mary was understood as the exact opposite of (and

antidote to) Eve. In the medieval church, Mary was celebrated with four feasts—her Nativity (birth), the Annunciation (when the Angel Gabriel announced to her that she would give birth to the Messiah), the Purification (when she presented the baby Jesus in the temple and was herself cleansed after giving birth), and her Assumption (when she rose to Heaven). (The Purification is also called the Presentation in the Temple.) These events were frequently depicted in paintings and sculpture, especially in the Later Middle Ages, when devotion to Mary's cult increased and greater emphasis was placed on her role as intercessor with her son in Heaven.

APPENDIX: LISTS

LATE ROMAN EMPERORS

(Usurpers in italics)

Maximinus Thrax (235-238)
Gordian I (238)
Gordian II (238)
Balbinus and Pupienus (238)
Gordian III (238-244)
Philip the Arab (244-249)
Decius (249-251)
Trebonianus Gallus (251-253)
Aemilian (253)
Valerian (253-260)
Gallienus (253-268)
Claudius II Gothicus (268-270)
Quintillus (270)
Aurelian (270-275)
Tacitus (275-276)
Florian (276)
Probus (276-282)
Carus (282-283)
Numerianus (283-284)
Carinus (284-285)

In the West	In the East
Maximian (Augustus) (285-305)	Diocletian (Augustus) (284-305)
Constantius (Caesar) (293-305)	Galerius (Caesar) (293-305)
Constantius (Augustus) (305-306)	Galerius (Augustus) (305-311)
Severus (Caesar) (305-306)	Maximin (Caesar) (305-309)
Severus (Augustus) (306-307)	Galerius (Augustus) (305-311)
Constantine I (Caesar) (306-308)	Maximin (Caesar and Augustus) (305-313)

Maxentius (in Italy) (306-312)

Constantine I (Augustus) (307-337)   Licinius (Augustus) (308-324)

Domitius Alexander (in Africa) (308-311)
Constantine I and Licinius (313-324)
Constantine I (324-337)

Constantine II (337-340)
Constans (340-350)   Constantius II (337-361)
Magnentius (350-353)
Julian Caesar (355-361)   Gallus Caesar (361-364)
Julian Augustus (360-363)

Julian (361-363)
Jovian (363-364)

Valentinian (364-375)   Valens (364-378)
Gratian (367-383)   Theodosius I (379-395)
Valentinian II (375-392)
Maximus (383-388)
Eugenius (392-394)

Theodosius I (394-395)

Honorius (394-423)   Arcadius (395-408)
(Stilicho regent) (395-408)
                                          Theodosius II (408-450)
Constantius III (421)
John (423-425)   Marcian (450-457)
Valentian III (425-455)
Petronius Maximus (455)   Leo I (457-474)
Avitus (455-456)
Majorian (457-461)
Libius Severus (461-465)
Anthemius (467-472)
Olybrius (472)
Glycerius (473)

Julius Nepos (473-475)
Romulus Augustulus (475-476)

Zeno (474-491)
Anastasius I (491-518)
Justin I (518-527)
Justinian I (527-565)
Justin II (565-578)
Tiberius II Constantine (578-582)
Maurice Tiberius (582-602)

BYZANTINE EMPERORS AND EMPRESSES

Justinian I (527-565)
Justin II (565-578)
      Tiberius, Caesar and regent (574-578)
Tiberius II Constantine (578-582)
Maurice Tiberius (582-602)
Phocas the Tyrant (602-610)
Heraclius (610-641)
Constantine III Heraclius (641)
Heraclonas (Heraclius) Constantine (641)
      Martina, regent
Constans II (Constantine) Heraclius the Bearded (641-668)
Constantine IV (668-685)
Justinian II the Slit-Nosed (685-695, 705-711)
Leontius (Leo) (695-698)
Tiberius III Apsimar (698-705)
Philippicus Bardanes (711-713)
Anastasius II Artemius (713-715)
Theodosius III (715-717)
Leo III the Isaurian (717-741)
Constantine V Name of Dung (741-775)
      Artavasdus, rival emperor at Constantinople (741-743)
Leo IV the Khazar (775-780)
Constantine VI the Blinded (780-797)
      Irene the Athenian, regent
Irene the Athenian (797-802)
Nicephorus I the General Logothete (802-811)
Stauracius (811)
Michael I Rhangabe (811-813)

Leo V the Armenian (813-820)

Michael II the Amorian (820-829)

Theophilus (829-842)

Michael III the Drunkard (842-867)

      Theodora, regent (842-856)

Basil I the Macedonian (867-886)

Leo VI the Wise (886-912)

Alexander (912-913)

Constantine VII Porphyrogenitus (913-959)

      Nicholas Mysticus, regent (913-914)

      Zoë Carbonopsina, regent (914-920)

      Romanus I Lecapenus, coemperor (920-944)

Romanus II Porphyrogenitus (959-963)

Basil II the Bulgar-Slayer (963-1025)

      Theophano, regent (963)

      Nicephorus II Phocas, coemperor (963-969)

      John I Tzimisces, coemperor (969-976)

Constantine VIII Porphyrogenitus (1025-1028)

Romanus III Argyrus (1028-1034)

Michael IV the Paphlagonian (1034-1041)

Michael V the Caulker (1041-1042)

Zoë Porphyrogenita (1042)

Constantine IX Monomachus (1042-1055)

Theodora Porphyrogenita (1055-1056)

Michael VI Bringas (1056-1057)

Isaac I Comnenus (1057-1059)

Constantine X Ducas (1059-1067)

Michael VII Ducas (1067-1078)

      Eudocia Macrembolitissa, regent (1067-1068)

      Romanus IV Diogenes, coemperor (1068-1071)

Nicephorus III Botaniates (1078-1081)

Alexius I Comnenus (1081-1118)

John II Comnenus (1118-1143)

Manuel I Comnenus (1143-1180)

Alexius II Comnenus (1180-1183)

      Andronicus Comnenus, regent (1182-1183)

Andronicus I Comnenus (1183-1185)

Isaac II Angelus (1185-1195)

Alexius III Angelus (1195-1203)

Isaac II Angelus (again) (1203-1204)

Alexius IV Angelus, coemperor
   Alexius III Angelus, rival emperor
Alexius V Ducas Murtzuphlus (1204)
   Alexius III Angelus, rival emperor
Alexius III Angelus (in Thrace) (1204)
Theodore I Lascaris (at Nicaea) (1205-1221)
John III Ducas Vatatzes (at Nicaea) (1221-1254)
   Theodore Ducas, emperor at Thessalonica (1224-1230)
   John Ducas, emperor at Thessalonica (1237-1242)
Theodore II Lascaris (at Nicaea) (1254-1258)
John IV Lascaris (at Nicaea) (1258-1261)
   Michael VIII Palaeologus, coemperor at Nicaea (1259-1261)
Michael VIII Palaeologus (at Constantinople) (1261-1282)
Andronicus II Palaeologus (1282-1328)
   Andronicus III Palaeologus, coemperor (1321-1328)
Andronicus III Palaeologus (1328-1341)
John V Palaeologus (1341-1376; 1379-1391)
   Anna of Savoy, regent (1341-1347)
   John VI Cantacuzenus, coemperor (1347-1354)
Andronicus IV Palaeologus (1376-1379)
Manuel II Palaeologus (1391-1425)
John VIII Palaeologus (1425-1448)
Constantine XI Palaeologus (1449-1453)

POPES AND ANTIPOPES TO 1500* (Antipopes in Italics)

Peter (?-c.64)

Linus (c.67-76/79)

Anacletus (76-88 or 79-91)

Clement I (88-97 or 92-101)

Evaristus (c.97-c.107)

Alexander I (105-115 or 109-119)

Sixtus I (c.115-c.125)

Telesphorus (c.125-c.136)

Hyginus (c.136-c.140)

Pius I (c.140-155)

Anicetus (c.155-c.166)

Soter (c.166-c.175)

Eleutherius (c.175-189)

Victor I (c.189-199)

Zephyrinus (c.199-217)

Calixtus I (Callistus) (217?-222)

Hippolytus (217, 218-235)

Urban I (222-230)

Pontian (230-235)

Anterus (235-236)

Fabian (236-250)

Cornelius (251-253)

 * Only since the ninth century has the title of "pope" come to be associated exclusively with the bishop of Rome.

Novatian (251)
Lucius I (253-254)
Stephen I (254-257)
Sixtus II (257-258)
Dionysius (259-268)
Felix I (269-274)
Eutychian (275-283)
Galus (283-296)
Marcellinus (291/296-304)
Marcellus I (308-309)
Eusebius (309/310)
Miltiades (Melchiades) (311–314)
Sylvester I (314-335)
Mark (336)
Julius I (337-352)
Liberius (352-366)
Felix II (355-358)
Damasus I (366-384)
Ursinus (366-367)
Siricius (384-399)
Anastasius I (399-401)
Innocent I (401-417)
Zosimus (417-418)
Boniface I (418-422)
Eulalius (418-419)
Celestine I (422-432)
Sixtus III (432-440)
Leo I (440-461)
Hilary (461-468)
Simplicius (468-483)
Felix III (or II) (483-492)
Gelasius I (492-496)
Anastasius II (496-498)
Symmachus (498-514)
Laurentius (498, 501-c.505/507)
Hormisdas (514-523)
John I (523-526)
Felix IV (or III) (526-530)
Dioscorus (530)
Boniface II (530-532)

John II (533-535)
Agapetus I (535-536)
Silverius (536-537)
Vigilius (537-555)
Pelagius I (556-561)
John III (561-574)
Benedict I (575-579)
Pelagius II (579-590)
Gregory I (590-604)
Sabinian (604-606)
Boniface III (607)
Boniface IV (608-615)
Deusdedit (also called Adeodatus I) (615-618)
Boniface V (619-625)
Honorius I (625-638)
Severinus (640)
John IV (640-642)
Theodore I (642-649)
Martin I (649-655)
Eugenius I (654-657)
Vitalian (657-672)
Adeodatus II (672-676)
Donus (676-678)
Agatho (678-681)
Leo II (682-683)
Benedict II (684-685)
John V (685-686)
Conon (686-687)
Sergius I (687-701)
Theodore (687)
Paschal (687)
John VI (701-705)
John VII (705-707)
Sisinnius (708)
Constantine (708-715)
Gregory II (715-731)
Gregory III (731-741)
Zacharias (Zachary) (741-752)
Stephen II (752-757)

Paul I (757-767)

Constantine (II) (767-768)

Philip (768)

Stephen III (768-772)

Adrian I (772-795)

Leo III (795-816)

Stephen IV (816-817)

Paschal I (817-824)

Eugenius II (824-827)

Valentine (827)

Gregory IV (827-844)

John (844)

Sergius II (844-847)

Leo IV (847-855)

Benedict III (855-858)

Anastasius (Anastasius the Librarian) (855)

Nicholas I (858-867)

Adrian II (867-872)

John VIII (872-882)

Marinus I (882-884)

Adrian III (884-885)

Stephen V (885-891)

Formosus (891-896)

Boniface VI (896)

Stephen VI (896-897)

Romanus (897)

Theodore II (897)

John IX (898-900)

Benedict IV (900-903)

Leo V (903)

Christopher (903-904)

Sergius III (904-911)

Anastasius III (911-913)

Lando (913-914)

John X (914-928)

Leo VI (928)

Stephen VII (929-931)

John XI (931-935)

Leo VII (936-939)

Stephen VIII (939-942)

Marinus II (942-946)

Agapetus II (946-955)

John XII (955-964)

Leo VIII (963-965)

Benedict V (964-966?)

John XIII (965-972)

Benedict VI (973-974)

Boniface VII (1st time) (974)

Benedict VII (974-983)

John XIV (983-984)

Boniface VII (2nd time) (984-985)

John XV (or XVI) (985-996)

Gregory V (996-999)

John XVI (or XVII) (997-998)

Sylvester II (999-1003)

John XVII (or XVIII) (1003)

John XVIII (or XIX) (1004-1009)

Sergius IV (1009-1012)

Gregory (VI) (1012)

Benedict VIII (1012-1024)

John XIX (or XX) (1024-1032)

Benedict IX (1st time) (1032-1044)

Sylvester III (1045)

Benedict IX (2nd time) (1045)

Gregory VI (1045-1046)

Clement II (1046-1047)

Benedict IX (3rd time) (1047-1048)

Damasus II (1048)

Leo IX (1049-1054)

Victor II (1055-1057)

Stephen IX (1057-1058)

Benedict (X)(1058-1059)

Nicholas II (1059-1061)

Alexander II (1061-1073)

Honorius (II) (1061-1072)

Gregory VII (1073-1085)

Clement (III) (1080-1100)

Victor III (1086-1087?)

Urban II (1088-1099)

Paschal II (1099-1118)

Theodoric (1100-1102)
Albert (also called Aleric) (1102)
Sylvester (IV) (1105-1111)
Gelasius II (1118-1119)
Gregory (VIII) (1118-1121)
Calixtus II (Callistus) (1119-1124)
Honorius II (1124-1130)
Celestine (II) (1124)
Innocent II (1130-1143)
Anacletus (II) (1130-1138)
Victor (IV) (1138)
Celestine II (1143-1144)
Lucius II (1144-1145)
Eugenius III (1145-1153)
Anastasius IV (1153-1154)
Adrian IV (1154-1159)
Alexander III (1159-1181)
Victor (IV) (1159-1164)
Paschal (III) (1164-1168)
Calixtus (III) (1168-1178)
Innocent (III) (1179-1180)
Lucius III (1181-1185)
Urban III (1185-1187)
Gregory VIII (1187)
Clement III (1187-1191)
Celestine III (1191-1198)
Innocent III (1198-1216)
Honorius III (1216-1227)
Gregory IX (1227-1241)
Celestine IV (1241)
Innocent IV (1243-1254)
Alexander IV (1254-1261)
Urban IV (1261-1264)
Clement IV (1265-1268)
Gregory X (1271-1276)
Innocent V (1276)
Adrian V (1276)
John XXI (1276-1277)
Nicholas III (1277-1280)

Martin IV (1281-1285)
Honorius IV (1285-1287)
Nicholas IV (1288-1292)
Celestine V (1294)
Boniface VIII (1294-1303)
Benedict IX (1303-1304)
Clement V (at Avignon, from 1309) (1305-1314)
John XXII (at Avignon) (1316-1334)
Nicholas (V) (at Rome) (1328-1330)
Benedict XII (at Avignon) (1334-1342)
Clement VI (at Avignon) (1342-1352)
Innocent VI (at Avignon) (1352-1362)
Urban V (at Avignon) (1362-1370)
Gregory XI (at Avignon, then Rome from 1377) (1370-1378)
Urban VI (1378-1389)
Clement (VII) (at Avignon) (1378-1394)
Boniface IX (1389-1404)
Benedict (XIII) (at Avignon) (1394-1417)
Innocent VII (1404-1406)
Gregory XII (1406-1415)
Alexander (V) (at Bologna) (1409-1410)
John (XXIII) (at Bologna) (1410-1415)
Martin V (1417-1431)
Clement (VIII) (1423-1429)
Eugenius IV (1431-1447)
Felix (V) (also called Amadeus VIII of Savoy) (1439-1449)
Nicholas V (1447-1455)
Calixtus III (Callistus) (1455-1458)
Pius II (1458-1464)
Paul II (1464-1471)
Sixtus IV (1471-1484)
Innocent VIII (1484-1492)
Alexander VI (1492-1503)

CALIPHS

Early Caliphs

Abu-Bakr (632–634)
Umar I (634–644)
Uthman (644–656)
Ali (656–661)

Umayyads

Mu'awiyah I (661–680)
Yazid I (680–683)
Mu'awiyah II (683–684)
Marwan I (684–685)
'Abd al-Malik (692–705)
al-Walid I (705–715)
Sulayman (715–717)
Umar II (717–720)
Yazid II (720–724)
Hisham (724–743)
al-Walid II (743–744)
Yazid III (744)
Ibrahim (744)
Marwan II (744–750)

Abbasids★

al-Saffah (750–754)
al-Mansur (754–775)
al-Mahdi (775–785)
al-Hadi (785–786)
Harun al-Rashid (786–809)
al-Amin (809–813)
al-Ma'mun (813–833)
al-Mu'tasim (833–842)
al-Wathiq (842–847)
al-Mutawakkil (847–861)

al-Muntasir (861–862)
al-Musta'in (862–866)
al-Mu'tazz (866–869)
al-Muhtadi (869–870)
al-Mu'tamid (870–892)
al-Mu'tadid (892–902)
al-Muqtafi (902–908)
al-Muqtadir (908–932)
al-Qahir (932–934)
al-Radi (934–940)

★ Abbasid caliphs continued at Baghdad — with, however, only nominal power — until 1258. Thereafter, a branch of the family in Cairo held the caliphate until the sixteenth century.

Fatimids

'Ubayd Allah (al-Mahdi) (909–934)
al-Ka'im (934–946)
al-Mansur (946–953)
al-Mu'izz (953–975)
al-'Aziz (975–996)
al-Hakim (996–1021)
al-Zahir (1021–1036)
al-Mustansir (1036–1094)
al-Musta'li (1094–1101)
al-Amir (1101–1130)
al-Hafiz (1130–1149)
al-Zafir (1149–1154)
al-Fa'iz (1154–1160)
al-'Adid (1160–1171)

OTTOMAN EMIRS AND SULTANS

Osman (1299-1326)
Orhan (1326-1360)
Murad I (1360-1389)
Bayezid I (1389-1402)
Ottoman Civil War (1402-1413)
Mehmed I (1413-1421)
Murad II (1421-1444, 1446-1451)
Mehmed II the Conqueror (1444-1446, 1451-1481)
Bayezid II (1481-1512)

SOURCES

MAPS

PLATES

5.3 Gloria with Musical Notation, Saint-Evroult. Gloria de la notation musicale (12th cent.). Latin 10097, fol. 32v. Copyright © BnF. Reprinted by permission of Bibliothèque nationale de France.

5.4 Durham Cathedral, Interior. Nave looking east, Cathedral Durham, Great Britain. Anthony Scibilia / Art Resource, NY. Reprinted by permission of Art Resource.

5.5 Sant Tomàs de Fluvià, The Last Supper, Painted Vault. Romanic monuments: Paintings recently found and restored in San Tomàs de Fluvià (Toroella). Photograph by Heinz Hebeisen. Reprinted by permission of iberimage.

5.6 Vézelay, Anger and Lust. Capital from Vézelay with Devil, Lust and Despair. Copyright © Kathleen Cohen. Reprinted by permission of Kathleen Cohen and San José State University.

5.7 Leaning Tower (Bell Tower) of Pisa. Leaning Tower (Campanile), Pisa. Romanesque. Begun 1173. Tower of Pisa, Pisa, Italy. Scala / Art Resource, NY. Reprinted by permission of Art Resource.

5.8 Santiago de Compostela, Interior. Main altar in Churrigueresque style (1656–1703) with the effigy of St. James (Iago) (c.1211). Cathedral, Santiago de Compostela, Spain. Scala / Art Resource, NY. Reprinted by permission of Art Resource.

5.9 Fontenay Abbey Church, Interior. Nave looking east. Abbey, Fontenay, France. Anthony Scibilia / Art Resource, NY. Reprinted by permission of Art Resource.

6.1 Reliquary Casket for Charlemagne's Arm. Gilded copper and wood, 12th CE. Photograph by Arnaudet. Louvre, Paris, France. Réunion des Musées Nationaux / Art Resource, NY. Reprinted by permission of Art Resource.

6.2 Notre Dame of Paris, Exterior. Notre-Dame, exterior, right side, Paris, France. Scala / Art Resource, NY. Reprinted by permission of Art Resource.

6.3 Notre Dame of Paris, Interior. Notre-Dame, interior view of central nave toward altar. Notre-Dame, Paris, France Scala / Art Resource, NY. Reprinted by permission of Art Resource.

6.4 Lincoln Cathedral, Interior. Center nave of Lincoln Cathedral, looking east, 2nd quarter 13th century. Cathedral, Lincoln, Great Britain. Erich Lessing / Art Resource, NY. Reprinted by permission of Art Resource.

6.5 San Francesco at Assisi. The interior of the Upper Basilica from the east, after the earthquake of 1997. Interior, Upper Basilica of St. Francis, Assisi. Photo by Ghigo Roli, 2002. Franco Cosimo Panini Editore © Management Fratelli Alinari. Alinari / Art Resource, NY. Reprinted by permission of Art Resource.

6.6 Reims Cathedral, West Portal, Saint Joseph (c.1240). Photograph by Hürliman, Thomas, 1967. Copyright © Swiss Foundation of Photography. SODRAC 2007.

7.1 Pietro Lorenzetti, *Birth of the Virgin*. Lorenzetti, Pietro (c.1342). Birth of the Virgin. Museo dell'Opera Metropolitana, Siena, Italy. Scala / Art Resource, NY. Reprinted by permission of Art Resource.

7.2 Virgin and Child. Madonna and Child, Ivory (1330–1350). Reprinted by permission and courtesy of Loyola University Museum of Art, Martin D'Arcy S.J. Collection, Chicago, Illinois.

7.3 Jean Pucelle, *Hours of Jeanne d'Evreux*. Heures de Jeanne d'Evreux by Jean Pucelle. Fol. 15v/16r. I. Walther, N. Wolf: Codices illustres; Köln 2005, S. 208.

7.4 Tomb and Effigy of Edward II. Gloucester Cathedral, tomb of Edward II murdered in 1327 (1330s). Photograph by Angelo Hornak. Reprinted by permission of Angelo Hornak Library.

7.5 The Motet *S'Amours*. The Motet S'Amours (*c.*1300) MS H196, fol. 170r. Reprinted by permission of Bibloiothèque Universitaire de Médecine de Montpellier (Montpellier University Library of Medicine).

7.6 Saint John, "Dominican" Bible. Bible de Saint John "Dominican" (mid 13th century). Latin 16722m, fol. 205v. Copyright © BnF. Reprinted by permission of Bibliothèque nationale de France.

7.7 Saint John, "Aurifaber" Bible. Miniature initial of St. John. Aurifaber (mid 13th) Württ. Landesbibliothek, Stuttgart, Cod. Bibl. Qt. 8, 402v. Reprinted by permission of Württembergische Landesbibliothek.

7.8 Nicola Pisano, Pulpit (1265–1268). Fratelli Alinari, Firenze.

7.9 Giotto, Arena Chapel, Padua. Giotto di Bondone, Scrovegni Chapel. View of the interior, looking toward the altar (1304–1313). Scrovegni Chapel, Padua, Italy. Scala / Art Resource, NY. Reprinted by permission of Art Resource.

7.10 Giotto, *Massacre of the Innocents*, Arena Chapel. Giotto di Bondone, Massacre of the Innocents (1304–1313). Scrovegni Chapel, Padua, Italy. Scala / Art Resource, NY. Reprinted by permission of Art Resource.

8.1 Woodcut from *Der Ackermann aus Böhmen*. *Der Ackermann aus Böhmen* woodcut (*c.*1462). Herzog August Bibliothek Wolfenbüttel: 1462 Ethica 20, 10 recto.

8.2 Donatello, *David Standing on the Head of Goliath*. Fratelli Alinari, Firenze.

8.3 Brunelleschi, Foundling Hospital. Brunelleschi, Filippo, Foundling Hospital Portico. Ospedale degli Innocenti, Florence, Italy. Scala / Art Resource, NY. Reprinted by permission of Art Resource.

8.4 Raphael, *Entombment of Christ*. Raphael (Raffaello Sanzio) Entombment. Galleria Borghese, Rome, Italy. Erich Lessing / Art Resource, NY. Reprinted by permission of Art Resource.

Seeing the Middle Ages Meleager Sarcophagus, detail. Detail of relief on façade of Casino Algardi in Villa Doria Pamphilj, Rome. Reprinted by permission of Presidenza del Consiglio dei Ministri.

Seeing the Middle Ages The Workshop of Rogier van der Weyden, *The Carrying of Christ to the Tomb* (*c.*1460-1470). Weyden, Rogier (Roger) van der. Christ Being Carried to His Tomb Surrounded by the Virgin, Saint Mary Magdalene, Nicodemus and Joseph of Arimathea. Photo by Michèle Bellot. Louvre, Paris, France, Réunion des Musées Nationaux / Art Resource, NY. Reprinted by permission of Art Resource.

8.5 Leonardo da Vinci, *Last Supper*. Leonardo da Vinci, The Last Supper (1498), Post-restoration. S. Maria delle Grazie, Milan, Italy. Alinari / Art Resource, NY. Reprinted by permission of Art Resource.

8.6 Gentile Bellini, *Portrait of Mehmed II*. Gentile Bellini, The Sultan Mehmet II (1479). Copyright © The National Gallery, London. Reprinted by permission of The National Gallery Picture Library.

8.7 *History of Alexander the Great*, Tapestry. Serie di Alessandro Magno. Le imprese in Oriente. Reprinted by permission of Arti Doria Pamphilj.

8.8 Rogier van der Weyden, *Columba Altarpiece*. St. Columba Altarpiece (c.1455), Rogier van der Weyden (c.1399–1464 Netherlandish). Oil on panel, Alte Pinakothek, Munich, Germany. Reprinted by permission of SuperStock, Inc.

8.9 Jan van Eyck, *Man in a Red Turban*. Van Eyck, Portrait of Man (Self-Portrait?) (1433). Copyright © The National Gallery, London. Reprinted by permission of The National Gallery Picture Library.

FIGURES

5.1 Saint-Germain of Auxerre. Christian Sapin (dir.), *Archéologie et architecture d'un site monastique. 10 ans de recherche à l'abbaye Saint-Germain d'Auxerre* (Auxerre: Centre d'études médiévales, Paris: CTHS, 2000) (*Mémoires de la section d'archéologie et d'hisotire de l'art, vol. X*), Fig. 3, p. 10 and Fig. 371, p. 312. Reprinted by permission of Christian Sapin.

5.2 A Model Romanesque Church: Santiago de Compostela. John Beckwith, *Early Medieval Art* (New York: Thames & Hudson, 1964), p.163, ill.155. Reprinted by permission of Thames & Hudson Ltd.

5.3 Schematic Plan of a Cistercian Monastery. *Making of the West.* Lynn Hunt et al. Bedford / St. Martin's, 2001. Adapted from Wolfgang Braunfels *Monasteries of Western Europe.* Princeton, NJ: Princeton University Press, 1972, p. 75. © Dumont Buchverlag GmbH.

7.1 Single Notes and Values of Franconian Notation. From *Anthology of Medieval Music*, edited by Richard Hoppin. Copyright © 1978. W.W. Norton & Company, Inc.

Every effort has been made to contact copyright holders; in the event of an omission or error, please notify the publisher.

INDEX

Page numbers for illustrations are in italics.

bellatores, 156. *See also* knights; vassals

Bellini, Gentile (*c.*1429-1507), 331, 334
    Portrait of Mehmed II, *335*

Benedict, Saint (*d.*547)
    Rule of, 205, 211, 213, 254

beneficium, 231

Benevento. *See also* Italy
    Treaty of (1156), 233

Berbers, 149
    Almohads, 219–20
    Almoravids, 180, 193, 199, 220

Bergamo, 321

Bernard, Saint (*c.*1090-1153), 204, 211, 213–14, 216, 257, 328

Bernard Gui, 274

Bernard Saisset, 280

Bernart de Ventadorn (*fl.*1150-1180), 238

Bertran de Born (*fl.*2nd half of 12th c.), 240

Bible. *See also* Psalter
    "Aurifaber," *293*
    "Dominican," *292*
    Mosaic law of, 163

biology, 286

"Birth of the Virgin," *282*, 283

bishops, 159, 190, 228
    appointment and investiture of, 166 (*See also* Investiture Conflict)
    Ottonian, 166
    in Peace of God, 159
    in Truce of God, 159

Black Death, 306, 322–23

Black Sea region, 146

Boethius (480-524), 163
    works of, in translation, 163

Bohemia, 326

Bohemond (Norman ruler in Sicily), 195

Bologna, 203, 233, 325
    Black Death in, 306
    University of, 243

Bonaventure, Saint (1217-1274), 286–87

Boniface VIII, pope (1294-1303), 279–80
    Clericis Laicos (1296), 280
    Unam Sanctam (1302), 280

Boniface IX, pope (1389-1404), 325

Books of Hours, 283, 286
    definition of, 350
    of Jeanne d'Evreux, *284*, 294

Bosporous, 195

Bourges
    Pragmatic Sanction of (1438), 326

Bouvines, battle of (1214), 229

bowl (or *bacini*), North Africa, *187*

Brethren of the Common Life. *See devotio moderna*

British Isles, 225. *See also* England; Ireland; Scotland; Wales

Bruges, 183

Brunelleschi
    Foundling Hospital, 329, *330*

Bruno of Cologne, 210

bubonic plague. *See also* Black Death

Bulgaria, 143, 147, 310

Bulgars, western. *See* Bulgaria

bull
    definition of, 350

Burchard of Worms, 166

Burgundian tapestries, 334, 340

Burgundians, 314

Burgundy (late medieval duchy), 312, 314, 317, 331, 334, 340

burhs, 163

Buyids, 147–49, 179

Byzantine empire, 139–41, 143, 145, 179–81, 221
    end of (1453), 310
    themes in, 143

Byzantine Orthodoxy, 147

Byzantines, artistic influence
    in West, 166

Byzantium. *See* Byzantine Empire; Constantinople

Cicero, 166

    Pro Archia, 328

Cid, (The), 199

Cináed mac Ailpín (Kenneth I MacAlpin) (*d*.858), 152

Cincius Romanus (*d*.1445), 327–28

ciompi rebellion, 323

Cistercians, 211, 213, 239, 257

cities, 179, 216, 275, 286. *See also* communes

    crisis of in late Middle Ages, 297, 299

    development of Western, 160–61, 269–70

    Franciscans in, 253

    growth of, 183–84

city-states (Italian), 231, 233, 236

Clairvaux, 211

Clare, disciple of Francis, 254

Clement VII, pope, 324

cleric

    definition of, 350

clerical marriage, 187. *See also* Gregorian Reform

Clericis Laicos (1296), 280

Clermont, 194

Cluny, monastery of, 188

    Abbot Majolus of, 155

Cnut (Canute) king (*r*.[in England] 1016-1035), 163–64

coinage, 234

    gold, 269

collegiate church

    definition of, 350

Cologne, 166, 194

colonialism (European), 344

Columba Altarpiece (van der Weyden), *338–39*, 340

Columbus, Christopher (1451-1506), 345

Commedia (*Divine Comedy*) (Dante), 288

commenda, 185

commerce. *See* economy

commercial revolution, 182–85

common law (English). *See under* law

commons (in parliament), 278

communes, 185, 216, 231, 233, 235–36, 270, 272, 319. *See also* cities

    relations with guilds, 242

Comnenus dynasty, 221

    Alexius I Comnenus (*r*.1081-1118), 181–82, 195

compagnia, 185

La Comtessa de Dia (*fl.c.*1200?), 239

Concordat of Worms (1122), 191

condottieri, 325

conquistadores, 323, 345

Conrad III (*r*.1138-1152), 231

Constance of Sicily (wife of Henry VI), 233

Constance of Sicily (wife of Peter of Aragon), 235

Constantine IX Monomachos, emp. (*r*.1042-1055), 141, 181

Constantinople, 257, 266

    Black Death at, 306

    falls to crusaders (1204), 221, 223

    Great Palace of, 141

    Italians in, 221

    Macedonian Renaissance at, 141

Constitutions of Melfi (1231), 234

contado, 160, 233, 236

convents. *See also* monasteries

    Cistercian, 213

    friars', 253, 286

    women's, 166

conversos, 307, 327

Córdoba, 149, 161

    Great Mosque at, 150

    Corpus Christi, feast of, 281

cortes, 275, 277

Cortés, Hernán (1485-1547), 345

cortezia, 240

Council of Constance (1414-1417), 325–26

Council of Pisa (1409), 325

counts, Carolingian. *See also* aristocrats

courtly love, 240

Courtrai, battle of (1302), 270

courts (legal). *See* church courts; law

courts (political). *See also* aristocrats

    Byzantine imperial, 141–42, 181, 221

    episcopal, 166

    Islamic, 141

    Renaissance, 329–31

    Western princely, 237–42

    Western royal, 152, 161, 163, 166

Crete, 143, 223

Crimea. *See* Black Sea region

Croatia, 236

Crucifixion

    definition of, 350

Crusader States, 196–97, 209, 221, 256–57, 264

    Franciscans in, 253

Crusades, 256–57

    Albigensian, 256

    First (1096-1099), 193–95

    Fourth (1202-1204), 221, 257

    Northern, 257, 269

    against Ottoman Turks, 331

    Peasants, 194

    Second (1147-1149), 197, 216, 257

    Third (1189-1192), 228

curia, 189, 193, 205

currency. *See* coinage

Cyprus, 143, 228

da Gama, Vasco (*c.*1460-1524), 343–44

da Vinci, Leonardo. *See* Leonardo da Vinci

Dalasseni, 145. *See also* *dynatoi*

    Anna Dalassena, 181

    Theophylact Dalassenus, 145

Damascus, 197

Dance of Death, 308

Danegeld, 154, 198

Danes. *See* Denmark; Scandinavia; Vikings

Dante Alighieri (1265-1321)

    Commedia (*Divine Comedy*), 288

Danzig, 269

dar al-ilm, 150

David (Donatello), 329, *329*, 342

Decretum (Gratian), 193

Decretum (*c.*1020) (Burchard of Worms), 166

Denmark, 257

devotio moderna, 342

Diarmait Mac Murchada (Dermot MacMur-
    rough), 258

Dias, Bartholomeu (*c.*1450-1500), 343

Diet of Besançon (1157), 231

Diet of Roncaglia (1158), 233

Digenis Akritas, 145

Dijon, 314

Divine Comedy (Dante), 288

Divine Office

    definition, 353

doge, 319

dogma

    definition of, 351

Domesday Book, 198

Dominic, Saint (1170-1221), 254

Dominicans, 253–54, 265, 280, 286

Domrémy, 314

Donatello (*c.*1386-1466)

    David, 329, *329*, 342

Dorset, 306

Duns Scotus, John (*c.*1266-1308), 287

Dunstable, John (*c.*1385-1453), 317, 340

Durham cathedral, 207, *208*

dynatoi, 143, 145, 172, 181, 221

Eckhart, Meister, 287

economy, 211

    Abbasid, 151

    Cistercian, 214

    commercial revolution, 183–85, 267, 269

definition, 351

Geoffrey of Anjou (Plantagenet), 199

geometry (liberal art), 191, 203

Gerald of Wales (d.1223), 258

Germans, 236. *See also* names of individual tribes
    and German successor states

Germany, 164, 189, 240, 277, 287. *See also* Holy
    Roman Empire; Rhineland

  Beguines in, 254

  Black Death in, 306

  Cistercians in, 211

  communes in, 185

  devotio moderna in, 342

  Franciscans in, 253

  Gregorian reform in, 188, 191

  Hungarian raids into, 155

  Jews in, 194, 256, 308

  Ottonian, 166, 168–69

  Staufen, 231, 233, 235

  vagabonds in, 299

Géza, (r.c.972-997), 147, 155

Ghenghis Khan. *See* Chingiz Khan

Ghent, 321

Ghibellines, 270

gift economy, 188

Gilbert of Liège, 203

Gilbert of Poitiers (c.1075-1154)
  Glossa Ordinaria, 191

Giotto (1266-1337), 291, 294, *295–96*, 297. *See also*
  Padua, Arena Chapel
  Massacre of the Innocents, 296

Glossa Ordinaria, 204

gold coinage, 161, 269, 343

Golden Bull, 277

Golden Horde, 265–66

Gospel Book of Otto III, 169, *170*, *171*

Gothic art and architecture, 237, 244–45, 294, 329,
  334

grammar (liberal art), 203

Granada
  conquest of (1492), 327

La Grande Chartreuse, 210

granges, 214

Gratian, 204
  Concordance of Discordant Canons (Decretum),
    193

Great Council (Venice), 319

Great Famine (1315-1322), 299

Great Schism (1054), 190

Great Schism (1378-1417), 305, 324–25, 342

Greek (classical texts), 204, 331

Greenland, 152

Gregorian chant, 194

Gregorian Reform, 187–89

Gregory the Great, pope (590-604), 163
  Pastoral Care, 161

Gregory VII, pope (1073-1085), 189–91, 200

Gregory XI, pope (r.1370-1378), 324

grisaille
  definition of, 352

Groote, Gerhard (1340-1384), 342

Guelfs, 270

Guelfs and Ghibellines
  definition of, 352

Guifred, Guillem, 158–59

guilds, 185, 216, 237, 242, 270, 306, 323, 329

Guillaume de Lorris
  The Romance of the Rose, 288

Guinevere, queen (literature), 241

Gutenberg, Johann, 343

Habsburgs, 235

Haithabu, 161

al-Hakim, Fatimid caliph, 150

Hamdanids, 147

Hanseatic League, 269

Harmony of Discordant Canons (Decretum), 193

Hastings, battle of (1066), 198

English, 198
in European schools and universities, 203–5,
  287, 327–28
Islamic, 150, 180
in Macedonian Renaissance, 141
military ethos and, 150
Ottoman, 330–31
Ottonian, 150, 166
in poetry, 238–42
Renaissance, 328–30
interiority, 342
Investiture Conflict, 166, 190–91, 193
iqta, 149
Iran, 148, 179
  agriculture, 179
Iraq, 148, 221. *See also* Baghdad
Ireland, 163, 225
  conquest by England, 258
  Vikings in, 152
Isabella, queen (England), 312
Isabella, queen (Spain) (r. 1474-1504), 326, 344
Isabella d'Este (1474-1539), 340
Islam, 146
  conversion of Mongols to, 265
  Qur'an, 180
Islamic world, 139, 146, 149–50, 180, 195, 219–21,
  264. *See also* Ottoman empire
Istanbul, 331
Italic League, 321
Italy, 160, 270, 287, 291, 323
  Albigensians in, 254
  Angevin, 235–36
  Cistercians in, 211
  city-states of, 231, 233, 236
  communes in, 185, 193, 231, 242
  Franciscans in, 253
  Frederick I in, 232–33
  Hungarian raids into, 155
  Jews in, 273

Muslim raids into, 146
sumptuary legislation in, 308

Jacob van Artevelde, 321
Jacquerie, 322
James, Saint. *See* Santiago (Saint James) de Compostela
Janissaries, 310
Jean de Meun
  The Romance of the Rose, 288
Jeanne d'Arc, 314, 317, 342
Jeanne d'Evreux, 283
Jerome of Prague, 326
Jerusalem, 195
  kingdom of, 196, 221
Jews, 184. *See also* moneylending; trade (long dis-
  tance)
  blood libel, 256
  conversos, 327
  expelled from Constantinople, 143
  expulsion (in West), 255, 273, 327
  in Islamic world, 151
  in Kievan Rus, 146–47
  persecution of, 194, 256
  rumors about, 273, 308
jihad, 221, 310
Joan of Arc. *See* Jeanne d'Arc
João I, king (r. 1385-1433), 343
Johannes von Saaz, 308
John, king (England) (r. 1199-1216), 228–29
John II, king (France) (r. 1350-1364), 322
John the Fearless, duke (r. 1404-1419), 331
John Tzimisces, emp. (969-976), 143
John XXIII, pope (at Bologna) (1410-1415), 325, 328
Joseph, Saint. *See* Reims, portal sculpture
Judaism. *See* Jews
Juliana of Mont-Cornillon, 281
justice. *See* law
Justinian's law codes, 205

as university discipline, 204, 243

Mediterranean. *See also* trade (long distance)

navigation, 343

trade, 184, 267, 291, 310

Mehmed II the Conqueror (*r.* 1444-1446, 1451-
1481), 310, 331

portrait of, *335*

Meissen, 237

Meleager Sarcophagus, 333

Melisende, queen (*r.* 1131-1152), 196

mendicants. *See* friars

mercenaries, 299, 319

Byzantine, 143

condottieri, 325

Free Companies, 317, 322-23

Turkish, 149, 180

merchants, 183-85, 196, 221, 272, 278, 323. *See also*
Hanseatic League

Italian, 223

at Milan, 160

Merseburg, Thietmar, bishop, 166

Metz, 194

Mexico, 345

Michael VIII Paleologus, emp. (1261-1282), 266

Michelangelo, 333

Mieszko I (*r.* 963-992), 146

Milan, 160, 187, 190, 233, 321, 329

military saints, 145

ministerials, 277

minnesingers, 240

missionaries. *See under* Christianity

monasteries, 156

Bec, 227

Benedictine, 205

Carthusian, 210

as centers of town growth, 183

Cistercian, 204, 211, 213-14

Cluny, 155, 188

Saint-Germain, 205-6

monastic reform, 163

monastic rules. *See Rule of Saint Benedict*

moneylending, 185, 194, 255, 273, 299, 323

Mongols, 263-67, 310

Monologion (Anselm), 191

Monophysites, 143, 181

Montezuma, 345

Montpellier, 203-4

University of, 243

Mosaic law, 163

Moscow, 265

Black Death at, 306

Mosel river valley, 254-55

mosques, 150, 180

Motet, 288, 290, 340

Motet, "S'Amours," *289*

motherhood

in Cistercian spirituality, 214-16

al-Mufid (*d.* 1022), 151

Muscovy, 265

music, 203, 207, 213

motets, 288, *289,* 290, 340

notation, 207, 290

polyphonic, 288, 340

rhythm in, 290

staves, 207

troubadour, 239

Muslims, 142-43, 151-52. *See also* Islam; Shi'ites;
Sunni Islam

in Sicily, 154

al-Mutamin, 199

mystics, 287. *See also* Beguines; *devotio moderna*

Nancy, 317

Naples, 317

nation

ethnic designation, 326

in universities, 243

national churches, 325-26